JUVENILE DELINQUENCY

Second Edition

JUVENILE DELINQUENCY: A JUSTICE PERSPECTIVE

Second Edition

Ralph A. Weisheit
Illinois State University

Robert G. Culbertson
Northwest Missouri State University

WAVELAND
PRESS, INC.
Prospect Heights, Illinois

For information about this book, write or call:

    Waveland Press, Inc.
    P.O. Box 400
    Prospect Heights, Illinois 60070
    (708) 634-0081

Contents

Preface

Juvenile delinquency and the processing of delinquents through the juvenile justice system continues to stimulate considerable debate. Having failed to attain most of the broad objectives established by the historic statute creating the first juvenile court in Cook County, Illinois, we have witnessed an increased sense of frustration. On the one hand the public is angered by delinquency, but on the other hand there is little consensus as to what should be done with these offenders. Despite the volume of research, theorizing, and programs which address juvenile delinquency, there is a sense that we are only beginning to understand the issues involved. At the same time there have been a number of substantial changes in our approach to the problem.

Earlier efforts tended to concentrate on the offender and the broad issues related to causation. However, since the U.S. Supreme Court became involved in the delinquency problem in 1965, there has been a growing interest in studying both the juvenile offender, and the formal system which identifies and processes offenders. This change is dramatically illustrated in the merger of courses on juvenile delinquency with those on juvenile justice. The distinction between theoretical and policy concerns are becoming increasingly blurred. Ironically, our progress in the study of delinquency brings us full circle. The earliest significant American work on delinquency was conducted in the 20s and 30s by individuals who similarly blended theoretical and policy concerns and, in the process, laid the foundation for decades of "academic" and "practical" work.

This reader was developed to reflect the changing nature of the study of juvenile delinquency and juvenile justice, and to meet several needs in this important field of study. First, we have produced a supplementary text which reflects an interdisciplinary perspective. Second, the reader supplements the general discussions presented in textbooks with a more in-depth coverage of specific issues in delinquency — such as the influence of bio-logical factors, exploitation in a juvenile facility, and the treatment of violent juvenile offenders. Finally, we have provided several concise articles regarding general issues in the study of juvenile delinquency and juvenile justice. The articles cover the conflicting philosophies underlying the juvenile justice system, current knowledge about status offenders, the role of such social institutions as the family and the school in the onset and control of delinquency, and major policy issues which must be faced by decision-makers in the years ahead.

This second edition was needed because of changes in the juvenile justice system, such as the increased use of remanding juveniles to adult court and the use of house arrest. In addition, researchers have recently been rethinking long-standing issues in the field, including the role of gangs in crime and the use of the death penalty for juvenile offenders. This edition provides not only a discussion of these current issues, but goes farther than the first edition in showing the range and complexity of problems faced by those who work in the field of juvenile justice.

Our ultimate objective is to stimulate the interest of students in one of the more complex and fascinating aspects of deviant behavior that has serious implications for the offenders and for society as a whole. The reader will find the articles concise, informative and clearly presented.

R.A.W.
R.G.C.

Section I

THE DELINQUENCY PROBLEM AND THE JUSTICE SYSTEM

"The process of making the criminal, therefore, is a process of tagging, defining, identifying, segregating, describing, emphasizing, making conscious and self-conscious; it becomes a way of stimulating, suggesting, emphasizing, and evoking the very traits that are complained of." (Frank Tannenbaum, 1938). Tannenbaum's arguments against intervention reflect his belief that in the "dramatization of evil" social institutions make a substantial contribution to the delinquency problem.

The battle over the so called "delinquency problem," then, is quite old. On the one hand there are those in the Tannenbaum tradition who believe that the state should have little involvement in the lives of children, except in those instances when the behavior constitutes a serious violation of the law. On the other hand, there are those who believe that the state has a significant responsibility in the area of juvenile misconduct regardless of the nature of that misconduct.

In "Delinquency and Social Policy: A Historical Perspective," Paul Lerman addresses the complexities of this debate and identifies the competing and conflicting ideological perspectives. Tracing our current problems back to 1660, Lerman identifies the sources of confusion which have contributed to the lack of a clear distinction between problems related to poverty, welfare, dependency, and those related to crime. The end result of a long history of child saving is that youth can easily lose their freedom for long periods of time for behaviors that are not criminal. Since publi-

1

cation of Lerman's work, problems have become even more complicated as the juvenile justice system continues to reach out to "help" children through the use of long term institutionalization and jailing. Even in those states where detaining youth for status offenses violates the law, judges have found a way to circumvent the law through contempt proceedings. That is, while a judge may not be able to jail a child for failing to attend school, judges are jailing youth after they hold them in contempt of court for failing to obey a court order to attend school. This practice underscores Lerman's contention that each reform movement results in the incarceration of more children, not less. And, because we do not have consistent policy statements, serious offenses can be treated much too lightly and trivial offenses much too seriously.

John Murray's "Status Offenders: Roles, Rules, and Reactions," addresses some of the policy issues raised by Lerman. Specifically, Murray examines the two opposing views on status offenders. Some contend that the behavior of the status offender is indicative of more serious problems in the future, and that the rejection of traditional authority will lead to situations that encourage delinquent behavior. Others contend that status offenders and delinquents are, in fact, quite different and that delinquency is not an inevitable consequence of participating in a status offense. Rather, status offenses are seen as the expression of a more extreme form of the traditional clash of parental and peer values. These conflicting perspectives have serious implications for the juvenile justice system. While Murray finds some contradictions in the research, he concludes that status offenders are different than delinquents. First, on the short term, status offenders who recidivate, tend to do so as repeat status offenders. Second, when there is evidence of escalation of offense pattern, status offenders tend to become misdemeanants rather than felons. Regardless of the research documenting differences between delinquents and status offenders, it is likely that history will prevail and there will be continued efforts to find mechanisms to deal harshly with status offenders. It is probably more important that status offenders have tested the authority of the home or the school than having done something that is injurious to others. We tend to assume that authority is exercised properly. That parents may be abusive, or that school officials may be dilatory in dealing with learning problems is seldom the issue. Instead, the focus is on disobedience and lack of respect by the students. The common sense extention of this perspective, of course, is that the inevitable outcome is delinquency, and probably serious delinquency. Having reached these conclusions, we invoke the very processes which will make certain our predictions come true. We then bring the status offender in contact with the delinquent and we accomplish something the youth probably could not have accomplished alone— the learning of delinquent value systems, techniques of neutralizing delinquent behaviors, and justifying the very behavior we complain so much about.

In "Violent Juveniles and Proposed Changes in Juvenile Justice: A Case of Overkill?" Richard Schuster examines another significant policy issue—the impact of reforms in the juvenile justice system on violent offenders. Schuster challenges the notion that there has been an increase in youthful violence. Rather, he points to media coverage and the extent to which it affects our perceptions of reality. Because of the perceived rise in violent crime, massive changes have been proposed in some state legislatures. Schuster argues that the commission of a violent offense does not necessarily indicate that the youth has a pattern of violent behavior. To the contrary, his research indicates that violent offenses make up only a small part of these youths' arrest records. The implications of Schusters' research are important. First, "violent youths" are more often "youths with a violent offense." Second, policy decisions based on media presentations which ignore the failures of juvenile justice systems in large cities, may result in reforms that are inappropriate for many other communities—or, a classic case of overkill. While care must be exercised in generalizing from Schuster's work to other cities, one cannot ignore the potential for new policy decisions based on myth, distorted perceptions and political demagoguery. This is not intended to lessen the seriousness of violent juvenile behavior. At the same time, it is important that public policy reflect the needs for correction rather than a disguised effort to compensate for bureaucratic inefficiency, inability of control agencies to deal with crime in general, and the general need to do something regardless of the outcome.

In the final chapter, M.A. Bortner examines the "Remand of Juveniles to Adult Court." The get-tough approach to handling juvenile offenders, which again became popular in the 1980s, led many states to change their statutes and make it easier to transfer troublesome youth to the adult system. It has been argued that such transfers are justified in order to protect the public from the most dangerous juvenile offenders. Bortner's examination of cases remanded to adult court challenges this belief. She finds that following their conviction in adult court, most transferred youth are released into the community on probation. Further, she argues they are not so much dangerous as intractable or difficult to treat. Often, waiving these youth to adult court is not done because it is in the best interest of the youth, but because it allows juvenile authorities to get rid of cases which raise questions about the effectiveness of the juvenile justice system.

1

Delinquency and Social Policy

A Historical Perspective

Paul Lerman

Delinquency Definition and the Ideal of Liberty

Many Americans, when they think about delinquency, probably conjure up an image of criminal behaviors. However, the actual American definition of delinquency, as revealed by our correctional practices and statutes, ever since the founding of the Plymouth Bay Colony, has always included other reasons for legally punishing or incarcerating youth.

As might be expected, the colonists used the law of their native land as a basis for forming an American response to wayward youth. According to English law, juveniles above the age of seven were subject to criminal statutes and sanctions; however, both in England and in the colonies, youth under fifteen were usually treated less severely than adults. Beginning about 1660, the laws of the Massachusetts colony began to invoke the criminal process to support adult authority. A preamble to one of the 1660 laws stated:

> It appeareth, by too much experience, that diverse children and servants doe behave themselves disobediently and disorderly, towards their parents, masters, and Governors....[1]

Based on a speech delivered Feb. 22, 1976, at Rutgers University, at the Conference on Juvenile Justice and Delinquency Prevention.

Paul Lerman, "Delinquency and Social Policy: A Historical Perspective," *Crime and Delinquency,* 23:4 (October 1977), pp. 383-393. Copyright © 1977 by Sage Publications, Inc. Reprinted by permission of Sage Publications, Inc.

The law gave a magistrate the power to summon before him "any such offender, and upon conviction of such misdemeanors,...sentence him to endure such corporal punishment, by whipping or otherwise, as in his judgment the merit of the fact shall deserve, not exceeding ten stripes for one offense."[2]

The laws of 1660 also made lying by children and failure to observe the Sabbath punishable offenses. Besides these laws, Massachusetts and other colonies had special laws regarding indentured servants and apprentices, so that masters could apply to the courts for measures to control youth who fornicated, contracted to marry, or gambled at cards or dice. In addition to these special restrictions on youth, juveniles were also subject to the Poor Laws which condemned idleness, begging, and vagrancy and used criminal penalties to enforce obedience.

These kinds of behaviors were included in the first attempt at a correctional definition of "delinquency" by the House of Refuge founded in 1825, the first institution specifically designed for juvenile offenders. In a memorial to the public appealing for funds, the Society for the Reformation of Juvenile Delinquents, the founding organization, stated:

> The design of the proposed institution is, to furnish, in the *first place,* an asylum, in which boys under a certain age, who become subject to the notice of our Police, either as vagrants, or houseless, or charged with petty crimes, may be received...[and] subjected to a course of treatment, that will afford a prompt and energetic corrective of their vicious propensities....[3]

New York legislation granted the institution a state charter and gave the self-perpetuating managers the right to "receive and take into the House of Refuge...all such children as shall be taken up or committed as vagrants, or convicted of criminal offenses...." Committing bodies could include judges, police magistrates, and the commissioner of the Almshouse and the Bridewell, providing the youth were "proper objects."[4] The New York legislature thereby concurred in the broad correctional definition set forth by the reformers in their public appeal.

In 1826 Boston established a House of Reformation for Juvenile Offenders. The incorporation act gave the House directors the power,

> ...at their discretion, to receive and take into said house all such children who shall be convicted of criminal offenses or taken up and committed under and by virtue of an act of this Commonwealth "for suppressing and punishing of rogues, vagabonds, common beggars, and other idle, disorderly and lewd persons," and who may...be proper objects therefor....[5]

Both the Boston and the New York statutes authorized the use of jails and prisons for youth who were not deemed "proper objects." However, by 1857, when the first national convention of refuge superintendents (from New York, Boston, Rochester, Cincinnati, Philadelphia, New Orleans, Baltimore, Pittsburgh, Chicago, and St. Louis) met in New York, there were seventeen juvenile reformatories, housing about 20,000 children admitted under policies and statutes that comprehended virtually every childhood misfortune.[6]

By the onset of the Civil War, a juvenile classified as a "proper object" of reformation could be covered by statutes that stemmed from three sources: (1) American adaptation of Elizabethan poor laws that covered idleness, begging, vagrancy, and destitution; (2) Puritan-inspired definitions of offenses peculiar to childhood and the apprentice status — in modern sociological language, juvenile status offenses; and (3) state adaptations of common-law criminal offenses. These three sources contributed, in actual correctional practice, to the lack of clear distinction between the problems of poverty, child welfare, and crime. In general, young America used the coercive power and punitive sanctions of the criminal law to handle many problems that were clearly noncriminal. In the nineteenth century, the reformatory performed the social functions of a juvenile almshouse, a workhouse, and a house of correction.

Sympathy for the plight of children whose fathers had been killed in the Civil War fostered a movement to build special asylums for poor and homeless youth, thereby diverting some youth from a reformatory experience. In addition, the "placing out" system, particularly in rural areas, was used to rescue children from "corrupting" living conditions. The spread of the free common schools also served to occupy some idle youth during the day. While these efforts may have diverted many idle and dependent youth from reformatories, the earlier statutes remained on the books in the older states, and the new Midwest and Western states, early in their statehood, enacted a broad correctional conception of delinquency through a variety of statutes that legitimated institutionalization in specific facilities.[7]

With the creation of the first juvenile court in Chicago, at the turn of the twentieth century, there was an attempt to codify existing Illinois statutes by adding a dependency and neglect category distinct from a criminal delinquency classification. In actual practice, however, distinctions among dependents, neglected children, status youth, and criminal offenders were often blurred: all categories could be — and actually were — detained in the same institution, even though the legislation and some judges gave a new emphasis to reforming "worthy" children in their own homes. The 1899 law, for example, made it possible for a youth to be held in detention or sent to a state training school if he was destitute; or if he was homeless, abandoned, or dependent; or if he had improper parental care; or if he was begging or receiving alms; or if he was living in a house of ill fame or with any vicious or disreputable person; or if he was in an unfit place.[8]

Following the lead of Illinois, other states also made certain that the jurisdiction of the court was sufficiently broad to encompass, as a "proper object" for detention or reformation in a training school, a broad array of poor law, juvenile status, and criminal characteristics. These broad terms were justified in 1901 by a Chicago child-saving committee, which urged that the legal definition of "condition of delinquency" be amended to include items that were implicit in the original dependency and neglect category or had been used in practice—"incorrigible"; "growing up in idleness and crime"; or "knowingly associating with thieves or vicious or immoral persons." The committee argued that "the amendment is intended to include all children that are in the need of government and care."[9] Since the use of local jails and prisons was forbidden, any separate juvenile correctional facility was deemed to be a place of government and care of the incorrigible and idle as well as a place of custody for the criminal offender. The reformers were successful in enacting a statutory definition of delinquency that had been implicit in practice for about 250 years.

The reformers believed that by deliberately equating the delinquent with any child "in need of government and care" they could use the police powers of the state to save children who might escape a narrow legal construction of dependency and neglect. To provide this control and care, they pushed through the legislature the creation of the first all-juvenile detention facilities, establishment of a truancy and parental school, provisions for paid probation officers, and state subsidies to existing religious institutions. They also initiated, before World War I, the creation of small pensions for worthy widows to allow them to keep their children at home. The court, with its broad jurisdictional boundaries, was primarily designed to serve the intake functions of a coercive welfare agency within the context of a modern juvenile quasi-criminal court.

Until the early 1960's, no statute in any state explicitly acknowledged the legal or correctional difference between status offenders and criminal offenders. About fifteen years ago a new legal category, Person in Need of Supervision, known as PINS, was created in New York and California as a noncriminal basis of juvenile court jurisdiction, distinct from a narrower definition of dependency and child neglect. By 1974 thirty-four states distinguished between criminal-type delinquency and at least some of the status offenses, but only eleven states explicitly prohibited institutionalizing status offenders in state training schools that housed criminal offenders.

The movement to remove the vestiges of Poor Law and juvenile status characteristics from the correctional definition of "delinquency" recently received added support from the federal Juvenile Justice and Delinquency Prevention Act of 1974. A state receiving block grants under the Act must give assurance that, within a specified time, no status offender will be detained in or committed to an institution set up explicitly for criminal delinquents. While this movement to narrow the boundaries of delinquency definitions and practices is laudable, whether youth will actually fare better under the new labels is still uncertain. Recent evidence indicates that PINS youth are more likely than delinquent youth to be detained in a facility as part of their court processing, are detained longer, and, if institutionalized, stay for longer periods. Whether American can learn to treat all arrested truant, idle, incorrigible, promiscuous, and runaway youth less harshly than their truly delinquent brothers and sisters is still uncertain at this time.[10]. In a country that prizes the ideal of liberty, it is ironic that youth can still lose their freedom so easily, and for such lengthy periods, for behaviors that are clearly not criminal and that would not even be admitted before an adult criminal court.

Delinquency and Justice for All

The evidence that noncriminal delinquents can be, have been, and are dealt with harshly is related to another American theme, "justice for all." Since 1824, when the House of Refuge was empowered to institutionalize a variety of youth—without distinction between the criminal and the non-criminal—for indeterminate periods, American juvenile laws and practices have flouted two basic components of a reasonable conception of justice: (1) Any deprivation of liberty, or other state-imposed penalty, should be graded proportionately to the degree of social harm a person has done or clearly threatens to do to members of a community. (2) Offenses or harms that are comparable should be dealt with by punishments that are equal.[11]

Before the Revolution of 1776, juveniles were treated like adults. In the reform legislation that swept the former colonies immediately after the War of Independence, imprisonment and fines replaced the pillory, the stocks, and other forms of corporal punishment. Borrowing ideas from European classical criminology (associated with Beccaria) and the general environment of the Enlightenment, Americans reformed their criminal codes with the aim of securing equality of judicial handling. Children benefited from these reforms, even though they were also thrust into the same local jails and prisons as adults.[12]

About 1820, when the House of Refuge was under discussion administrators of the local Bridewell were trying to separate youth from adults during the day, furnish some in-jail instruction in reading and writing, and care differently for their younger charges.[13] According to the keeper of the Bridewell, the period of confinement ranged from a few days to a year or more, with many remaining several months. Though the charges were mainly for "trifling offenses," many remained longer than customary "because of a want of residence."[14]

Instead of seeking residences for the vagrant, apprenticeships for the un-employed, and schools for the ignorant, the Society for the Reformation of Juvenile Delinquents decided to attack the problems of child welfare, poverty, and delinquency with a new social invention—an all-purpose workhouse and reformatory designed to reshape moral character coercively and render children obedient to their superiors. Only after a child had met the strict reform standards of the Refuge superintendent—during a stay ranging from a year to three years—would he be bound out as a laboring apprentice or sent out on a whaling ship. The reformers argued that agents of government should be the "fathers of the people," should "stand towards the community in the moral light of guardians of virtue."[15] In carrying out their guardianship inside the Refuge, they were not reluctant to use the stripes, solitary confinement, bread and water, and other correctional penalties.

In exchange for receiving a new and quite punitive "father," juveniles gave up their traditional rights under criminal law. Commitment to the Refuge meant that vagrancy and "trifling offenses" could be dealt with the same as more serious offenses since they could be viewed as signs of "vicious propensities." Many resolutions were proposed at the first national convention of House of Refuge superintendents in 1857 but only one was chosen for adoption—for fear of stifling any autonomous correctional initiatives. Not surprisingly, the superintendents agreed that they should have "unqualified control over the treatment and disposition of inmates for the length of their minority."[16] Children were deprived of legal restraints on the type, degree, and duration of punishment that agents of government could impose, and all parental rights were abrogated for the duration of the child's minority. In many cases, parents did not even know where youth had been placed after a long stay at Refuge.

Juvenile court legislation at the turn of the twentieth century continued this tradition of deliberately refraining from establishing any definition of degrees of delinquency or limits on the type, degree, and duration of penalties. While the indeterminate sentence has, in some jurisdictions, given way to eighteen-month renewable placements (or sentences) or three-year dispositions, no state has enacted legislation that limits its power in accordance with traditional norms of justice.

The historical legacy continues to confound the handling of juvenile status and trivial, petty offenders, the bulk of the delinquency population, and it neutralizes the common-sense moral distinction made by most Americans when they compare the harm done by a mugger of the elderly to a shoplifting spree at a local store. We have devised a system where the serious offense can be treated much too lightly and the trivial much too seriously. We now have 150 years of evidence that relinquishing substantive justice in exchange for a correctional regime that does not correct is a bad bargain. Even if our institutional programs were effective, one could still argue that just dispositions should take precedence over efforts at reformation. Recognition of the legal and moral concept of degrees of criminal delinquency could promote the ideal of "justice for all," including children.

The Modern Social Control System: The Ideal and the Actual

The overreach of the delinquency definition and the failure to specify degrees of offense highlight the profound discrepancy between formal declarations of liberty and justice and our societal practices. This disparity between the ideal and the actual deserves to be examined further, since the current degree of discrepancy tells us a good deal about the modern American approach to controlling, regulating, and treating delinquency.

Enforcement of the law in America is local and has always varied in scope and degree. As a result, many youthful misbehaviors have been either overlooked by police or ignored by judges. In practice, police and judges have exercised discretion in softening the breadth and harshness of our laws. Until recently, reformers were usually not satisfied with this tendency toward underenforcement since identifying, correcting, and reforming youth at the earliest possible age was deemed important. The founders of the House of Refuge complained that local judges were reluctant to convict youth because they were unwilling to mix the young with older, hardened criminals. Seventy-five years later, when the modern juvenile justice system was created in Chicago, reformers complained that judges were reluctant to correct youth because they had to send youngsters to jails pending disposition of their cases. If the laws were not strictly enforced how could "guardians of virtue" become "fathers of the people" or take legal control of all children "in need of government and care"?

Both of these important movements in juvenile reform, the refuge movement and juvenile court movement, did help to separate youth from workhouse and criminal adults. But in the process of doing this, they created new forms of broad social control over youth. It is quite likely that *more* youth were incarcerated *after* each reform than *before* it. The Refuge Movement founders were the initiators of our reformatories, industrial and training schools, truancy and parental schools, and other *long-term* juvenile correctional facilities. The juvenile court movement founders were the initiators of *short-term* detention facilities, where youth could be properly studied and governed before a determination of whether they needed longer government and care.

Given the breadth of our nation's definition of juvenile delinquency and a continual growth in youth population, the juvenile court's available resources were continually strained to meet the demand for coercive child-saving. Underenforcement, informal adjustment of cases, and high probation caseloads were adaptive mechanisms utilized to deal with the fundamental problems of a potentially limitless demand for reformation of the young and the limited supply of resources. Other aids to the overburdened juvenile social control system were inadvertently provided in the support programs of Aid to Dependent Children, mental health, and child welfare, which siphoned off Poor Law and juvenile status offenders who comprised part of the potential "delinquent" population. States and counties, of course, have varied in their use of alternative resources and underenforcement mechanisms, so that many juvenile facilities still house a mixed population of delinquent, dependent, neglected, and status offense children.

Accompanying all of these diverse trends have been assertions by correctional leaders that we have moved progressively from a policy of revenge and restraint to rehabilitation and reintegration of the juvenile offender. Some academics also have given support to this assessment.[17] Unfortunately, the dispartiy between these lofty intentions and actual practice is much greater than we have wished to believe. In 1967 the nation was presented with the results of the first nation-wide study of correction. The data provide a means of understanding how our juvenile policy operates from a national perspective.[18]

The figures of this national study clearly indicate that about *one-half* of the youth formally reported as arrested by local police departments were not sent to court — these cases were informally adjusted by the police. However, approximately *two-thirds* of arrested youth experienced a detention lockup for an average stay of twelve days. This means, of course, that more youth were detained than appeared on an official court calendar to have the charges formally assessed. The number of detention lockups surpassed the number of children appearing in court and the number receiving probation treatment. We can reasonably infer that *short-term restraint* (social control), not rehabilitative and reintegrative service, is the actual dominant public policy response toward youth.

This dominance of community-based institutionalization was first measured with 1965 data. However, it could not have occurred without the intervention of a new social control device, the specially constructed local juvenile detention facility associated with the rise of the juvenile court. This multipurpose facility has a variety of euphemistic names — reception center, diagnostic clinic, juvenile hall, and receiving home — but its essential quality is quite familiar to youth: it is a juvenile version of the local jail.

Recent data suggest that a greater emphasis on due process inside the courtroom and a verbal commitment to diversion and community-based programs have not halted the growth and reliance on detention lockups. A recently completed survey conducted by Rosemary Sarri and her team of University of Michigan researchers disclosed that in 1973 at least 100,000 children spend at least one day in an adult jail and that nearly 500,000 other youth were admitted to local detention facilities[19] — an increase of 50 per cent over the 1965 figure, much more than the growth in the youth population facing the risk of detention.

A recent study offers some clues to the difficulty of trying to reverse the steady rise in local detention rates. In 1967, the chief judge of the Cuyahoga County (Cleveland, Ohio) juvenile court launched a determined effort to reduce detention. He comments about his efforts as follows:

> Social workers, probation officers and police officers, who had previously for all practical purposes made the decision as to the necessity of detaining the child, reacted strenuously to our screening process....
>
> Naturally, these criticisms, those from within the court and more especially those from outside agencies, militated against acceptance of our new policy....
>
> The social agencies which staunchly proclaimed their non-punitive philosophy wanted us to detain children as part of their "treatment" process....
>
> Helpful in discouraging one of the social agencies from the overuse of detention was our new requirement that an official complaint must be filed concerning each child placed in the detention home....
>
> It had been a common practice for a probation officer to place a child in detention who was uncooperative, who failed to keep appointments, who truanted from school, or who, upon a complaint of the parents, was considered out of control at home.... The 380 children admitted by probation officers in 1967 was reduced to 125 in 1971, a reduction of 60 percent....
>
> As we began our initial effort to reduce population, we found that many children were being detained, awaiting acceptance by various state, county, and private facilities who, often arbitrarily and for their own convenience, imposed quotas and admission requirements on the court.[20]

This unusually frank report indicates that detention can be used as a multi-purpose resource for a variety of arbitrary social control and administrative reasons. For three years (1967-69) Judge Whitlatch was unable to demonstrate empirically that the chief judge could administratively regulate the use of detention by police, probation officers, treatment agencies, and correctional organizations. Finally, in 1970 and 1971, his detention reduction policy began to show signs of success — particularly with police and his own probation staff. However, a separate reading of the 1971 Annual Report of the Cuyahoga County Court reveals that more local youth still received detention compared to formal probation — 3,439 to 2,387.[21]

Summary and Conclusions

We continue to compound the original delinquency problem by permitting systems of juvenile control to expand under broad laws that operate under arbitrary discretionary standards. Many of the standards and the outcomes appear unreasonable and unjust when subjected to close scrutiny. Left to operate according to the unstated policy, the system tends to result in a dominance of social control. Merely adding more fiscal and organizational resources to the existing system — as during the last decade — can only further the relative dominance of social control over efforts at treatment. This incremental policy of merely adding more resources has resulted in excessive expense — in both dollars and social values — without offsetting benefits.

During the first seventy-five years of this century, we created a modern juvenile control system to regulate the conduct and character of America's youth. We accomplished this while believing that we were primarily engaged in saving or rehabilitating youth. The image of a nonrestraining society was set forth while we constructed new institutions that were classified as detention facilities, residential schools, diagnostic centers, and reception clinics. During this time we also created probation and other less coercive services, but the dominance of our continued reliance on institutionalization is clearly revealed by national and state data. In the last quarter of this century will we continue to maintain the discrepancy between reality and our intentions or will we begin the troublesome task of determining where arbitrary social control ends and justice and non-coercive help begin?

Footnotes

[1] Joseph M. Hawes, *Children in Urban Society: Juvenile Delinquency in Nineteenth Century America* (New York: Oxford University Press, 1971), p. 14.

[2] *Id.,* p. 41.

[3] Society for the Reformation of Juvenile Delinquents, *House of Refuge Documents* (New York: Mahlon Day, 1832), p. 21. Hereafter cited as *Refuge Documents.*

[4] Hawes, *op cit. supra* note 1, p. 41; Robert S. Pickett, *House of Refuge* (Syracuse, N.Y.: Syracuse University Press, 1969), p. 58.

[5] R.H. Bremner, J. Barnard, T.K. Hareven, and R.M. Mennel, *Children and Youth in America: A Documentary History,* 2 vols. (Cambridge, Mass.: Harvard University Press, 1970), Vol. I, p. 681.

[6] David Rothman, *The Discovery of the Asylum* (Boston: Little, Brown, 1971), p. 209.

[7] Bremner et al., *op. cit. supra* note 5, Vols. I, II.

[8] *Id.,* Vol. II, p. 507.

[9] Hawes, *op. cit. supra* note 1, p. 185.

[10] P. Lerman, "Child Convicts," *TransAction,* July-August 1971, pp. 35-44, 72.

[11] P. Lerman, "Beyond *Gault*: Injustice and the Child," in Paul Lerman, ed., *Delinquency and Social Policy* (New York: Praeger, 1970), p. 237.

[12] Rothman, *op. cit. supra* note 6, pp. 30-57.

[13]Pickett, *op. cit. supra* note 4, p. 57.

[14]*Refuge Documents, op. cit. supra* note 3, p. 15.

[15]*Id.,* p. 13.

[16]Rothman, *op. cit. supra* note 6, p. 293.

[17]L.T. Empey, *Alternatives to Incarceration* (Washington, D.C.: U.S. Dept. of Health, Education and Welfare, 1967).

[18]President's Commission on Law Enforcement and Administration of Justice, *Task Force Report: Corrections* (Washington, D.C.: U.S. Govt. Printing Office, 1967), pp. 121, 129.

[19]*Youth Reporter* (monthly newsletter, Youth Development Office, U.S. Dept. of Health, Education and Welfare), November 1973, p. 2.

[20]W.C. Whitlatch, "Practical Aspects of Reducing Detention Home Population," *Juvenile Justice,* August 1973, pp. 21, 22, 23.

[21]*Cuyahoga County Juvenile Court Annual Report,* 1971, pp. 26-27.

[22]Lerman, *supra* note 10.

2

Status Offenders
Roles, Rules, and Reactions

John P. Murray

Context

Status offenders are youngsters who have been brought to the notice of the courts or police because they have engaged in behavior which, although not illegal for adults, is proscribed for juveniles. Behavior such as truancy, running away from home, or being ungovernable, as well as other specific acts such as drinking or curfew violations are perhaps the more common examples. The judicial labels attached to status offenders include "Persons in Need of Supervision" (PINS), "Minors in Need of Supervision" (MINS), or "Children in Need of Supervision" (CHINS). In each instance, however, the relevant state statute defines a set of behavioral categories that are considered sufficiently worrisome to warrant intervention. For example, the New York State Family Court Act defines a "person in need of supervision" as:

> A male less than 16 years of age and a female less than 18 years of age who does not attend school in accord with the provisions of Part I, Article 65, of the Education Law, or who is incorrigible, ungovernable, or habitually disobedient and beyond the lawful control of the parent or other lawful authority, or who violates the provisions of Sec. 221.05 (Unlawful Possession of Marijuana) of the penal law.

1983 Status Offenders: A Sourcebook. Reprinted by permission of Boys Town Center.

The New York state law is similar to one in force in California which states that "any person under the age of 18 years who persistently or habitually refuses to obey the reasonable and proper orders or directions of his parents, guardian, custodian, or school authorities, or who is beyond the control of such person... is within the jurisdiction of the juvenile court which may adjudge such person to be a ward of the court." (The California act originally included the broad mandate "...or who from any cause is in danger of leading an idle, dissolute, lewd, or immoral life..." but this was repealed in 1976.)

The New York and California statutes are examples of fairly recent revisions of laws relating to status offenders. Earlier laws, such as that enforced in South Dakota until 1968, were even more specific about activities that could bring the youngster within the purview of the juvenile court. For example, proscribed activities in South Dakota included patronizing a public poolroom where the game of billiards or pool was being carried on for pay or hire; habitually wandering around any railroad yards or tracks; smoking cigarettes or using tobacco in any form; writing or using vile, obscene, vulgar, profane, or indecent language; or being guilty of indecent, immoral, or lascivious conduct.

Characteristics

What are the behaviors and the characteristics of the youngsters who are alleged to be status offenders? A recent study of the New York City Family Court (Weisbrod, 1981) included a factor analysis of the reasons given for petitioning the family court to intervene in the lives of young persons and found five main factors: One category was called "out late," which included cases of staying out late at night or keeping late hours, disobedience, or incorrigibility; the second was called "away for sex," and included cases of running away and sexual acting out allegations; the third factor was a cluster of activities called "out-of-control," such as stealing from the home and in general being in need of supervision; the fourth factor was named "drug set" and included cases of drug use and allegations of undesirable companions; and the final category covered allegations of truancy. The researchers found that age, sex, ethnic background, and family structure differentiate these five categories of PINS petitions:

> *Out-late.* The youngsters in this category were likely to be living in households with mother only, and in which no one was employed and where the residents were dependent upon public assistance. There were no age, sex, or ethnic differences in comparing this subcategory to the total sample of PINS.

A way-for-sex. These youths tended to be younger than those in the other categories (24% were 13 years old compared to only 17% in other PINS offense categories). This charge was primarily brought against girls (71% female in this category versus 42% female in the general sample). Moreover, there was a heavy representation of Spanish surname juveniles in the away-for-sex cases (54%).

Out-of-control. The youngsters in this category were younger (10% under 12) and were more likely to be black (57%) and male (69%) than in the general sample of status offenders. In addition, they were more likely to live with their mothers only and less likely to live in households where no one was employed.

Drug set. The "drug set" cases were much older than the other PINS groups (52% were 15 years old, 84% were 14 or over). There were no sex or ethnic differences in this category compared to other categories, but these youngsters were slightly more likely to live in a household with only the mother.

Truancy. Finally, the "truancy" cases, when compared with the general sample of status offenders, were more likely to be male (58% versus 42% in the general PINS sample) and white (16.5% versus 11% general). Moreover, truancy allegations were less likely to be brought against Hispanics (39% versus 44% general), and the families were more likely to be intact (23% versus 19% general).

Other studies have focused upon particular subgroups of status offenders, such as runaways, and have found that while these are problem youngsters in conflict with their families, they may not be extremely deviant in comparison with other adolescents. For example, Miller and his associates (Miller, Miller, Hoffman, & Duggan, 1980) found that about 13% of a general sample of high school youth had run away from home and returned while another 20% had considered running away at some time. They also found that the phenomenon of running away is not limited to any one socioeconomic or ethnic group. National surveys, such as that conducted by Brennan (1978), found that the typical runaway is likely to be between the ages of 15 and 17 (80%) and that boys (53%) outnumber girls.

Are Status Offenders Similar to Delinquents?

There is perhaps no more central — and controversial — issue in the policy debate about status offenders than the relationship between status offenders and delinquents.

Some jurists and social scientists feel that youngsters who are truant, ungovernable, or respond to difficult family situations by running away are rejecting the traditional authority of home or school. This rejection of authority, they assert, may in itself lead to more serious forms of misbehavior. Additionally, youngsters who are bereft of adequate parental or educational supervision as a consequence of running away or truancy may simply find themselves in situations that encourage delinquent behavior.

On the other hand, those researchers and others in the juvenile justice system who feel that status offenders and delinquents are quite different, argue that status offenders have more in common with the typical adolescent than with the youngster who engages in serious criminal behavior. They note that adolescence is a time when young people are sorting out their values, social roles, and lifestyles and, not uncommonly, experiencing some conflict with authority figures, be they parents or principals. At worst, they assert, status offenders may be expressing only a more extreme form of the traditional clash of parental and peer values.

These two opposing views of status offenders have quite serious implications for the ways in which the juvenile justice system might respond to such youngsters. If it is accurate to suggest that status offenders are at-risk for becoming delinquent — or perhaps are actually predelinquent — then it would seem logical to recommend early intervention to prevent more serious misbehavior. Moreover, this intervention might be best directed by the juvenile court since it is the agency charged with responsibility for delinquent youths. On the other hand, some jurists have argued that even in this instance, the "rule of law" would not authorize the juvenile court to intervene in predelinquency. However, the issue becomes even more complicated if one adopts the view that status offenders are manifesting family-based conflicts that are not likely to escalate into serious or delinquent acts. In this latter case, the nature of the intervention and the agency best suited to the task become a major point of discussion.

In order to evaluate these conflicting views of the nature of status offenders, it is helpful to review the background characteristics and offense patterns of these youngsters. In doing so, it will be apparent that various types of research offer differing insights.

Background Characteristics

In order to understand the nature of the relationships between status offenders and delinquents, it is useful to begin with an analysis of the demographic characteristics of youngsters who are clearly involved in the juvenile justice system (those identified in offender studies) and then contrast this description with one that emerges from studies of nonoffender populations (Epidemiological or Cohort studies).

Offender Studies

It is a truism that youngsters who become involved in the juvenile justice system tend to be drawn disproportionately from families with fewer economic and social resources. However, it is still relevant to ask whether the delinquents and status offenders who are so involved come from different backgrounds. The major demographic markers of interest are age, sex, ethnicity, and family structure.

Age. With regard to age, the three studies that provide comparable information for status offenders and delinquents (South Carolina, Staten Island, and New York-KMBQ) suggest that the status offenders included in these studies might be slightly younger than the delinquents. For example, among the 5,700 youngsters in the South Carolina study, the modal age for status offenders is 15 while the modal age for delinquents is 16. Similarly, the modal ages for status offenders and delinquents in the Staten Island study were 15 and 16 respectively. In the New York-KMBQ study, the average age for status offenders was 13 years 7 months and for delinquents 13 years 10 months.

Sex. Differences in the ratio of males to females represented in the status offender category were minimal in all sample locations with the exception of Chicago where females accounted for 61% of those charged with status offenses. However, in all three geographic areas of the country, delinquents were predominantly male. This is more true in New York City where males accounted for between 86% and 92% of the delinquent charges, but the pattern is also evident in Chicago and South Carolina where males accounted for 76% and 60%, respectively, of the delinquents studied.

Ethnicity. Differences in ethnic composition are more difficult to evaluate in this collection of studies because differential court involvement of various ethnic groups is, in part, dependent upon the ethnic composition of the particular community. However, in the Brooklyn and Bronx New York Family Court study, white youngsters were involved in only about 9% of the delinquent and status offender cases although whites account for 53% of the population of these boroughs. On the other hand, blacks and Hispanics who make up only 47% of the population account for more than 90% of the delinquent and status offense cases. Moreover, within these geographic areas and ethnic groups, there seems to be a tendency for Hispanics to become involved in status offenses more often than delinquency. One of the researchers (Weisbrod, 1981) noted that the ethnic differences may be linked to sex differences in that Hispanic parents are more likely to ask the juvenile court to intervene in behalf of their daughters to control sexual activity (a status offense charge of ungovernable).

Family. These data suggest that status offenders are more likely to come from single-parent families while delinquents are more likely to be drawn from two-parent, intact families. However, the preponderance of both status offenders and delinquents come from other than two-parent families. This is but another way of stating the obvious finding that youngsters involved with the juvenile court tend to be drawn disproportionately from families under stress.

Personality. In addition to the broad surveys of large courts described above, several smaller and more specialized studies have compared the characteristics of delinquents and status offenders who were referred for psychological services by the court or probation department. One study (Hays, Solway, & Schreiner, 1978) evaluated the intellectual characteristics of 15- to 16-year-olds who were adjudicated murderers or petitioned status offenders and found that the 39 status offenders were significantly brighter than the 25 juvenile murderers.

A second study (Fjeld, Newsom, & Fjeld, 1981) evaluated 92 of the 198 youngsters referred for psychological services by the Hamilton County Juvenile Court in Chattanooga, Tennessee, during 1975-1976. The youngsters were selected for study if they were 13 years or older, had lived in the court's area for at least six months, could read at the sixth grade level or better, and had an IQ greater than 80. Most of the 106 who were excluded from the study were rejected because of low intelligence and poor reading ability. The 92 cases accepted and 106 rejected were only a subset of the 1,000 cases screened by the court during the study period. Nevertheless, the pattern of findings in this highly selected sample is similar to that described in more extensive court populations: Males were more likely to be delinquent while females were more likely to be status offenders, and status offenders were both brighter and younger than delinquents.

It seems likely that there are some recurring differences in the backgrounds and life circumstances of status offenders and delinquents. For example, in the case of delinquents, regardless of single- or two-parent family structure, they *do* have a family to which they may return. For status offenders, it is often the case that the parent or parents have initiated the court or police action and so these youthful "runaways, truants or ungovernables" are in double jeopardy—out of favor with the law and out of favor with their families.

Questions about the background characteristics of status offenders are important because they have implications for the way in which these youngsters might best be served. But, an equally important question is whether these background differences are paralleled in differential patterns of criminal and noncriminal offenses.

Offense Patterns

Analyses of the offense patterns of status offenders and delinquents have been focused upon two major issues: recidivism rates and "escalation" in seriousness from initial to subsequent offenses. Some who feel that status offenders are different from delinquents suggest that there is very little escalation in the offense patterns of status offenders and, correspondingly, very little "de-escalation" in the offenses of delinquents. Conversely, those who feel that status offenders are similar to delinquents are concerned about the recidivism rates of the two groups and predict that, over time, status offenders will escalate their acts into delinquent offenses. Of course, these two predictions may not be mutually exclusive in that those youngsters who have repeated involvement with the police and courts may comprise a group that is quite different from the once-only offenders, whether they be status or delinquent.

In order to evaluate these conflicting claims, information is again needed from studies that provide baseline rates on status and delinquent acts as well as studies that track the offense careers of youngsters involved in the juvenile justice system.

Recidivism and Escalation

The claim that status offenders have comprised a sizeable number of the clientele of juvenile courts and probation offices seems indisputable. The corollary claim that status offenders are so prevalent because they come back so often, stay so long, and become more nasty over time is one that needs closer examination.

One of the earlier studies that compared the offense patterns of status offenders and delinquents is Thomas' (1976) review of the court records of 2,092 youth brought before the Portsmouth and Virginia Beach juvenile courts during 1970-1974. The researcher was able to track the youngsters' "progress" through the juvenile justice system in terms of repeated court appearances during the five-year study period. In particular, Thomas was interested in recidivism rates and types of repeated offenses for youths charged with status offenses, misdemeanors, or felonies.

Thomas found that the most frequent initial charge was that of misdemeanor (1,053 or 50.3% of the sample) followed by status offense (572 or 27.3%) and felony (467 or 23.3%). In addition, he found that there were clear differences in the likelihood that these three types of offenders would reappear in the court records. Although only about 28% of the total sample returned to court at least once, those initially charged with a status offense had a recidivism rate of 38% followed by felons (32%) and those arrested for misdemeanors (22%). Over the subsequent five years, Thomas was able to track the young offenders through as many as three court appearances and thus evaluate the "progress" of youngsters whose first contact with the juvenile justice system was for a status offense rather than a delinquent charge. Thomas titled his report "Are Status Offenders Really

So Different?'' and his short answer was, "no." However, other studies, and Thomas' own data, raise serious questions about the adequacy of the "no difference" hypothesis.

Other studies provide even more compelling evidence that status offenders are different from serious delinquents. For example, Clarke (1975) reanalyzed some findings from the longitudinal study of a Philadelphia birth cohort (Wolfgang, Figlio, & Sellin, 1972) in an effort to assess recidivism, chronicity, and seriousness of offenses for youths initially charged with status offenses as opposed to serious or non-serious delinquency. About 35% of the almost 10,000 males included in the study acquired a police record during the study period covering their 10th to 18th birthdays. The three main classes of offenses were: Status offense (truancy, running away, disobedient at home); Other NonIndex offense (sex offenses, liquor law and traffic violations, disorderly conduct); and Index offense (serious offenses against persons or property).

The results of this analysis suggest that status offenders are among the least likely to become recidivists. Similarly, first-time Status youngsters were the least likely to become chronic offenders. The mean number of serious criminal offenses (Index offenses) and the mean cumulative seriousness scores were far lower for the first-time Status offenders than for either NonIndex or Index offenders. This pattern of findings was similar for both white and nonwhite males although the levels of police involvement were higher for nonwhite youth.

A more recent study (Kobrin, Hellum, & Peterson, 1980; Kobrin & Klein, 1982) provides an even more differentiated picture of status and delinquent youths. In the course of evaluating the effectiveness of diversion programs for juvenile status offenders, Kobrin and his colleagues assembled a sample of more than 3,000 youngsters from eight locations around the country. Each youngster had been brought to the attention of the police or juvenile court for the commission of a status offense during a one-year period. The youths were included in the study regardless of prior offense records (although there was some variation in selection across study locations) and were followed for a six- to 12-month period to evaluate subsequent offense patterns. In addition, a search of police and court records was conducted to assess prior offense patterns.

Of the 3,017 youngsters, 1,567 (52%) had no prior offense, while 2,073 (69%) had no subsequent offenses. Almost half of the sample (43%) were once-only status offenders. The recidivism rate for first-time offenders in this study (subsequent status and delinquent/mixed offenses as a percentage of the none prior) was about 17%. The recidivism rate for repeat status offenders was 43% (subsequent status and delinquent/mixed offenses as a percentage of prior status only offenses) while the recidivism rate for repeat delinquent/mixed youngsters was 48% (subsequent status and delinquent/mixed as a percentage of prior delinquent and mixed).

Beyond the issue of recidivism, however, is the major question of escalation of offenses, the development of delinquent careers in these status offenders. In order to examine the escalation hypothesis, we need to exclude those who did not have any subsequent offenses recorded against them. To examine the careers of hard-core repeat offenders, we might also exclude the youngsters who had no prior offenses. Of those whose prior offenses were status offenses, 55% (80) return as status offenders; for those whose prior offenses were delinquent or mixed, 71% (378) return as delinquent or mixed offenders. Thus, while there may be some shifting of offenses for first-time offenders, among recidivists there is evidence of reduced escalation and increased specialization of offense careers.

A longer term study of recidivism rates and offense patterns of youthful offenders is provided by an analysis of 2,574 youths committed to the Georgia Department of Youth Services (Scanlon & Webb, 1981). The researchers followed the offense careers of these youngsters by monitoring entry into the Georgia adult prisons during the period 1975 to 1980. Some of the main findings were that 26% of the juvenile offenders became adult offenders, but only 6% of the 680 recidivists were originally juvenile status offenders.

Summary

The offense patterns of status offenders, misdemeanants, and delinquents can be differentiated in terms of the frequency and nature of subsequent offenses.

Studies that have attempted to evaluate the scope of the status offender problem for courts, police, and social service agencies have generally found that misdemeanants and serious delinquents are by far the more numerous and compelling clients of these agencies. For example, the FBI Uniform Crime Reports for 1975 indicate that status offenders accounted for only 15% of all arrests, compared with 46% misdemeanants and 39% serious delinquents. Similarly, longitudinal studies in Philadelphia found that status offenders accounted for only 23% of the youngsters who attained a police record during their teens.

At the same time, studies of self-reported involvement in status offenses have found that upwards of 90% of the youngsters admit to engaging in behavior which would be considered a status offense if known to police or courts. Thus, status offense behavior may be quite common during adolescence. Of course, in their more extreme forms, these actions can bring the youngster into serious conflict with authorities in a manner that accounts for more than one-quarter of the juvenile court caseload.

Are status offenders worth the effort of intervention by the court or other agencies? This is but another way of asking about the seriousness of status offenses—do status offenders re-enter the juvenile justice system, do they escalate their acts to more serious delinquency, and is it necessary to intervene through the courts? Available evidence suggests that status offenders do re-enter the system with recidivism rates ranging from a low of 17% to upwards of 50%. Those who exhibit noncriminal behavior continue to be a problem for the police and courts because they return so often.

But, do they return in a more worrisome way—do status offenders escalate into delinquents? The answers are mixed, but at least in the short term, status offenders who do recidivate tend to do so as repeat status offenders. Where there is evidence of escalation, it is usually status offenders becoming misdemeanants rather than felons. For example, the study of youths entering the Georgia adult prison system found that those whose juvenile offenses consisted of status or alcohol/drug offenses engaged in the least serious adult crimes.

Is intervention necessary? Whether and how to intervene in the lives of status offenders will be discussed in the next section. However, it seems clear that there is a need to reevaluate the allocation of the limited resources of the juvenile justice system. Although status offenders *are* worth the effort, as are all troubled youth, perhaps they need a different type of effort.

References

Clarke, S.H., "Some implications for North Carolina of recent research in juvenile delinquency," *Journal of Research in Crime and Delinquency,* 12(1): 51-60, (1975).

Fjeld, S.P., Newsom, L., and Fjeld, R.M., "Delinquents and status offenders—The similarity of differences," *Juvenile and Family Court Journal,* 32(2): 3-10, (1981).

Hays, J.R., Solway, K.S., and Schreiner, D., "Intellectual characteristics of juvenile murderers versus status offenders," *Psychological Reports,* 43(1): 80-82, (1978).

Kobrin, S., and Klein, M.W., *National Evaluation of the Deinstitutionalization of Status Offender Programs,* Vols. 1 and 2, Washington, D.C.: United States Department of Justice, (1982).

Kobrin, S., Hellum, F.R., and Peterson, J.W., "Offense patterns of status offenders," in D. Shichor and D. Kelly (Eds.), *Critical Issues in Juvenile Delinquency,* Lexington, MA: Lexington Books, (1980).

Miller, D.L., Miller, D., Hoffman, F., and Duggan, R., *Runaways—Illegal Aliens in Their Own Land: Implications for Service,* New York: Praeger Publishers, (1980).

Scanlon, J.R., and Webb, L., "Juvenile offenders who become adult criminals," *Criminal Justice Review,* 6(1): 1-5, (1981).

Thomas, C.W., "Are status offenders really so different? A comparative and longitudinal assessment," *Crime and Delinquency,* 22(4): 438-455, (1976).

Weisbrod, J.A., *Family Court Disposition Study,* New York: Vera Institute of Justice, (1981).

Wolfgang, M.E., Figlio, R.M., and Sellin, T. *Delinquency in a Birth Cohort,* Chicago: University of Chicago Press, (1972).

3

Violent Juveniles and Proposed Changes in Juvenile Justice
A Case of Overkill?

Richard L. Schuster

"Crime in the streets" is a theme that permeates our image of modern urban America. Opinion polls have shown that the vast majority of respondents felt that crime has been increasing and many said that major personal crimes (violent crimes) were a major factor in the rise of national crime.[1] Uniform Crime Report statistics confirm the public perception of rising violent crime. In addition, the news media has presented Americans with the image of violence as perpetrated by a violent delinquent who is a breed apart from earlier generations in their willingness to engage in wanton and vicious personal attacks.[2] The rise of juvenile violence and especially the exploits of urban gangs was a common lament of the media in the 1970s.[3] However, doubt exists concerning the "true" extent of juvenile violence in America. In a recent review of the data and literature on the subject, Doleschal and Newton conclude: "The perceived increase in youthful violence in the United States today appears to stem from the interest by the mass media in the problem of crime rather than to reflect any real increases."[4]

Unfortunately, *perceptions* of reality are often more important than

Richard L. Schuster, "Violent Juveniles and Proposed Changes in Juvenile Justice: A Case of Overkill?", *Juvenile and Family Court Journal,* November, 1982. Reprinted with permission.

reality itself. Because of the perceived rise in juvenile crime, especially violent crime, state legislatures have proposed, and in some cases, passed, legislation that would dramatically alter the juvenile courts and/or the juvenile justice system.[5] These "reforms" are generally aimed at treating juvenile offenders more like adult offenders. Some of the more common proposals are: the elimination of confidentiality of juvenile records; the imposition of equal sentences for adults and juveniles charged with the same kind of crime; the elimination of juvenile court jurisdiction for specified offenses; the lowering of the maximum age for juvenile court jurisdiction; the raising of the maximum age to which a juvenile may be kept in a juvenile institution; the use of adult institutions for sentencing; and the transfer of the authority to file waiver petitions from the juvenile court judge to the district attorney's office.

The assumption of many of these "reforms" is that serious juvenile offenses, especially violent offenses, would be curbed by reducing what is seen as the "protection" and "coddling" of heinous offenders by the juvenile courts. This would be accomplished by placing juveniles into the adult criminal justice system. These reforms would dramatically alter the nature and purpose of the juvenile court system for all youths and, if the trend is expanded, ultimately turn the juvenile court into an adult, adversary proceedings.[6] Strasburg notes that very little information exists concerning the scope and nature of violent juvenile actions which would be affected by the proposed changes.[7] Before such changes are undertaken the following unanswered question must be empirically answered: Do violent juveniles, especially serious and/or repetitive offenders, constitute a significant enough proportion of juvenile offenders to justify the radical restructuring or possible dismantling of the juvenile court system?

This study is designed to shed some light on the number of officially recognized violent acts and violent youths in relation to the larger juvenile population. The literature on violent juvenile offenders has been limited but is now expanding. Doleschal and Newton review most of the writings that now exist.[8] Noticeably absent are studies which measure the extent of violent involvement within an entire juvenile or delinquent population. Most studies are either case histories, a select sample of violent youths, or reports of the level of *delinquency* as measured by the number of offenses or arrests for a particular period of time. Few studies attempt to measure the number of *delinquents* in a population let alone the number of violent delinquents or violent acts.

An effective method of determining the extent of delinquent involvement is the cohort study because this technique allows the researcher to trace the entire delinquent career of all youths passing through their pre-adult years. Three cohort studies have recently been done but none adequately measure the "violence problem." Wolfgang, Figlio and Sellin's now classic Philadelphia study did not focus specifically on violence and most of the data is at the offense level.[9]Furthermore, the 1945 cohort does not represent the current generation of youth. The Vera study does focus on violence but includes only a maximum of six arrests so entire juvenile careers are not examined.[10] Polk's Oregon study has not centered on violence in a cohort but emphasizes school performance and delinquency.[11] Thus a cohort study that concentrates on a violent cohort is still needed.

Methodology

The population for this study was all Franklin County, Ohio, youths who had at least one contact with the Columbus City Police Department for a violent offense (murder, manslaughter, armed and unarmed roberry, aggravated and simple assault, rape, sexual imposition and molesting) and who were born in the years 1956 through 1958.[12] An employee of the Columbus Police Department searched all juvenile records from January 1, 1956, to Dec. 31, 1976, for any youth who had been in contact with the police for any of the above violent offenses. When the file of such a youth was encountered his case records or investigative reports for all contacts, violent or not, were photocopied and sent to the project office. The 1956 to 1976 time frame covers the entire juvenile "careers" of all three birth cohorts (1956, 1957, 1958) from birth to 18th birthday—the end of juvenile court jurisdiction in Ohio.

Much discussion in criminology has centered around the use of official statistics as representative of "delinquent involvement." This study does not purport to measure all violent behavior but rather the extent of juvenile violence behavior that would be handled by the juvenile justice system. Since the proposed "reforms" would directly affect only youths who were detected and "disposed" by the system, this study is justified in its use of only officially detected "violent offenders."

Findings

In 1970 the Franklin County 1956-1960 birth cohorts numbered 84, 792 persons and the same Columbus cohorts totaled 50,297.[13] The 1956-1958 cohort figures were estimated to be 50, 875 for Franklin County and 30,178 for Columbus.[14] The 811 youths arrested constituted 1.6 percent of the total age-eligible cohort (2.7 percent for the Columbus cohort). This means that about 2 percent of all age-eligible youths were ever arrested for any violent act—a very small proportion of the youth population.

Unfortunately, statistics were not available for the total number of youths born in 1956-1958 who had any contact with the juvenile justice system. If one assumes that about one-third of all age-eligible youths were ever in contact with the law, this means that approximately 16,000 youths (10,000 for Columbus) were delinquent.[15] The 811 violent youths then represent 5.1 percent of all age-eligible delinquents in Franklin County (8.1 percent of Columbus delinquents).

Most of these youths were arrested for minor violent acts. Two hundred twenty-one youths or 27.2 percent of the total violent population were arrested for "serious" violent offenses (murder/manslaughter, rape/sexual imposition, aggravated assault or armed robbery). Needless to say 221 youths who commit serious injury crimes are 221 too many, but they represent a fraction of the at-large population. This seriously violent group constitutes 0.4 percent of the 1956-1958 Franklin County age-eligible cohort (0.7 percent of the Columbus cohort). Of the 1956-1958 age-eligible delinquents this group represents 1.4 percent of Franklin County's group and 2.2 percent of the Columbus group.

Only 21 youths (2.6 percent of the 811 violent youths) were arrested two or more times for "serious" violent offenses during their juvenile careers. These 21 youths, who could be called truly violent, made up 0.04 percent (0.07 percent in Columbus) of the age-eligible cohort and 0.1 percent of the estimated Franklin County (0.2 percent in Columbus) delinquent cohort. In short, the officially repetitive, seriously violent offender constitutes a very small proportion of the youth or delinquent population.

Turning from the proportion of the "violent" youths in the population to their arrest offenses shows that violence is not a major part of these violent offenders' careers. These 811 youths were arrested a total of 3,373 times (mean of 4.2 arrests) and were charged with 4,445 offenses (mean of 5.48 charges per person.) Of the 3,373 arrests 985 (29.2 percent) were for violent offenses or an average of 1.2 violent arrests per person.[16] There were 1,087 violent offenses charged (24.5 percent of all charges and a mean of 1.3 violent charges per person). The range of all arrests was from one arrest to a maximum of 23 arrests and for violent arrests from one to a maximum of six. As Table 1 indicates, the majority of youths (55.9 percent) were arrested three or less times for any offense and the vast majority (83.5 percent) for only one violent offense. Table 2 gives the distribution of all 3,373 arrests and shows that non-violent arrests make up a significant majority (70.8 percent) of all arrests.

Table 1

Distribution of Violent Youths by
Number of All Arrests and All Violent Arrests

Number Arrests	Percent of Juveniles (All Arrests)	Percent of Juveniles (Violent Arrests)
1	29.5	83.5
2	16.2	12.7
3	10.2	3.0
4	10.6	0.7
5	7.0	-------
6	4.2	0.1
7	4.7	
8	5.1	
9	3.3	
10	2.7	
11-15	5.1	
16-23	1.5	
Total	100.1	100.0
(N)	811	811
Mean	4.2	1.21
Median	3.4	<1

These figures show that violent offenses make up only a minor part of these youths' arrest records. These 811 youths were arrested for 272 "serious" violent offenses. These serious offenses made up only about one-quarter (27.6) percent of the 985 violent arrests and a small fraction (8 percent) of the arrest total. Simple assaults represented the largest category (38.2 percent) of the violent offenses followed by unarmed robbery (26.2 percent). Even among the violent offenses, less serious offenses predominate the distribution.

Table 2

Distribution of All Arrests

	Number	Percent
Violent Offenses		
assault	376	11.1
robbery (unarmed)	258	7.6
robbery (armed)	106	3.1
aggravated assault	90	2.7
molesting	79	2.3
rape	40	1.2
sexual imposition	21	0.6
murder	15	0.4
	985	29.2
Other Violent Offenses	106	3.1
Property Offenses		
petit theft	315	9.3
breaking and entering	240	7.1
auto theft	147	4.4
burglary	104	3.1
trespassing	63	1.9
grand larceny	63	1.9
receiving and concealing	61	1.8
other property	66	2.0
	1,059	31.4
Drug Offenses		
glue sniffing	65	1.9
other drugs	58	1.7
	123	3.6
Public Order Offenses		
malicious destruction of property	95	2.8
suspicious person	85	2.5
disorderly conduct	48	1.4
intoxication	39	1.2
other	89	2.6
	356	10.6
Status Offenses		
curfew	288	8.5
truant from home	215	6.4
incorrigible	78	2.3
other status	163	4.8
	744	22.1
TOTAL	3,373	100.0

Discussion

The findings of this study provide several implications. First, researchers and practitioners should be aware that the concept of "violent delinquent" or "dangerous offender" is subject to misuse. Technically, all 811 youths caught in the web of this study were "violent youths," but a more accurate statement for the majority of these people would be that they are "youths with a violent arrest." A large proportion of these violent arrests were for minor events with little harm resulting such as hair-pulling incidents and neighborhood fist-fights. For other youths a violent arrest was a small part of a wider range of delinquent activities. These youths could more appropriately be called "thieves," "truants" or "incorrigibles" than "violent." The label of "violent offender" should not be indiscriminately applied to anyone arrested for any violent offense.

Second, media presentations may have distorted the extent and nature of the violence problem. Articles such as *Time's* "Youth Crime Plague" imply that wanton violence among teen-agers is a widespread problem and that only drastic action will save our society. The data of this study show that the proportion of youths ever arrested for any serious violent offense is very small in comparison to the total cohort or delinquent populations. Official statistics do show predatory crime rising among juveniles, and the 220-odd serious violent offenders in this study do represent a significant social problem, but the violent "crime plague" does not seem to be of epidemic proportions, at least not in Columbus, Ohio.

Third, many of the "reforms" proposed for the juvenile justice system will subject all youths — violent and non-violent, serious and petty — to the adult criminal justice system or an adult-like system with concomitant problems of labeling and formality. While changes in the juvenile system intended to make it more like the adult system may have an affect on 17-year-old murderers and 16-year-old rapists, they will also impact on 12-year-old truants, 8-year-old petty thieves and 10-year-old trespassers. Does the public seriously want minor juvenile offenders, especially those who are very young, to experience the rigors of the adult criminal justice system? (Has the adult system been that successful in halting adult violence that it is a model for the juvenile system?) Given the very small proportion of serious violent offenders in the delinquent population, the data of this study imply that wholesale changes to the juvenile justice system may be a classic case of overkill.

Fourth, Columbus may or may not be a representative city from which to draw conclusions concerning the level of violent incidents and the numbers of violent youths. Any generalizations should be made carefully. It can be argued that much of the "violence problem" seems to emanate from the large metropolitan areas but generalization of their problems to all juvenile justice systems is also problematic. The "failures" of the systems in large cities to deal with violent juveniles may be an inherent function of the size, complexity and bureaucratic inefficiency of their juvenile justice systems rather than the inadequacies of juvenile justice *per se.* Unfortunately, the proposed "reforms" will affect *all* juvenile justice systems in a particular state. Thus, legislative action to change New York City juvenile courts will also affect rural, upstate New York as well. While Columbus, Ohio, may or may not reflect the seriousness of violent delinquency in such cities as New York, Boston, Philadelphia, Miami, Los Angeles and Dallas, neither do these cities necessarily reflect the extent of violence in the rest of their states. Legislators would do well to keep this in mind when contemplating sweeping changes in the juvenile justice system.

In conclusion, the findings of this study do not support the media-generated belief in widespread, serious juvenile violence — at least not officially detected violence. Reforms predicated on this fear that would essentially transform the juvenile justice system into an adult system are ill-advised, though this is not meant to be taken as an affirmation for the entire juvenile justice system. Instead, measures that would deal specifically with the minority of "hard core" or vicious individuals would be more consistent with the data. Such measures could include greater use of the waiver system already established in all states or a modification of that system. Whatever changes that are made should be based on an informed knowledge of the extent of juvenile crime, not sensational accounts of particularly heinous events that are generalized to the whole delinquent population.

Footnotes

[1] James Garofalo, *Public Opinion About Crime* (Washington, D.C.: U.S. Government Printing Office, 1977), p. 15.

[2] Paul A. Strasburg, *Violent Delinquents* (New York: Monarch, 1978), p. 2.

[3] Donna Martin Hamparian et al., *The Violent Few* (Lexington, Mass.: Lexington Books, 1978), pp. 11-12.

[4] Eugene Doleschal and Anne Newton, "The Violent Juvenile: A Review," *Criminal Justice Abstracts* 10, no. 4 (1978): 539-573.

[5] "No More Kid Gloves for Young Hoodlums," *U.S. News and World Report* March 5 (1979): 24.

"Treating Kids Like Adults," *Newsweek* April 16 (1979): 54.

H. Ted Rubin, *Juvenile Justice: Policy, Practice and Law* (Santa Monica, Calif.: Goodyear Publishing Co., 1979), pp. 19-27.

[6] For a discussion of the nature, philosophy and changing directions of juvenile courts, see the following:

Martin R. Haskell and Lewis Yablonsky, *Juvenile Delinquency* (Chicago: Rand MacNally, 1978), pp. 25-64.

Lamar T. Empey, *American Delinquency: Its Meaning and Construction* (Homewood, Ill.: Dorsey Press, 1978), pp. 88-96, 440-483.

For a discussion of the attempts to reshape the philosophy of the court, see:

Rubin, *Policy, Practice and Law,* pp. 19-30.

[7]Strasburg, *Violent Delinquents*, p. 3.

[8]Doleschal and Newton, "Violent Juvenile."

[9]Marvin E. Wolfgang, Robert M. Figlio, and Thorsten Sellin, *Delinquency in a Birth Cohort* (Chicago: The University of Chicago Press, 1972).

[10]Strasburg, *Violent Delinquents*.

[11]Kenneth Polk, "Teenage Delinquency in Small Town America," Research Report No. 5 (National Institute of Mental Health, 1974).

[12]The boundaries of the city of Columbus shifted significantly over the two decades covered by this study. An accurate determination of the residency of some youths was virtually impossible, so youths from all of Franklin County, of which Columbus is a part, were included. Since only Columbus police records were used, this technique may slightly overrepresent Columbus delinquents or underrepresent Franklin County delinquents. One-hundred seventy youths lived in Franklin County in "split" census tracts during the course of this study, of which an estimated 80 (10 percent of the violent population) were probably Franklin County residents. In comparison, 40 percent of the 1956-1958 birth cohorts were Franklin County residents in 1970. For these reasons base population statistics for both Columbus and Franklin County will be reported for all appropriate statistics.

[13]U.S. Bureau of the Census, *Census of Population and Housing: 1970 Census Tracts* (Final Report PHC (1)-50 Columbus, Ohio, SMSA) (Washington, D.C.: U.S. Government Printing Office, 1970).

[14]The one-third figure for the number of delinquents in the Columbus cohorts may be too high since it is based on statistics from a more crime-prone city — Philadelphia. However, Polk's findings for a rural and small-town region — an area one would project to be less "criminal" — show that one-fourth had an official record. Polk's figure would be even higher if traffic offenses had been included, as they were in the Philadelphia study.

Polk, "Teenage Delinquency."

[15]Wolfgang et al., *Birth Cohort*.

The most serious offense, in legislative terms, in a multiple-charge arrest was coded to represent the entire event. In cases in which a violent and non-violent offense were charged the violent offense was automatically assumed to be the "most serious."

[16]Wolfgang et al.'s Philadelphia data show that less than 5 percent of their 10, 214 arrests were for serious violent offenses. Unfortunately, the study does not report on the number of *youths* arrested for violent offenses. This low figure could be taken as a rough support for the current study in that serious violent arrests represent a very small proportion of all delinquent involvement.

References

"Coming: Tougher Approach to Juvenile Violence." *U.S. News and World Report* June 7 (1976): 65-67.

4

Remand of Juveniles to Adult Court

M. A. Bortner

Due to their age and inexperience, juveniles have traditionally been depicted as less culpable than adult offenders, less committed to a criminal lifestyle, and more amenable to rehabilitative intervention. Accordingly, treatment, not punishment, has been portrayed as the most appropriate method of dealing with juvenile offenders (Bortner, 1982; Cicourel, 1968; Emerson, 1969). Despite this rehabilitative orientation, all states have established procedures for remanding juveniles to adult court for prosecution.[1] This is an extremely consequential and controversial action, one that strips individuals of the allegedly protective status of "juvenile" and subjects them to the punitive forces of the adult criminal justice system. These remanded juveniles are the exception to the rehabilitative ideal espoused by the juvenile justice system (Flicker, 1981).

The controversies surrounding the remand of juveniles to adult court reflect the more general crisis engulfing the juvenile justice system. The violent and repetitive offenders frequently considered for remand epitomize pervasive public concern about juvenile involvement in serious crime, as well as increased public scrutiny of juvenile justice philosophy and methods of treatment. The question of whether

M.A. Bortner: Associate Professor of Justice Studies at Arizona State University. I would like to thank Kay Korman for her assistance in the preparation of the manuscript and David Altheide, Gray Cavender, John Johnson, and Pat Lauderdale for their thoughtful and critical reading of previous drafts of this article.

M.A. Bortner, "Traditional rhetoric, organizational realities: Remand of Juveniles to adult court," *Crime & Delinquency,* Vol. 32 Number 1 (January 1986) pp. 55-73, Copyright 1986 by Sage Publications, Inc. Reprinted by permission of Sage Publications, Inc.

juveniles should be prosecuted and punished as adults and, if so, which juveniles should be treated thusly reflects growing discontent with the traditional treatment orientation of the juvenile system. This also reflects the emerging strength of a more punitive, retributive orientation toward delinquents (Wizner, 1984: 42-43).

The predominant rationale for the negation of the rehabilitative ideal (via transfer to adult court) has been that, although juveniles as a class are treatable, particular juveniles by virtue of their behavior do not merit such a protected status. Accordingly, public interest mandates the waiver of jurisdiction by the juvenile court. This justification for remand implies that the more dangerous and intractable delinquents can be identified and that their removal to the adult system will increase the safety afforded the general public (Gardner, 1973; Gasper and Katkin, 1980; Reid, 1974).

Despite the crucial nature of this issue, we have few empirical studies that address the assumptions underlying remand, and few that examine the organizational and political dimensions of this process. We have little evidence regarding the histories of those juveniles remanded, their fate within the adult court system, or the potential impact of their remand on public safety (Eigen, 1981; Hays and Solway, 1972; Keiter, 1973; Snyder, et al., 1978). Only recently have preliminary national data become available regarding one of these dimensions, the adult dispositions of remanded juveniles, and these data do not support traditional rationale and rhetoric (Hamparian, et al., 1982: 112-141).

Methodology

The present study examines the remand process within a western metropolitan county, a jurisdiction in which the rate of remanded juveniles has tripled since 1979, whereas the rate of delinquency referrals, including major felonies, has remained stable. Judicial transfer is the decision-making procedure for remanding juveniles to adult court within this jurisdiction. The prosecutor initiates the consideration of a particular case for remand; probation officers, psychological and psychiatric personnel make recommendations; and the final decision is made by a juvenile judge. To argue successfully that a juvenile should be transferred to the adult court, the prosecutor must first demonstrate that there is sufficient evidence to believe that the juvenile was involved in the alleged offense. Probable cause must be established, with preponderance of evidence as the necessary level of proof. He or she then must demonstrate that the juvenile is not amenable to treatment within the juvenile system, meaning that the juvenile justice system has no further treatment resources to offer this particular juvenile.

The present study provides an organizational analysis of the decision-making process and examines the case histories of a cohort of 214 juveniles remanded to the adult court during 1980 and 1981.[2] The prosecutor's files provided the following information regarding the case histories of the 214 remanded juveniles:

the charges on which the juveniles were remanded; the charges on which they were convicted in adult court; the adult court sentences; and the juveniles' age, gender, and race. Further information regarding the juvenile court's remand decision was available for 145 of the remanded juveniles, including the recommendations of court personnel (probation and intake officers) and psychological experts (psychologists and psychiatrists) regarding whether or not the juvenile should be remanded to adult court.

The organizational analysis is derived from interviews and participant observation over a period of four years, including membership on the state juvenile corrections advisory board, testimony before the state legislative juvenile justice committee, and participation in panel discussions regarding serious and violent juvenile offenders at the governor's conference on juvenile crime. Intensive interviews were conducted with key juvenile court decision makers, including the chief juvenile prosecutor, the judges responsible for the ultimate decisions to remand juveniles in the sample (the presiding and associate juvenile judges), and the chief juvenile court administrator. The analysis of both the case histories and the interviews with key decision makers suggests that the nature and complexion of remand are changing, and that current realities differ markedly from traditional rhetoric.

Traditional Rationale: Protection of the Public

The most pervasive rationale for the remand of juveniles to adult court is that such action provides greater protection to the public than does juvenile justice processing (Gasper and Katkin, 1980). This is an assumption for which there is little empirical validation (Hamparian, et al., 1982). It is also an assumption the key concept of which— "protection of the public" — is ill-defined (Alers, 1973).

It may be argued that the adult arrest record that remanded juveniles receive, as well as the high probability of an adult conviction record, will deter young offenders from future crimes, thus enhancing public safety.[3] Also, the placement of juveniles on adult probation may promote public safety due to its qualitatively different nature when compared to juvenile probation; that is, the sanction for probation violation on the adult level (imprisonment) may have a greater deterrent potential. Nevertheless, these two provisions do not represent the increased protection envisioned by advocates of juvenile remand, for the dominant interpretation is one that equates protection of the public with incarceration (Gasper and Katkin, 1980). For, as all decision makers who were interviewed acknowledge, advocates of remand have touted incarceration as the major vehicle to increased public safety and have portrayed incarceration as the major objective of the remand process.

If protection of the public is defined as incarceration, these data demonstrate that remand does not, in fact, provide extensive protection. Nor does remanding juveniles culminate in a high percentage of incarceration or long periods of incarceration. In the present sample, in only 61.7% of the cases did any post-conviction incarceration occur. And this statistic is misleadingly high, for only 30.8% (66) of the remanded juveniles received prison as their primary disposition; 0.9% (2) received jail as their primary disposition; and the remaining individuals who were incarcerated received jail sentences not as their primary disposition but as a condition of probation (64 individuals, 29.9% of the sample, or 47.4% of those placed on probation). The most common disposition was probation (see Table 1).

The terms of incarceration were generally low: less than nine months for those who received jail sentences and five years or less for those sentenced to prison. Of those given jail terms, 33% (22) were sentenced to three months or less; 34.8% (23) to 4-8 months; and 28.8% (19) were sentenced to a year. Of those sentenced to prison, 10.6% (7) received less than two years; 34.8% (23) received 2-4 years; 27.3% (18) received five years; 16.7% (11) received 6-10 years; and 10.6% (7) received over ten years' imprisonment. The above figures indicate the sentences meted out, but the actual time served prior to release on parole for those imprisoned would be considerably less.

Clearly, a significant number of juveniles remanded to adult court are returned to the community immediately or shortly after conviction. The possible reasons for this are several. The chief ones include their first-time offender status in the adult system, the relatively minor nature of their offenses, and the brevity of their

Table 1

Adult Court Dispositions

Primary Disposition*		
Probation	135	(63.1)
Prison	66	(30.8)
Jail	2	(0.9)
Fine	2	(0.9)
Dismissed	9	(4.2)
Total	214	(100)
Conditions of Probation*		
Restitution and reimbursement	84	(62.2)**
Jail	64	(47.4)
Probation fee	26	(19.3)
Community service	22	(16.3)

NOTE: Percentages are in parentheses.

* The majority of adult court dispositions have several elements. For example, an individual's sentence may include probation with numerous conditions of probation, i.e., a jail sentence, restitution, or community service. Primary disposition refers to the central component of the disposition, which is usually probation or imprisonment.

** Percentages refer to percentage of total (135) placed on probation. One individual may have several conditions of probation.

offense histories *compared to adult offenders* (Greenwood, et al., 1980). Also, juveniles' youthfulness and resulting vulnerability to the harshness of prison life, the lack of facilities and programs oriented toward young offenders, and the overcrowding of the adult system may affect judicial decisions. Regardless of the reasons, remanded juveniles are not being incarcerated uniformly nor for long periods of time.

It must be noted that acknowledgement of the moderate rate of incarceration is not to advocate that remanded juveniles *should* be incarcerated nor is it to argue that such action would, in fact, enhance public safety. Rather, within the present context, the moderate rate of incarceration is important because it demonstrates the discrepancy between the popular rationale for remand and the actual consequences of such action. Accordingly, protection of the public via incarceration is disclosed as more rhetorical imagery than contemporary reality.

Identifying the Dangerous and Intractable

As well as arguing that the transfer of particular juveniles to adult court enhances public safety, advocates of remand assume that the decision-making process provides for the identification of the most dangerous and intractable delinquents (Braithwaite and Shore, 1981; Gasper and Katkin, 1980; Sargent and Gordon, 1963). Accordingly, scarce resources are reserved for those viewed as most likely to benefit from treatment within the juvenile system.

The judges, chief prosecutor, and chief administrator alike view the remand process as a mechanism for identifying those juveniles for whom the juvenile justice system is inappropriate. Ostensibly, due to their age, sophistication, or long histories of failed rehabilitative efforts, these juveniles are viewed as not amenable to the juvenile justice system's espoused goals. The chief administrator provides this characterization:

> They're the ones that cause the biggest problems to the juvenile justice system, both in detention facilities and in department of corrections facilities, because they're too sophisticated, too hardened, or too uninterested in what's going on there to benefit from it. So it's really a waste of the money, a waste of taxpayers' money, because they're just not going to take anything out of the system that's positive . . . . To make the juvenile justice system viable, you have to have an escape valve.

Essentially, remand of juveniles to adult court is a statement that particular juveniles are viewed as beyond the rehabilitative scope and treatment capacity of juvenile justice. But, traditional rhetoric notwithstanding, there is little evidence to suggest that those juveniles remanded are, in fact, the most dangerous or intractable delinquents.

It might be expected that the basic criterion of offense seriousness would provide a measure of juveniles' dangerousness. To the contrary, analysis of the offenses for which these juveniles were remanded does not indicate that they are unequivocally dangerous. Unlike popular images of remanded juveniles as violent offenders, the present juveniles were more likely to be accused of property offenses. Only 55% (117) of the juveniles were charged with felonies against persons; 61% (130) were charged with property felonies; and less than .5% (11) were charged with drug offenses.[4]

The assumption that juvenile justice personnel can identify the most dangerous and intractable delinquents is subject to a major criticism that has plagued the entire juvenile justice system, namely, that the ability to predict juvenile behavior and effectively rehabilitate is unproven (Feld, 1984; Kittrie, 1971). Demonstrated predictive and rehabilitative success is rare within juvenile justice, and there is little reason to believe that the juvenile system can accurately predict which juveniles are, indeed, beyond rehabilitative efforts and should therefore be remanded in the name of public safety.

Those most intimately involved in the remand decision do not agree regarding juveniles' amenability to treatment within the juvenile system. In the 145 cases for which information regarding the juvenile court's remand decisions are available, probation officers and intake personnel recommended against remand in 9% (13) of the cases. And in the 130 of these cases for which such data are available, psychological experts (psychiatrists and psychologists) recommended against remand to the adult court in 24% (31) of the cases.

All of the decision makers interviewed initially professed confidence in the system's ability to identify those juveniles who should be remanded. Due to the number of experts involved in the decision-making process, the volume of information reviewed prior to the final decision, and the image of these juveniles as the most serious and repetitive offenders, top decision makers uniformly expressed confidence in the identification process. When questioned further, however, and requested to compare remanded juveniles with individuals charged with similar offenses but retained within the juvenile system, decision makers were divided regarding whether remanded juveniles represent "the worst" juveniles within the system. The chief prosecutor and chief administrator were most firm in their conviction that remanded juveniles are clearly those meriting punitive treatment within an adult court system. The judges were reticent to describe remanded juveniles as "the worst" and acknowledged that they see "worse" juveniles who are not even being considered for remand. They suggest that an organizational factor is responsible for this apparent inconsistency:

> There's probably a lot of kids that are sent to the State Department of Corrections (juvenile institutions) by me that probably would have been transferred (to adult court) by me had somebody requested that. The only change is that the prosecuter doesn't request it, so I don't do it [Associate Judge].
>
> By and large, yes, I feel the kids being transferred are appropriate for transfer.
>
> (Are they the worst kids in the system?)

No. There are some kids who are worse than those who are being transferred who are not because no transfer is requested, because they're too young, because they've managed to avoid the judge having the opportunity to make the decision. But there are some kids who are still in the system who are bad asses, who shouldn't ought to be here, but some of them just haven't been caught yet [Presiding Judge].

Because judges cannot initiate the remand process, prosecutorial decisions not to request transfer or to withdraw the request before it reaches a judge for final decision eliminate judicial consideration of remand. Some of the "worst" juveniles may not be remanded because the prosecutor does not request it. The chief prosecutor estimates that in half of the cases originally set for remand consideration, he and his deputy prosecutors subsequently withdraw the request and the juveniles are kept within the juvenile system. Of those cases that go to a remand hearing, the judges decide to remand over 90% of the juveniles. The prosecutor exercises extreme power, as stated by the presiding judge: "Most of the decisions are not made by the judge, because most are made by withdrawing the request to transfer."

The prosecutor's official criteria for deciding in which cases to file a request for remand are based on a formula incorporating age, offense, and referral history in order to identify "dangerous and repetitive offenders." The criteria for *withdrawing* requests for remand are unofficial and, as acknowledged by the chief prosecutor, have not been officially articulated or codified, nor are they emphasized in discussions of remand policy. When questioned regarding the criteria for withdrawing remand requests, the chief prosecutor emphasizes offense, referral history, age of offender, and recommendations against transfer by probation officers or psychological/psychiatric experts. But he also referred to less specific issues such as "options available to the community," evidentiary and legal strength of the case, and "prosecutorial needs."

A juvenile may be permitted to stay in the juvenile system because she or he is willing to testify in the prosecution of an adult co-suspect. The "high-profile" nature of a case, for example, the fact that it has received widespread media and public attention, may figure prominently in the decision to remand. A 17-year-old who is not admitting to guilt may be remanded because the remaining time available in the juvenile system would be consumed in proving guilt rather than "providing treatment." One juvenile may be remanded primarily because the companion case of a juvenile co-suspect is being remanded. Or remand consideration may be withdrawn in exchange for a guilty plea and consent to incarceration on the juvenile level.[5]

Decision makers portray the remand process as one in which legal considerations, such as severity of offense and past record, make possible the selection of the most dangerous and intractable juveniles for remand. But when the daily application of these guidelines is examined, the process is revealed as highly discretionary. The evidence is far from conclusive that even those originally set for remand consideration represent the most dangerous and intractable juveniles, but such an argument would be more convincing than the assertion that those juveniles who actually go to a remand hearing and those actually remanded to adult court are the most dangerous and intractable. There are far too many organizational and political considerations and practicalities that enter into the decision-making matrix for such an argument to be supported.

Alternative Explanations of Remand

It cannot be demonstrated that those juveniles who are remanded are singularly dangerous or that they are intractable. Neither can it be demonstrated that the remand of these particular juveniles enhances public safety through incarceration or deterrence.[6] The lack of compelling evidence in support of the traditional rationale for remand necessitates alternative explanations of its increased use.

Within the jurisdiction under study, there are several salient organizational dimensions that contribute to a climate in which remand has become an acceptable and sometimes preferred manner of processing an increasing number of juveniles. The major explanation for the increase in number and rate of remands proffered by decision makers interviewed is a 1979 State Supreme Court ruling that terminated juvenile court jurisdiction when juveniles reach age 18. Prior to this ruling, the juvenile justice system could retain jurisdiction over individuals until age 21.[7] The increase in the number and rate of remands since that ruling has been dramatic. The remand rate in 1979 (prior to the ruling) was 32.71 remands per 10,000 referrals to juvenile court. By 1981, the rate had more than tripled to 115.59 remands per 10,000 referrals to juvenile court. Decision makers stress the limitations placed upon the juvenile justice system by the State Supreme Court's termination of their jurisdiction over juveniles at age 18. The fact that 85.5% of those juveniles remanded were 17 years old indicates that remand is invoked primarily with those juveniles approaching legal adulthood.

Controversies regarding the state's correctional institutions for juveniles also are relevant to the issue of remand. In 1980, due to limited bed space, the average length of incarceration was less than four months, with violent offenders averaging incarceration periods of eight months. The perceived lack of punishment for juvenile offenders was a major issue of debate within the state legislature, the media, and statewide juvenile justice agencies.

In 1980 the state department of corrections instituted guidelines that compute minimum-maximum sentences based on offenses for which a juvenile has been adjudicated over a two-year period prior to commitment to the department of corrections. Violent offenders receive top priority for incarceration, and, due to limited bed space, a major consequence of this policy has been a decreased average length of incarceration for nonviolent offenders. Although this emphasis on the confinement of violent offenders is ostensibly a response to expressed public concern for safety, it has created an atmosphere in which a correctional policy designed to provide incapacitation of violent offenders may contribute to the remand to adult court of property offenders, even younger individuals, who might have previously been retained within the juvenile system.

Of the decision makers interviewed, the chief prosecutor was the only one to indicate that the lack of correctional facilities for juveniles strongly influences his decision making regarding remand. The lack of bed space, lack of programs, and lack of evidence that juveniles will be rehabilitated in the juvenile system contribute to the prosecutor's conviction that remand to adult court is more appropriate for many juveniles than is juvenile court processing. In contrast, the judges do not identify correctional resources as a major factor in their decision to remand. The presiding judge characterizes this issue as "just one of many things" of which he is aware and considers in deciding to remand; the associate judge suggests that although the "inadequacies of the department of corrections" may have some effect on him "subconsciously," it is not a major factor in the remand decision.

Thus decision makers emphasize the impact of the Supreme Court's ruling on their remand practices and, to a lesser extent, acknowledge the impact of the perceived inadequacies of juvenile correctional facilities. These factors are extremely relevant to explaining the increase in remands, especially from the perspective of juvenile justice decision makers. But these factors and the general phenomenon of increased remand can be more fully understood and illuminated when they are situated within the context of more encompassing dilemmas that confront individuals within contemporary juvenile justice.

The juvenile justice system is a 90-year-old experiment in substantive justice a legal institution, the espoused goals of which are to provide individualized treatment for children while providing protection to the community (Matza, 1964). However, critics chastise the system for its failure to provide documentable rehabilitation of juveniles and for failing to protect the public. The increased use of remand is at least a partial response to the critique of the rehabilitative ideal embodied in juvenile justice, as well as a highly visible response to the retributionist critique that assails the juvenile system for not punishing juveniles and in so doing undermining the moral force of the legal system (Kittrie, 1971; Rothman, 1980; Platt, 1977).

Essentially, the increased willingness of these juvenile justice decision makers to remand juveniles to adult court reflects their sensitivity to and desire to diminish perceived criticisms of the entire juvenile justice system. For in many ways those juveniles considered for remand, the violent and repetitive offenders, are viewed as epitomizing the crisis. As the chief prosecutor suggests, "In their hands lies the future of juvenile justice."

The prosecutor articulates these sentiments most strongly when he portrays the juvenile justice system as a system that has failed to "impose moral condemnation for criminal behavior," and asserts that the goals of the justice system should be "moral condemnation, normative reinforcement, and incapacitation." He further argues that the major objective of the justice system should be the protection of the community, not the rehabilitation of juveniles. In this key decision maker's view, remand is a mechanism for making repetitive and violent juvenile offenders accountable for their behavior, and, in so doing, generating credibility for the juvenile system.

Although the judges do not view the juvenile system as failing in its rehabilitative mission and express far more support for that philosophy and goal than does the chief prosecutor, they too acknowledge changing priorities within the juvenile system. The associate judge suggests, "The interest of the community has now become more important than the individual child's interest."

Although decision makers frequently made reference to community pressures, the exact nature and level of those pressures are unascertained. Considerable legislative discussion has revolved around juvenile justice, focusing particularly upon violent juveniles and the need for more protection of citizens through increased periods of incarceration on the juvenile level and increased remand. And, although unsuccessful to date, perennial bills are introduced in the legislature that advocate lowering the age of jurisdiction for the juvenile system and implementing a mandatory remand process in which all juveniles charged with felonies against persons would be remanded automatically.

The key decision makers within this jurisdiction vary in their response to legislative, media, victim, and public pressures. All express an increased sensitivity to public "demands" for greater punishment of serious juvenile offenders, but only the chief administrator and chief prosecutor acknowledge that such pressures motivate their attitudes and policies regarding remand. Elected on a bipartisan basis, the judges claim that they are relatively free from pressures outside their own predilections regarding the needs of the community and juveniles.

The position of the prosecutor is markedly different. Not only does he express greater concern with public pressure, but he is identified by other decision makers as the focal point of public criticism and the major respondent to such criticism. As the associate judge suggests,

> I imagine the prosecutor's free of pressure himself, except his perception that there is pressure. I don't imagine that the people out there know the system (I'm not talking about the legislature, I'm talking about the people). I don't know that they are aware of the procedure except in the most cursory of ways. I don't imagine they're beating down the door saying "do this" or "do that," in a particular case maybe, but not average. But the prosecutor may perceive that that's a wish of the public and *the perception is the reality* many times.

The role of the prosecutor is pivotal. The highly political nature of the office is reflected in the stress the prosecutor places upon public outcry for more punitive sanctioning of juveniles. The prosecutor also exercises the greatest discretion regarding remand decisions. The most political actor in the juvenile court setting has the greatest power to respond to perceived public demand for remand.

The extent to which remanding more juveniles will actually satisfy vocal critics of the juvenile system as well as the rate of remand sufficient to satisfy them are questions on which decision makers differ. De-emphasizing the influence of external forces on their decision making, both judges suggest that even greatly increasing the number of remands will not completely satisfy critics. The presiding judge admits that remanding more juveniles will probably not satisfy critics because such criticisms stem from a general lack of empathy for the goals of individualized treatment as a whole; thus remanding particular juveniles will not abate that criticism. The associate judge depicts a similar impasse:

> Nothing's going to satisfy them. They're insatiable. There are people who get themselves reelected time after time by appealing to the base instincts of the public, and they don't tend to change. As a matter of fact, a lot of them do this in good faith. They're demagogues in good faith, good faith demagogues, because they really believe this. Statistics, facts, whatever, to the contrary, are not going to change their mind and it's not going to affect the public. No matter what the courts do in the criminal area — they speed up the trials, they change the rules, throw everybody in jail, remand everybody — it's not going to change the public's perception of the system, because their perception is that it doesn't function properly, whether it does or not.

The primary issue involved in the remand of juveniles to adult court is the juvenile justice system's need to reestablish its efficacy as an institution, namely, by evidencing a sensitivity to vocal critics. Although remand represents a court of action ostensibly directed toward protection of the public, it is a policy integrally related to the juvenile system's interest in organizational maintenance. This interest in the preservation of the system is preeminent, even if the specific action of remand deflects the system from pursuing and accomplishing its original and professed goal of rehabilitating these particular juveniles (Balbus, 1977: xviii, 22-25). Remand protects institutional authority by removing high-risk cases from juvenile court responsibility, thus reducing potential organizational troubles and public criticism that might damage institutional legitimacy. Not unlike policies fashioned to deal with diverse "social problems," the increased use of remand is not so much the result of a more scientific understanding of the problem but, rather, it represents a more efficient means of organizational management (Scull, 1977: 344-345).

In an era of fiscal uncertainty when the juvenile justice system is confronted with the necessity of reasserting its worth, maintaining its uniqueness, and redefining its mission, remanded juveniles provide a symbolic avenue for the reaffirmation of the juvenile system's commitment to public safety and rehabilitation for *most* juveniles (Butler, 1972; Conrad, 1981; Feld, 1979; Galliher and Cross, 1982; Sargent and Gordon, 1963). In evidencing a willingness to relinquish its jurisdiction over an admittedly small percentage of its clientele, and by portraying these juveniles as the most intractable delinquents and greatest threat to public safety, the juvenile system creates an effective public gesture of retribution and punishment in the name of responsiveness to public concerns.

The chief administrator of the court clearly articulates this concern with criticisms of the entire juvenile justice system and a fear of "losing the franchise":

> Where we seem to get in the most trouble is when we mishandle, according to the public and the police and the politicians and prosecutors, when we mishandle the serious cases. Okay. They're not uninterested in what you're doing with the shoplifters and the beer drinkers and the kids who are joy-riding in their cars, and things like that, but, boy, you just mishandle one assaultive kid, or one rapist, or one armed robber—by mishandle I mean make a disposition that people just shake their head and don't understand, that's what I call mishandle—that does more damage to the juvenile justice system and puts you in jeopardy of losing all of your franchise than the mishandling of 650 burglary cases. . . . Now if you took the number of kids who were 16 and 17 in that violent offense category and automatically or somehow remanded them to adult court, we'd be talking about less than 500. If you took those 500 kids out, the franchise that we have to deal with the other 19,500 would never be in jeopardy again.

The remand of juveniles purported to be the most dangerous is far more than a symbolic gesture toward law and order demands of the media and legislature, for it is also a mechanism for staving off criticisms of the entire juvenile system. Increased remand of juveniles is an acceptable course of action to a great extent because of the unattractiveness of alternatives (Scull, 1977: 347). The untenable alternatives to remand are either to develop successful methods of dealing with serious juvenile offenders or to acknowledge the system's inability to rehabilitate, thus incurring greater criticism regarding the efficacy of the entire system.

Essentially, the juvenile system is relinquishing control over and responsibility for that group of juveniles seen as their most serious failures, those with whom the rehabilitative ideal has had least success. No longer a last resort for dealing with an extreme few (Emerson, 1981), or even the admission of failure of the rehabilitative ideal (Feld, 1979), remand is rapidly becoming a routine manner of processing troublesome clientele, those juveniles who epitomize the current organizational and political uncertainties of the system (Emerson and Messinger, 1977: 132). This action simultaneously advances the system's territorial interest in preserving jurisdiction over the vast majority of juveniles (Balbus, 1977).

Remanded juveniles are the negation of the rehabilitative ideal, but this failure is viewed not as damning evidence regarding the viability of the juvenile system. To the contrary, it is interpreted and portrayed as evidence of the intractability and failure of individual juveniles (Emerson, 1981; Matza, 1964; Parenti, 1978). When questioned regarding whether remand is an indication that the juvenile system has failed, decision makers uniformly respond that the major responsibility lies with the individual juveniles.

We failed and the kid failed. We own half of that problem and the kid owns the other half. But the failure has got to be acknowledged. We do fail. There isn't any doubt in my mind that there are some kids that no matter what we do we can't reach them. The whole topic of remand is so situational that it's hard, to make a generalization that a remand kid even is a failure on the part of the juvenile system [Associate Judge].

Rather than being viewed as an admission of failure of the juvenile system, the remand of juveniles with enormous symbolic value has come to represent the wise exercise of discretion by the juvenile court, as well as good managerial efficiency by reserving limited resources for those juveniles most "amenable to treatment." The underlying assumption of rehabilitation is preserved as is the integrity of the juvenile system, while the remand of individual juveniles provides symbolic solace for a fearful community and a temporary reprieve for a troubled juvenile system.

Conclusion

The remand of juveniles to adult court has traditionally been justified as providing protection to the public by identifying the most intractable and dangerous delinquents. The present analysis suggests that political and organizational factors, rather than concern for public safety, account for the increasing rate of remand. In evidencing a willingness to relinquish jurisdiction over a small percentage of its clientele, and by portraying these juveniles as the most intractable and the greatest threat to public safety, the juvenile justice system not only creates an effective symbolic gesture regarding protection of the public but it also advances its territorial interest in maintaining jurisdiction over the vast majority of juveniles and deflecting more encompassing criticisms of the entire system.

Footnotes

[1] The remand process is also referred to as "transfer," "certification," "unfitness hearing," and "waiver of jurisdiction." For a comprehensive review of the various methods for remanding juveniles to adult court see Hamparian, et al., *Youth in Adult Courts: Between Two Worlds* (1982).

[2] The chief of the juvenile division of the county prosecutor's office originally identified 228 juveniles as having been remanded in 1980-1981, but no information regarding adult court processing was available in the adult division of the prosecutor's office for fourteen of those individuals. Due to the fact that neither computer nor physical files contained information regarding these individuals, it is assumed that no action was taken on these cases at the adult court level.

[3] Only 4.2% (9) of the juveniles had all charges dismissed in adult court, due perhaps to the careful screening of cases on the juvenile level and the fact that a finding of probable cause is a necessary element of remand in this jurisdiction (also see Eigen, 1981).

[4] Felony, property offenses included breaking and entering, burglary, felony theft, forgery, fraud, larceny, theft of a motor vehicle, possession of a stolen vehicle, trafficking in stolen goods, criminal simulation, extortion, and possession of stolen property.

Additional evidence regarding the prior records of the remanded juveniles does not suggest that they are clearly distinguishable from other juvenile offenders. The juvenile histories available for 145 of the 214 individuals do not disclose extensive records of major delinquency and, interestingly, they disclose a marked lack of violent activities. Of those juveniles for whom prior records were available, 34.5% had between 1 and 5 prior referrals to court; 29.7% had 6-10 prior referrals; 21.4% had 11-15 prior referrals; 8.3% had 16-20 prior referrals; and 6.2% had over 20 prior referrals to juvenile court. The number of prior referrals to court for the majority is relatively low. Almost half, 48.3%, have fewer prior referrals than do those juveniles committed to the juvenile division of the department of corrections (average of 8.4 prior referrals to juvenile court).

The data available indicate that prior juvenile court referrals are predominantly for property offenses: 37.1% involved felony property offenses and an additional 21.2% involved other property offenses. Only 9.8% of the prior referrals to juvenile court involved major offenses against persons. Drug violations were involved in 3.8% of the prior referrals; 13.1% involved status offenses (offenses unique to juveniles such as incorrigibility, truancy, runaway, curfew violations); and 9.2% involved justice system violations such as parole or probation violations, court holds, warrants, false information, and dependency. It is important to note that the foregoing statistics pertain to referrals to juvenile court, that is, alleged involvement in delinquent activity. If the portrait were based solely on adjudications (those offenses for which juveniles had been found guilty), the prior records of these remanded juveniles would appear even less serious.

[5] Critics of the remand process also suggest that this decision might be based on the juvenile's gender, race, or social class, rather than offense or prior record (Hall, et al., 1981). Preliminary indicators suggest that the racial identity of the juvenile may be particularly salient. Black juveniles are greatly overrepresented in those remanded (23.7%) when compared both to those referred for serious offenses (9.4% black) and those committed to the department of corrections (10.9% black). The percentage of remanded juveniles who were white (52.2%) is similar to those committed to the juvenile department of corrections (52.8% white), but is disproportionately low when compared to the percentage of those referred for serious offenses (62.4% white). The percentage of remanded juveniles who were Mexican American (20.6%) is disproportionately low compared to those referred for serious offenses (25.2% Mexican American) as well as to those committed to the department of corrections (29.3% Mexican American). In regard to gender, the percentage of remanded juveniles who were male (94.7%) was slightly greater than the percentage of those referred for serious offenses (91.6%) and those committed to the department of corrections (91.6%). Thus, although this is a preliminary indication, both gender and race may have an impact upon the decision to remand.

[6] The decision makers vary in their assessment of the deterrent capacity of remand. The chief prosecutor suggests that "the word is out on the street" and even some of the most hard-core delinquents are deterred due to the possibility of remand. The presiding judge "hopes" that the fear of remand might act as a deterrent, but the associate judge asserts that the possibility of remand does not deter juveniles, mainly because "they don't think like the rest of us," that is, they don't think in terms of the possible consequences of their acts.

[7] Those juveniles who were wards of the state (committed to the department of corrections) prior to their eighteenth birthday could be incarcerated until age twenty-one.

References

Alers, M. 1973. "Transfer of jurisdiction from juvenile to criminal court." *Crime & Delinquency* 19: 519-526.

Balbus, I.D. 1977. *The Dialectics of Legal Repression: Black Rebels Before the American Criminal Courts*. New Brunswick, NJ: Transaction.

Bortner, M.A. 1982. *Inside a Juvenile Court: The Tarnished Ideal of Individualized Justice*. New York: New York University Press.

Braithwaite, L., and A. Shore. 1981. "Treatment rhetoric versus waiver decisions." *Journal of Criminal Law and Criminology* 72: 1867-1891.

Butler, K.D. 1972. "Juvenile court waiver: The questionable validity of existing statutory standards."
   St. Louis University Law Journal 16: 604-618.
Cicourel, A.V. 1968. *The Social Organization of Juvenile Justice*. New York: Wiley.
Conrad, J.P. 1981. "Crime and the child," pp. 179-192 in J.C. Hall, et al. (eds.) *Major Issues in Juvenile
   Justice Information and Training*. Washington, DC: Department of Justice.
Eigen, J.P. 1981. "Punishing youth homicide offenders in Philadelphia." *Journal of Criminal Law and
   Criminology* 72: 1071-1093.
Emerson, R.M. 1969. *Judging Delinquents: Context and Process in Juvenile Court*. Chicago: Aldine.
_____. 1981. "On last resorts." *American Journal of Sociology* 87: 1-22.
Emerson, R.M., and S.L. Messinger. 1977. "The micro-politics of trouble." *Social Problems* 25: 121-134.
Feld, B. 1979. "Reference of juvenile offenders for adult prosecution: The legislative alternative for
   asking unanswered questions." *Minnesota Law Review* 62: 515-616.
_____. 1984. "The decision to seek criminal charges: Just deserts and the waiver decision." *Criminal
   Justice Ethics* (Summer/Fall): 27-41.
Flicker, B. 1981. "Prosecuting juveniles as adults: A symptom of a crisis in the juvenile courts," pp.
   351-377 in J.C. Hall, et al. (eds.) *Major Issues in Juvenile Justice Information and Training*.
   Washington, DC: Department of Justice.
Galliher, J.F., and J.R. Cross. 1982. "Symbolic severity in the land of easy virtue: Nevada's high
   marihuana penalty." *Social Problems* 29: 380-386.
Gardner, M.C. 1973. "Due process and waiver of juvenile court jurisdiction." *Washington and Lee
   Law Review* 30: 591-613.
Gasper, J. and D. Katkin. 1980. "A rationale for the abolition of the juvenile courts' power to waive
   jurisdictions." *Pepperdine Law Review* 7: 937-951.
Greenwood, P.W., J. Petersilia, and F.E. Zimring. 1980. *Age, Crime and Sanctions: The Transition
   from Juvenile to Adult Court*. Santa Monica, CA: Rand.
Hall, J.C., D.M. Hamparian, J. Pettibone, and J.L. White (eds.). 1981. *Major Issues in Juvenile Justice
   Information and Training: Readings in Public Policy*. Columbus, OH: Academy for Contemporary
   Problems.
Hamparian, D.M., L.K. Estep, S.M. Muntean, R.R. Priestino, R.G. Swisher, P.L. Wallace, and J.L.
   White. 1982. *Youth in Adult Courts: Between Two Worlds*. Washington, DC: Department of Justice.
Hays, J.R., and K.S. Solway. 1972. "The role of psychological evaluation in certification of juveniles
   for trial as adults." *Houston Law Review* 9: 709-715.
Keiter, R.B. 1973. "Criminal or delinquent? A study of juvenile cases transferred to the criminal court."
   Crime & Delinquency 19: 528-538.
Kittrie, N.N. 1971. *The Right To Be Different: Deviance and Enforced Theory*. Baltimore, MD: Johns
   Hopkins University Press.
Matza, D. 1964. *Delinquency and Drift*. New York: John Wiley.
Parenti, M. 1978. *Power and the Powerless*. New York: St. Martin's.
Platt, A. 1977. *The Child Savers: The Invention of Delinquency*. Chicago: University of Chicago Press.
Reid, B. 1974. "Juvenile waiver: The inconsistent standard." *American Journal of Criminal Law* 2:
   331-347.
Rothman, D.J. 1980. *Conscience and Convenience: The Asylum and its Alternatives in Progressive
   America*. Boston: Little, Brown.
Sargent, D.A., and D.H. Gordon. 1963. "Waiver of jurisdiction: An evaluation of the process in the
   juvenile court." *Crime & Delinquency* 9: 121-128.
Scull, A.T. 1977. "Madness and segregative control: The rise of the insane asylum." *Social Problems*
   24: 337-350.
Snyder, R.V., W.H. Kent, C.F. Klejbuk, D.L. McCorkle, and D.L. Libby. 1978. *The Transfer of Juveniles
   to Adult Court in Pennsylvania*. Harrisburg: Pennsylvania Joint Council on the Criminal Justice System.
Wizner, S. 1984. "Discretionary waiver of juvenile court jurisdiction: Arbitrariness." *Criminal Justice
   Ethics* (Summer/Fall): 41-50.

Section II

SOURCES OF
DELINQUENCY

What leads one youth to become delinquent while another does not? This question, as old as delinquency itself, has been approached from a variety of perspectives and has led to the development of numerous "cures" for the problem. To date, there is no simple and elegant answer to this basic question, but a lively debate continues. The three articles selected for this section represent those areas on which much recent attention has been directed and around which much controversy has been generated. The first article, which highlights research on the link between nutrition and delinquency, illustrates the growing interest in biological factors by academicians and by practitioners alike. When used in conjunction with sociological and psychological theories, the consideration of biological influences promises to add significantly to our understanding of delinquency. The second article focuses on the influence of family factors on delinquency. The family was the focal point of early American research on delinquency and recent research reflects a renewed interest in family variables particularly such factors as child abuse, broken homes, and working mothers. The final article focuses on gangs, the community conditions which lead to the formation of gangs, and the manner in which gangs change as the members mature. These three articles represent only a portion of the current ideas on what factors lead to delinquency, but they do represent areas in which a great flurry of research activity is now taking place.

Bernard Rimland and Gerald Larson, in "Nutritional and Ecological

Approaches to the Reduction of Criminality, Delinquency and Violence,'' question psycho-social approaches to the rehabilitation of offenders, and argue that some crime is caused by biological malfunction of the brain. To focus on the personality structure of the offender, or the social environment from which the offender comes without concurrently examining the biological-ecological-chemical aspects of the problem is to ignore a great deal of evidence on the delinquency problem. Rimland and Larson have brought together an excellent collection of studies to document their perspective. In addition to examining a number of nutritional issues, the authors have also examined issues related to pollution and the extent to which maternal smoking, lead poisoning and other toxic materials impact on the lives of youth, enhancing the potential for delinquency.

Travis Hirschi, in "Crime and Family Policy," argues that the family may be the most important influence in the delinquency process. Describing the research conducted by the Oregon group, Hirschi notes that they went into the homes of families with potentially delinquent and nondelinquent children and observed the patterns of interaction. The process by which delinquent behavior is controlled is quite simple: monitor behavior, recognize deviant behavior, and, punish such behavior. However, in examining this process we come to grips with some very basic issues in the delinquency process. For example, Hirschi notes that some parents do not recognize criminal behavior in their children. Hirschi examines a number of additional issues including working mothers, child abuse and single-parent families and proposes a novel solution that reflects the importance of teaching and the educational process. At the same time, he acknowledges the limitations of this approach and the extent to which the state can intervene in family situations. And therein lies a major problem. While we may be able to identify the kinds of family problems that enhance the potentials for delinquency, there may not be an effective remedy which would involve the state.

In the final article in this section, "How Do Gangs Get Organized?," John Hagedorn examines the nature of gang activity and the factors which lead groups of young people to define themselves as a gang. Much of the stage for gang activity is set by economic and social conditions in the local community. Hagedorn argues that the law enforcement perspective on gangs is often built on false stereotypes which have little to do with the reality of gang life. Further, many law enforcement policies actually make the gang problem worse by giving gang members a sense of unity and public visibility.

5

Nutritional and Ecological Approaches to the Reduction of Criminality, Delinquency and Violence

Bernard Rimland and Gerald E. Larson

Abstract

An upsurge in crime and violence, much of which has been characterized as senseless, has attracted much attention and concern in recent years. The traditional approaches toward the treatment of offenders, through counsel‧ ing and psychosocial rehabilitation, have in repeated studies been found to be useless or counterproductive. These futile methods assume antisocial behavior to be primarily sociogenic in origin. This paper takes the view that much crime, particularly violent crime, is caused by biological malfunction of the brain. The strong and well-known association between learning disabilities and antisocial behavior suggests that both learning problems and problems with the law may stem from a common cause—brain malfunction. A number of demonstrated causes of brain malfunction in youth are discussed. Maternal smoking, poor nutrition, toxic metal and other chemical exposure, and food allergies are among the adverse factors considered. Several biological remedial interventions are proposed, including megavitamin therapy. Megavitamin therapy has been proven useful in treating various behavioral disorders in a number of recent double

Bernard Rimland and Gerald E. Larson, "Nutritional and Ecological Approaches to the Reduction of Criminality, Delinquency and Violence." From *Journal of Applied Nutrition,* Vol. 33, No. 2 — 1981. Reprinted with permission.

blind studies, and opposition to it by the medical establishment may consequently be expected to diminish in the near future.

Our main point is that biogenic factors may play a substantial and important role in causing crime, and that these influences have been ignored for too long.

These influences include, but are not limited to:

Nutrition, including
1. Excess sugar intake
2. Ingestion of food additives
3. Need for increased vitamins and minerals
4. Ingestion of phosphates
5. Food allergy effects on behavior

Pollution, including
1. Ingestion or inhalation of lead and other toxic metals
2. Ingestion of pesticides and herbicides inadvertently added to food or water supplies
3. Inhalation of fumes from various environmental sources
4. Exposure to artificial light and other sources of radiant energy
5. Medical interventions, such as prenatal estrogen and induced delivery

Substance abuse, including
Deliberate use of alcohol, lysergic acid diethylamide (LSD) and other drugs (including use during pregnancy)

In the following sections some of these purported causal factors will be discussed, and we will describe certain biologically based remedial techniques intended to offset them, at least in some individuals.

Biological Factors in Crime and Violence: Nutritional

After years of neglect, there has been a recent, though still small, upsurge of interest in the biological approach to correcting deviant behavior. Two recent books by Hippchen[1] and Schauss[2] will provide the interested reader with a wealth of information on the topic.

Hypoglycemia. Hypoglycemia means "low blood sugar," but the mental problems which are attributed to hypoglycemia appear in fact to be the result of abnormal fluctuations in the blood sugar level. Such fluctuations are brought about largely by the excessive consumption of sugar-containing foods, to which the human body has difficulty in adjusting. Evolution produced a brain which utilizes glucose (blood sugar) for energy. Eating large amounts of sucrose (table sugar) triggers an intricate process in the body metabolism which results, in some cases, in a severe disruption of the brain's glucose metabolism. The quick energy supplied by sucrose can in the long run be expensive to one's physical and behavioral health.

Many specialists in the nutrition-behavior area regard sugar as the arch villain in provoking an increase in juvenile crime and disruption and in causing degradation of learning skills. Sugar consumption has risen rapidly during recent years, the current per capita consumption being about 130 pounds per year, which averages about 6 ounces per day. As with other additives, however, some individuals consume many times that amount. Schauss, in his study of the dietary habits of delinquents, found some who ingested sugar at the rate of 400 pounds per year.[3]

Although a vast amount of literature exists on the adverse psychological effects of excessive sugar[4], most of the evidence is anecdotal or circumstantial. Few controlled studies have been done, because it is hard to control diets (especially of those who crave sweets), because foods that contain sugar also contain fats and additives, and for various other reasons. Kershner and Hawke[5] conducted a study in which the dietary intake of hyperactive and learning disabled students was controlled. They obtained parent ratings on 13 factors, such as hyperactivity, aggression, and attention span, for 20 students before and after a 6.5-month trial of a high protein, low carbohydrate, sugar-free diet. The children improved significantly on all 13 factors rated.

Food additives. Food additives are another ecological factor that has gained a great deal of attention in recent years as a probable cause of hyperactivity and learning disabilities. The relationship was first reported by Feingold in 1973[6], and has since been the subject of a great deal of investigation and controversy. Some investigators have reported studies confirming Feingold's work, while others reported little if any behavioral disruptions in children given artificial food colorings and flavors. At present, the controversy seems to be resolving strongly in Feingold's favor. The experimental studies that reported little effect had used only about 27 mg of artificial additives per day to test for additive effects. Swanson and Kinsbourne[7] decided that the earlier experimenters had asked the wrong question: "Does taking the amount of additives ingested by the average child cause hyperactivity?" Instead, Swanson and Kinsbourne asked: "Does taking the amount of additives typically ingested by the hyperactive child cause hyperactivity?" They determined that hyperactive children typically ingested 100 to 150 mg per day of additives. On 100 or 150 mg, very noticeable effects were seen.[8] Studies on both children and laboratory animals have confirmed adverse effects of additives on learning as well as on the activity level.[9]

"Junk Food." Lonsdale and Shamberger[10] have shown that the type of diet ingested by many American teenagers, which includes a high percentage

of vitamin- and mineral-deficient, sugar- and additive-laden "junk foods," can, in some cases, lead to symptoms of beriberi (thiamine deficiency). Among the symptoms they noted in their subjects were personality changes such as increased irritability and aggressiveness. They stated:

> Access to easily assimilable sweet beverages could represent a modern danger which is insufficiently emphasized in American society and may well be responsible for personality traits and symptomatology that are regularly overlooked and considered to be "the personality of a growing child or adolescent."

Liggio[11] studied a group of children in Italy whose diets completely lacked animal protein, consisting, instead, primarily of bread, potatoes, and pasta. As a result, the children were restless, impulsive, inattentive, and had poor memories. Those children who were provided with the recommended 100 grams of meat daily showed considerable behavior improvement. Langseth and Dowd have also reported amelioration of disturbed behavior in children upon dietary improvement.[12]

Another interesting report of the effect of improved diet upon behavior in a military correctional facility was discussed by Schauss:[13]

> On 1 November 1978, white flour was removed from the confinees' diet and was replaced with whole wheat bread. On 3 February 1979, granulated sugar was removed from the confinees' diet. This consisted of removal of all pastries, cakes, ice cream, soft drinks, and Kool-Aid from the confinees' diet. (The confinees are allowed a teaspoon of sugar in their coffee (or tea) and drink milk or water.) Since this time, the medical log shows that a definite decrease in the number of confinees at sick call and on medication has occurred and that disciplinary reports from the period this year are down 12 percent from the same time-frame of last year.

It was also reported that the behavioral improvements were maintained, and that the attitude of tension, frustration, and anxiety which ordinarily pervades correctional facilities was greatly reduced. Schauss, a criminologist, and Reed, a probation officer, have reported a degree of success in using their dietary management methods on criminal offenders that far exceeds the negligible levels achieved by traditional approaches.[14]

Both sugar and white flour contain very little nourishment other than calories. The process of refining wheat to make white flour from the whole wheat removes 87 percent of the fiber, 98 percent of vitamin B-6, 84 percent of the magnesium, 81 percent of the manganese, etc. The brain, which must have these nutrients in order to function properly, evolved over a period of hundreds of thousands of years during which vitamins and minerals were not removed from foods through misguided "refining" processes. It is thus not surprising that some individuals who consume highly refined foods such as white sugar and white flour may suffer problems in learning and behavior. Variations as great as 2000 percent among normal people in vitamin requirements are not unusual.[15]

Phosphates. Within the past few years a controversy has erupted in Germany about the behavioral toxicity of foods containing phosphates.[16]

Phosphates are contained in many foods, and it is reported that some children become hyperactive when given such foods, or when given a challenge dose of 75 mg of phosphate in capsule form or mixed with foods. Hafer[17] stated that if a phosphate-sensitive child is given a phosphate-free diet for several weeks, then given the challenge dose of phosphate, the symptoms of minimal brain damage, including hyperactivity, (MBD) will ensue within 1 hour, usually within 15 minutes. Phosphate containing foods include:

> Practically all processed or canned meats, including hot dogs, ham, bacon, etc.
> Processed cheeses
> Many, perhaps most, baked products, because of the use of phosphate baking powder
> All cola drinks, and many other soft drinks
> All instant soups, puddings, etc.
> Various toppings, seasonings, etc.

Given the pervasiveness of phosphates in the diet, it is not surprising that the problem should be considered controversial. It is of interest that Adelle Davis suggested that excess of phosphates can be harmful.[18] She recommended supplementing the diet with calcium and magnesium to help offset the effects of excess phosphorus.

Cerebral Allergies and Chemical Intolerances. It is well known that allergies may cause such symptoms as hay fever, asthma and hives. Since it is so widely recognized that the nasal membranes, the lungs and the skin can be affected by a food or other substance to which some individuals are intolerant, it is surprising that there should be controversy as to whether the brain, the most intricate and biochemically complicated organ in the body, could also be affected by allergies. Yet there has indeed been controversy. Only in the past few years has there begun to be some acceptance, within the medical profession of the idea of cerebral allergies.

Individuals who have cerebral allergies to wheat, beef, milk, corn and other common foods are likely to experience chronic problems such as headaches, feelings of unreality, and lack of control over their behavior, sometimes resulting in violence or, surprisingly, specific compulsions such as to steal or commit arson. Individuals who are allergic to or who cannot tolerate substances not commonly eaten or encountered, such as, perhaps, oysters, walnuts, or formaldehyde, may experience unexpected and uncontrolled episodes of aberrant behavior with intervening periods of trouble-free behavior.

Biological Factors in Crime and Delinquency: Pollution

Maternal Smoking

Smoking among women is a form of ecological pollution that has grown enormously in the years since World War II, and that appears likely to have an adverse effect on the intellectual competence and behavior of children.[19a] According to a 1979 report from the U.S. Surgeon General, more women than men aged 17 to 24 now smoke. Cigarette smoking among women became common during World War II, about 25-30 years after it became a common practice for men to smoke. In 1950, deaths among women from lung cancer occurred at the rate of 4.0 per 100,000. By 1970, the figure was 9.5 per 100,000 and, by 1977, it had risen over 300 percent to 14.9 per 100,000. By 1983, the projected number is about 23 deaths per 100,000, thus equalling the number of deaths due to breast cancer. The Surgeon General's report also noted that babies born to women who smoked during pregnancy were, on the average, 6 ounces lighter than babies born to comparable non-smokers, and the more the women smoked, the greater the reduction in birth weight. Women who smoke double their risk of having a low birth-weight baby.[19b] Small birth size and prematurity are known concomitants of impaired intellectua! level. Another recent study indicates that the negative effects of smoking continue even if women quit before pregnancy. Naeye[20], in his study of 50,000 pregnancies, reported abnormally large areas of dead tissue in the placentas of both smoking mothers and women who had been smokers in the past. Such damage to the placenta interferes with the nutrition of the fetus. In his comparison of 2,476 hyperactive children with 12,511 normal children, Nichols[21] found maternal smoking during pregnancy to be the most important of the 42 factors he studied.

While space does not permit its discussion, maternal drinking has also been implicated as a cause of retardation and other difficulties.

Lead and Other Toxic Metals

Of all the ecological pollutants that adversely affect intelligence and behavior, lead is perhaps the most widely recognized. It has long been known that high blood lead levels in children lead to hyperactivity, aggressiveness, and mental retardation. Only recently, however, has it been recognized that much lower levels of lead in the body may also have adverse cognitive and behavioral effects. Clinical lead toxicity is usually thought of as being found only in persons with unusual exposure to high levels of lead, such as smelter workers or children who eat flakes of heavily leaded paint from inner city slum dwellings. There are, however, many other sources of environmental lead, including some that are almost impossible to avoid, such as lead from soldered tin cans or automobile exhausts. Automobile exhaust lead is especially dangerous, because the particle size is very small, and the route of intake—lung tissue—is highly sensitive to even small amounts of lead.[22a] Psychological impairment due to lead appears to be much more prevalent than has heretofore been thought. The lead burden of the human body is increasing at a rapid rate due to industrialization. Ericson, Shirahata, and Patterson[22b] found that the bones of ancient Peruvian Indians contained less than 1/500th as much lead as is contained in the bones of persons who have died recently.

One method of determining the levels of lead and other metals in the body is through hair mineral analysis, a sensitive laboratory process in which a small sample of hair is tested. In a study of subclinical lead toxicity, Moore and Fleishman[23] determined that degradation in hand/eye coordination on a pursuit rotor task could clearly be seen at a mere 10 parts per million of lead in the hair. These authors noted that this was "probably less than the average lead burden in the U.S., and implies far more widespread toxicity than had been previously supposed."

Of special interest is the repeated finding that delinquent and disruptive behavior is associated with high lead levels. Needleman, and his colleagues[24] conducted a study in which both psychological test performance and classroom behavior were evaluated in children with elevated lead levels. They reported that the performance of high-lead-level children was significantly worse than that of the low-lead-level children on all of the following factors on a teachers' behavioral rating scale: distractability, lack of persistence, dependability, hyperactivity, impulsiveness, frustration level, daydreaming, inability to follow simple instructions, and overall functioning.

Although lead is the metal that has received the most attention, other metals can also be neurotoxic, and are being increasingly implicated as causes of physical and behavioral disorders. It has been reported that mercury, cadmium, copper, and, to some extent, aluminum have provoked "mental" problems. The increased use of copper plumbing throughout the U.S. since World War II is of special interest, since it has been found that excess copper may cause a variety of problems, including depression, irritability, and hyperactivity. It has also been reported that copper acts synergistically with artificial food additives, so that individuals with high copper levels may become hyperactive at even low levels of these additives.[25]

Pihl and Parkes[26a], on analyzing hair samples from 31 learning-disabled and 22 normal students, reported that they could classify the two groups with 98 percent accuracy by using only the hair mineral content to predict learning disability. Cadmium was the mineral most closely related to learning disability. Pihl has subsequently reported in an unpublished study that violent criminals have higher levels of both hair lead and cadmium than nonviolent criminals.

Attempts have been made to control lead and other forms of pollution. Decreased use of lead in gasoline and paint, educational campaigns on the dangers of smoking and drug use, and legislation aimed at getting "junk food" out of schools and residential institutions represent limited attempts to correct the problems. There are other areas in which little or no progress is being made. The Environmental Protection Agency has estimated that 90 percent of the 57 million tons of toxic waste produced annually in the U.S. is disposed of by environmentally unsound methods.[26b]

Treatment

While it may seem that an individual with longstanding brain dysfunction is a poor prospect for remediation, the chances for improvement are in fact quite substantial. Even if the individual incurred his handicapping condition prenatally or in infancy, there is a reasonable probability that the efficacy of brain function can be increased. Although it is unlikely that remediation can bring the individual damaged prenatally or in infancy to his full potential, it is nevertheless possible that worthwhile improvement can be achieved. It may be, for example, that the "damage" increases the brain's need for a certain substance to a level that would not ordinarily be reached by eating a normal diet, but that might be reached by using potent nutritional supplements.

An obvious step is to reduce or stop the intake of noxious substances that cause brain impairment. It is commonly known that such substances as alcohol, marijuana, and LSD can cause such impairment. Only recently, however, has evidence begun to accumulate indicating that a wide variety of other substances such as food additives, lead, and cadmium can also have adverse effects. We have already discussed the benefits to hyperactive/learning disordered persons of discontinuing the consumption of artificial food colorings and flavorings. We have also referred to studies in which sugar and additive laden foods were removed from the diet, with good behavioral consequences.[27]

The heavy metals, such as lead, cadmium and mercury, remain in the body, and can continue to be troublesome, even after the individual has ceased ingesting or inhaling them. They are especially likely to be troublesome if the individual's diet is low in zinc, calcium, and iron. There are medical and nutritional procedures for reducing the body level of heavy metals, through the process of chelation.[28] Chelation therapy consists of administering substances orally or by injection that capture (chelate) the molecules of lead or other contaminants. In their study of hyperactive children whose blood lead levels were in the elevated, yet "nontoxic" range, David, Clark, and Hoffman reported marked behavioral improvement when chelation therapy was applied to the subgroup that had no known cause for their behavioral problems.[29] The children whose problems stemmed from non lead-related causes did not show such improvement.

There are a number of nonprescription chelating compounds on the market. Most of these contain various nutrients, including large quantities of vitamin C, which is a good chelating agent. Stone[30] reported a number of studies showing the value of vitamin C in protecting against poisoning by heavy metals, drugs, toxic gases, and other pollutants. For example, when vitamin C was used to treat 17 subjects with chronic lead poisoning, all showed improvement within a week: "Most of the men enjoyed normal sleep, lost the irritability and nervousness, and no longer had tremors."

A certain, and as yet indeterminable, proportion of learning- and behavior-disabled individuals can be helped by discontinuing their intake of noxious substances, or by removing deposits of noxious substances from their bodies through chelation therapy. In a great many other instances, however, it will also be necessary to increase the brain's concentration of the substances that it uses during its normal functioning; that is, by improving nutrition.

Improving nutritional intake can be accomplished in two ways. The first is by excluding junk food and restoring to the individual's diet natural foods high in protein and low in refined carbohydrates.

For most individuals, the use of such a diet, particularly when supplemented by a good quality multiple vitamin and mineral tablet, will provide adequate nutrition.[31] In such cases, the individual is said to have had a vitamin deficiency. There is, however, a certain and not insubstantial proportion of the population whose learning and behavior disorders stem from the need for a much larger intake of vitamins and minerals than they can reasonably expect to obtain from even a superior diet.[32] Whether such individuals need larger than normal amounts of these nutrients because of a genetic defect, a handicapping condition incurred prenatally or during childhood, or for some other reason, their primary hope for improved functioning may lie in the intake of vitamin supplements in quantities that are perhaps many times as large as those needed by normally functioning individuals. The use of such large amounts of vitamins as a means of remediation is known as megavitamin therapy. Individuals who have a greater need for one or more vitamins than can be met by the usual dietary interventions are said to have a vitamin dependency condition.

Megavitamin therapy has been the center of a good deal of dispute and debate during the past 30 years. The controversy peaked in the early 1970s, with the publication of a series of often vitriolic attacks and counterattacks by groups favoring or opposing this approach. The dispute seems to be subsiding, as more objective data have become available, and as each side has adjusted its stance in response to criticism.

Evidence favoring megavitamin therapy is now accumulating at a fast rate and, with little doubt, it will, in a few years, be a widely accepted form of treatment for learning and behavior disorders. (For a recent review, see Kahan.[33] Any serious consideration of options available for controlling antisocial behavior should therefore include the possibility of employing, or at least investigating, the use of megavitamin therapy.

Most of the controversy surrounding the use of megavitamin therapy in treating learning disabilities has centered around the use of high dosage levels of the B vitamins. A substantial body of evidence, however, shows that vitamin C also has beneficial effects upon mental functioning. Kubala and Katz[34] investigated the relationship between blood levels of vitamin C and IQ, using four groups of students as subjects. They found that high blood levels of the vitamin were associated with above average IQ in all four groups. Supplementing the students' diet with citrus juice raised the IQ of the low vitamin C groups by 3.4 points, but had no effect on the group already high in vitamin C.

The Czechoslovakian government has done extensive work with vitamin C. In one study of vitamin C supplementation on 12,000 coal miners, remarkable improvements were noted in a variety of mental and physical measures.[35] Of particular interest was the significant decrease in accidents, which was attributed to increased alertness. Further investigation showed that vitamin C administration improved such "psychomotor reactions" as tapping speed and reaction time.[36]

Vitamin C supplementation, like supplementation with the B vitamins and the various nutrient minerals, is not only safe but can confer many additional benefits beyond the improvement in mental functioning described above. As noted earlier, Stone[37] has cited numerous studies showing that vitamin C protects against heavy metal toxicity. It also protects against other organic and inorganic toxins, heat and cold stress, physical shock and trauma, various kinds of infections, as well as radiation.

Iron is another nutrient that has been implicated in learning disabilities.[38] In a 1971 report to the Food and Nutrition Board, "tests of attentiveness and ability to focus on, orient to, and sustain interest in a learning task revealed significant differences between children with iron deficiency anemia and those who were not anemic.[39] A recent FDA press release (30 May 1980) noted that "an expert advisory committee reported to the FDA that iron deficiency is a leading nutrition problem in the United States," and advised that selected foods be fortified with iron. According to the Department of Health, Education & Welfare (DHEW), white male youths aged 15-19 years from low income families and black youths aged 18-19 years have average iron intakes that are 17 and 25 percent below dietary standards, respectively.[40]

With the possible exception of vitamins A, E and D, which may, in rare cases, be harmful when taken in large amounts, megavitamins are quite safe. (Vitamins A and D are not used in the megavitamin treatment of learning disabilities in any event).[41] Several recent reports in the medical literature have erroneously claimed danger from megavitamin therapy and have caused unwarranted concern about safety. One widely-cited study by Herbert & Jacob[42] claimed that high levels of vitamin C ingestion resulted in the destruction of vitamin B-12. This report was inaccurate, since the authors had simply used the wrong laboratory method for measuring B-12.[43] Another widely cited report, which claimed that "megavitamin therapy" was dangerous, described a four-year-old child who became ill from taking excessive vitamin A and recovered when he stopped taking the vitamin A.[44] As it turned out, this report had nothing to do with megavitamin therapy; the teachers of the child had reported seeing him eating candy-flavored vitamins on the school playground.

Poor diet seems to have a cascading effect, with each problem causing and aggravating other problems. As mentioned earlier, Lonsdale and Shamberger[45] reported a widespread thiamine deficiency, not yet at the beriberi level, in American teenagers as the result of their consumption of junk foods. Aggressiveness and irritability were reported as common symptoms. Supplementation with megadoses (150-300 mg/day) of vitamin B_1 reversed the symptoms, sometimes in a matter of weeks. Alcoholism, another serious problem, also seems to be aggravated by junk foods. In a study conducted at Loma Linda Medical School, laboratory rats fed a "typical American teenage diet" consumed five times as much alcohol as did rats given conventional human food. Adding coffee increased the consumption of alcohol to six-fold, but supplementing the teenage diet with vitamins produced a significant decrease in alcohol consumption.[46] Vitamin supplements have also been shown to reduce the level of intoxication resulting from alcohol consumption.[47]

While there is yet much to learn, it seems obvious that the field of nutrition has a great deal to offer, if we are seriously interested in stemming the rising tide of crime and violence.

Footnotes

[1]Hippchen, L.J. (ed.), *Ecologic-Biochemical Approaches to Treatment of Delinquents and Criminals,* New York, Van Nostrand Reinhold, (1978).

[2]Schauss, A.G., *Diet, Crime, and Delinquency,* Berkeley, CA, Parker House, (1980).

[3]Schauss, A.G., *Orthomolecular Treatment of Criminal Offenders,* Berkeley, CA, Michael Lesser, M.D., (1978).

[4]Dufty, W., *Sugar Blues,* New York, Warner Books, (1975).

Rodale, J.I., *Natural Health, Sugar, and the Criminal Mind,* New York, Pyramid, (1968).

Wallace, J.F., and Wallace, M.J., "The effects of excessive consumption of refined sugar on learning skills, behavior, attitudes, and/or physical condition in school-aged children," A booklet prepared for Parents for Better Nutrition, Medford, OR, (1978).

Yudkin, J., *Sweet and Dangerous,* New York, Wyden Press, (1972).

[5]Kershner, J., and Hawke, W., "Megavitamins and learning disorders: A controlled double-blind experiment," *Journal of Nutrition,* 109:819-826, (1979).

[6]Feingold, B., *Why Your Child is Hyperactive,* New York, Random House, (1973).

[7]Swanson, J.M., and Kinsbourne, M., "Food dyes impair performance of hyperactive children on a laboratory learning test," *Science,* 207:1485-1487, (1980).

[8]Ibid.

[9]Shaywitz, B.A., Goldenring, J.R., and Wool, R.S., "The effects of chronic administration of food colorings on activity levels and cognitive performance in normal and hyperactive developing rat pups," *Neurobehavioral Toxicology,* 1:4-47, (19??).

Weiss, B., Williams, J.H., Margen, S., Abrams, B., Caan, J., Citron, L.J., Cox, C., McKibben, J., Ogar, D., and Schultz, S., "Behavioral responses to artificial food colors," *Science,* 207:1487-1489, (1980).

[10]Lonsdale, D., and Shamberger, R.J., "Red cell transketolase as an indicator of nutritional deficiency," *American Journal of Clinical Nutrition,* 33:205-212, (1980).

[11]Liggio, F., ["Interference in the performance of the mental activities due to the wrong diet which lacks the protein factor of animal origin and nervous disorders which are complementary and reversible"], *Acta Neurologica,* 24(4):548-556, (1969).

[12]Langseth, L. and Dowd, J., "Glucose Tolerance and Hyperkinesis," New York, The New York Institute for Child Development, Inc., (1977).

[13]*Op. Cit,* note 2.

[14]*Op. Cit,* note 1.

Reed, B., Testimony before the Select Committee on Nutrition and Human Needs, United States Senate, 95th Congress, 1st Session, 22 June 1977.

Op. Cit, note 3.

Schauss, A.G., "A critical analysis of the diets of chronic offenders: Part I," *Journal of Orthomolecular Psychiatry,* 8:149-157, (1979).

Schauss, A.G., "A critical analysis of the diets of chronic offenders: Part II, *Journal of Orthomolecular Psychiatry,* 8:222-226, (1979).

Op cit., note 2.

[15]Williams, R.J., *Biochemical Individuality,* New York, Wiley, (1956).

Williams, R.J., and Rimland, B., "Individuality." In *Encyclopedia of Psychiatry, Neurology, and Psychoanalysis,* New York, Van Nostrand, (1977).

[16]Hafer, H., *Nahrungsphosphat als Ursache fur Verhaltensstorungen und Jugendkriminalitat,* Heidelberg, Kriminalistik Verlag, (1979).

[17]*Ibid.*

[18]Davis, A., *Let's Get Well,* New York, Harcourt Brace Jovanovich, (1965).

[19a]Dunn, H.G., McBurney, A.K., Ingram, S., and Hunter, C.M., "Maternal cigarette smoking during pregnancy and the child's subsequent development: II. Neurological and intellectual maturation to the age of 6½ years," *Canadian Journal of Public Health,* 68:43-50, (1977).

Rapp, D.J., "Nutrition in the vision of children," *Journal of the American Optometric Association,* 50:1107-1111, (November 1979).

[19b]Richmond, J.B., "A perspective on primary prevention in the preschool years." Address to the National Center for Clinical Intern Programs, Washington, D.C., (December 1979).

[20]Naeye, R.L., "The duration of maternal cigarette smoking, fetal and placental disorders." *Early Human Development,* 2:229-37, (1979).

[21]Nichols, P.L., "Early antecedents of childhood hyperactivity," Bethesda, MD. National Institute of Health, (May 1980).

[22b]Clinton, M., "The intoxications," In T. Harrison (ed.), *Principles of Internal Medicine,* New York, Blakiston, (1950).

[22b]Ericson, J.E., Shirahata, H., and Patterson, C.C., "Skeletal concentrations of lead in ancient Peruvians," *New England Journal of Medicine,* 946-951, (26 April 1979).

[23]Moore, L.S., and Fleischman, A.I., "Subclinical lead toxicity," *Orthomolecular Psychiatry,* 4:61-70, (1975).

[24]Needleman, H.L., Gunnoe, C., Leviton, A., Reff, R., Peresie, H., Maher, C., and Barrett, P., "Deficits in psychologic and classroom performance of children with elevated dentine lead levels," *New England Journal of Medicine,* 300:689-695, (1979).

[25]Brenner, A. "A study of the efficacy of the Feingold diet on hyperkinetic children: Some favorable personal observations," *Clinical Pediatrics,* 16:652-656, (1977).

[26a]Pihl, R.O., and Parkes, M., "Hair element content in learning disabled children," *Science,* 198:204-206, (1977).

[26b]"Everybody's problem: Hazardous waste," SW-826, Washington, D.C.: Office of Water and Waste Management, United States Environmental Protection Agency, (1980).

[27]*Op. cit,* note 5.

Op cit, note 14 (last five references).

[28]Chisholm, J.J., Jr., & Barltrop, D., "Recognition and management of children with increased lead absorption," *Archives of Disease in Childhood,* 54:249-262, (1979).

Op. cit, note 2.

Walker, M., *Chelation Therapy,* Atlanta, '76 Press, (1980).

[29]David, O.J., Clark, J., and Hoffman, S., "Childhood lead poisoning: A Reevaluation," *Archives of Environmental Health,* 34: 106-111, (1979).

[30]Stone, I., *The Healing Factor: Vitamin C,* New York: Grosset and Dunlap, (1972).

[31]Williams, R.J., *The Physician's Handbook of Nutritional Science,* Springfield, IL, C.C. Thomas, (1975).

[32]*Op. cit,* note 15.

[33]Kahan, M., "Search and research: Summaries of megavitamin studies," Canadian Schizophrenia Foundation, Regina, Canada (1980).

[34]Kubala, A.L., and Katz, M.M., "Nutritional factors in psychological test behaviors," *The Journal of Genetic Psychology,* 96:343-352, (1960).

[35]Hejda, S., Smola, J., and Masek, J., "Influence of physiological vitamin C allowances on the health status of miners," *Review of Czechoslovak Medicine,* 22(2): 90-97, (1976).

[36]Masek, J., Hruba, F., Novakova, V., Honzak, R., and Kaucka, J., "Vitamin C and vigilance," *Review of Czechoslovak Medicine,* 22:209-215, (1976).

[37]*Op. cit,* note 30.

[38]Oski, F.P., "The nonhematologic manifestations of iron deficinecy," *American Journal of Diseases of Children,* 133:315-322, (1979).

[39]Berman, A., "Nutrition and learning," *Ladycom Magazine,* 53-56, (April 1980).

[40]Abraham, S., "Caloric and selected nutrient values for persons 1-74 years of age: First health and nutrition examination survey, United States, 1971-1974," Vital and health statistics, data from the National Health Survey, Series II, No. 209, Report No. PHN-79-1657 (Rockville, MD: National Center for Health Statistics (DHEW), June 1979).

[41]Rimland, B., "High dosage levels of certain vitamins in the treatment of children with severe mental disorders." In L. Pauling and D.R. Hawkins, (eds), *Orthomolecular Psychiatry,* San Francisco, W.H. Freeman, (1973).

[42]Herbert, V., and Jacob, E., "Destruction of vitamin B_{12} by ascorbic acid," *Journal of the American Medical Association,* 230:241-242, (1974).

[43]Pauling, L., *Vitamin C, the Common Cold, and the Flu,* San Francisco, W.H. Freeman, (1976).

⁴⁴Shaywitz, B.A., Siegel, N.J., and Pearson, H.A., "Megavitamins for minimal brain dysfunction: A potentially dangerous therapy," *Journal of the American Medical Association*, 238:1749, (1977).

⁴⁵*Op. cit,* note 10.

⁴⁶Register, U.D., Marsh, S.R., Thurston, C.T., Fields, B.J., Horning, M.C., Hardinge, M.G., and Sanchez, A., "Influence of nutrients on intake of alcohol," *Journal of the American Dietetic Association,* 61:159-162, (1972).

⁴⁷Myrsten, A.L., Kelly, M., and Goldberg, L., "Effects of intravenous administration of a multivitamin preparation on acute alcoholic intoxication," Report No. 315, Stockholm, Sweden, Psychological Laboratories, University of Stockholm, (1970).

6

Crime and Family Policy

Travis Hirschi

For many years the Oregon Social Learning Center has treated families with problem children—children who bite, kick, scratch, whine, lie, cheat, and steal. As might be expected nowadays, this group started with the assumption that the proper way to train children is to reward their good deeds and ignore their bad ones. The idea was, of course, that eventually the children would be so wrapped up in doing good that they would no longer consider doing evil. After much struggling with such families and (one supposes) their own training, these scholarly practitioners came to the conclusion that children must be *punished* for their misdeeds if they are to learn to live without them.[1]

This conclusion may come as no surprise to those millions of parents who have spent years talking firmly to their children, yelling and screaming at them, spanking them, grounding them, cutting off their allowances, and in general doing whatever they could think of to try to get the little bastards to behave; but it is exceedingly rare among social scientists, especially those who deal with crime and delinquency. Criminologists become interested in people only after they are capable of criminal acts. By then, people (especially delinquents) tend to be pretty much free of their parents and too big for spanking. Not only is it too late to do anything about the family situation; it is too late to learn much about what the family situation was like during the "child-rearing" years. As a result, we have many explana-

Travis Hirschi, "Crime and Family Policy." *Journal of Contemporary Studies,* Volume 6, Number 1, 1983. Reprinted with permission.

tions of crime that ignore the family, and those of us who consider the family important in crime causation cannot say much in detail about specific deficiencies in child-rearing practices that are associated with an increased likelihood of criminality.

But I am being too generous. The major reason for the neglect of the family is that explanations of crime that focus on the family are directly contrary to the metaphysic of our age. "Modern" theories of crime accept this metaphysic. They assume that the individual would be noncriminal were it not for the operation of unjust and misguided institutions.[2]

"Outdated" theories of crime assume that decent behavior is not part of our native equipment, but is somehow built in through socialization and maintained by the threat of sanctions. It is hard to imagine a family-based explanation of crime that would not take the latter position.

Yet in taking this view, the members of the Oregon group are swimming against the intellectual currents of our time, and are doing what few students of crime have had the time or inclination to do. They are actually going into the homes of families with potentially delinquent children and watching them in operation. And they are coming up with terms and ideas in many ways superior to those traditionally used to describe the situation one finds there.

For example, the traditional research literature reports that discipline, supervision, and affection tend to be missing in the homes of delinquents; that the behavior of the parents is often "poor"; that indeed the parents of delinquents are unusually likely to have criminal records themselves. This information is all well and good, and is enough to make us suspicious of those many explanations of crime that ignore the family, but it does not represent much of an advance over the firm belief of the general public (and those who deal with offenders in the criminal justice system) that "defective upbringing" or "neglect" in the home is the primary cause of crime.

Another large literature deals with the subtleties of child-rearing — what might be called the "fine tuning" side of socialization. This information, too, is valuable. It is good to know, for example, that one should not rage and storm around the house, but should in all cases provide the child with a model of reasoned self control. And I suspect most parents would be more than happy to follow such advice if their children were not so exasperating. But in talking about delinquency, we are not really talking about the difference between good and better behavior, but the difference between tolerable and intolerable behavior, and at this level there is not much we can take for granted.

In fact, the Oregon group starts pretty much from scratch. They tell us that in order for the parent to teach the child not to use force and fraud, the parent must (1) monitor the child's behavior; (2) recognize deviant behavior when it occurs; and (3) punish such behavior. This seems simple and obvious enough. All that is required to activate the system is affection for *or* investment in the child. The parent who cares for the child will watch his behavior, see him doing things he should not do, and correct him. Presto! A socialized, decent human being.

Where might this simple system go wrong? Obviously, it can go wrong at any one of four places. The parents may not care for the child (in which case none of the other conditions would be met); the parents, even if they care, may not have the time or energy to monitor the child's behavior; the parents, even if they care *and* monitor, may not see anything wrong with the child's behavior; finally, even if everything else is in place, the parents may not have the inclination or the means to punish the child. So, what may appear at first glance to be nonproblematic turns out to be quite problematic indeed. Many things can go wrong. According to the Oregon group, in the homes of problem children many things have gone wrong: "Parents of stealers do not track: ([they] do not interpret stealing...as 'deviant'); they do not punish; and they do not care."[3]

I am impressed by the simplicity, beauty, and power of this approach. I believe that it organizes most of what we know about the families of delinquents, and that it provides a framework for addressing many of the complicated questions about the place of the family in crime causation. I also believe that when we consider the potential effects of some governmental action on crime and delinquency, we should specifically consider its impact on the ability of parents to monitor, recognize, and punish the misbehavior of their children. When we conclude the action would have an adverse impact on the family, we should be extremely reluctant to endorse it *as a crime prevention measure.* When we conclude that the program would have no impact on the family, we should at least hesitate to endorse it: in fact, we should immediately entertain the suspicion that the policy in question may have unintended adverse consequences on the crime problem.

The Independent Adolescent

The classic example is of course employment policy. If one asks professors of criminology why the crime rate is so high, or if one asks students in criminology courses why a particular group has an unusually high rate of crime, they will almost invariably mention unemployment or underemployment first. If one points out that homicide, rape, and assault do not typically produce much in the way of income, undergraduates as well as professors can quickly figure out how to get to these crimes from joblessness by way of something like frustration or rage.

The appeal of such explanations of crime is phenomenal. Year after year they are favored by students. Year after year criminologists produce dreadful warnings of what is going to happen if kids are not able to find jobs.

The source of the appeal of these explanations has already been mentioned. They suggest that people would not "turn to crime" if something better were available. This clearly implies that "faulty training" or other family defects have nothing to do with crime. In point of fact, such explanations often suggest in a not too subtle way that the families of "criminals" have done a better job of socializing their children than other families in the same circumstances. After all, isn't it normal for parents to teach their children to want to better themselves, to aspire to the good things of life?

So we ignore family considerations and, as best we can, concentrate on providing kids with good jobs. What do we expect to happen? Employment of the adolescent would presumably not much affect the parents' ability to monitor his behavior. Adolescents are outside the home a good deal anyway, and the employer would to some extent act as a surrogate monitor. The parents' affection for the child may, if anything, be improved by the child's willingness to reduce the financial burden on the family, and work is certainly not going to affect the parents' ability to recognize deviant behavior. The only element we have left in our model of child-rearing is *punishment.* How, if at all, does the employment of the youth affect the family's ability to punish his deviant behavior?

The power of the family in this situation will depend on the resources available to it relative to the resources available to the child. It will also depend on the child's aspirations. If the child wants to go to college at the parents' expense, to continue to drive the family Buick on weekends, and is really only picking up pocket money on the job, the damage to parental control is presumably minimal. (Although even here it may not be negligible. Drugs cost money, and their purchase is facilitated by money that does not have to be accounted for.[4]) If the child does not want to go to college, his family does not own a car, and the money he earns provides him a level of living equal or superior to that of his family, he is by definition no longer dependent on them. His parents no longer have the material means to punish him, and the entire system of family control is vulnerable to collapse. Henceforth the adolescent is free to come and go as he pleases. Affection and monitoring had better have done the job already, because the "child-rearing" days are over. It is time to hope for the best.

This conclusion about the possible consequences of adolescent employment is more than a deduction from theory. It is also a finding from research. According to historians of the family and criminologists interested in comparing crime rates across developing societies, a major feature of recent times is the increasing independence of adolescents from the family made possible by expansion and differentiation of the labor market. This independence from the family results in increasing dependence of the adolescent on other adolescents. But adolescents cannot take the place of parents as socializing agents because they have little or no investment in the outcome, are less likely to recognize deviant behavior, and, most important, do not possess the authority necessary to inflict punishment.[5]

More to the point, research that looks directly at delinquents offers no support for the notion that they are economically deprived when compared to other adolescents in their immediate area. On the contrary, it finds that they are more likely to be employed, more likely to be well-paid for the work they do, and more likely to enjoy the fruits of independence: sex, drugs, gambling, drinking, and job-quitting.[6]

By looking directly at the family we are thus able to resolve one of the minor paradoxes of our time, the fact that crime is caused by affluence *and* by poverty. General affluence to some extent weakens the control of all families. It especially weakens the control of those families in which the adolescent is able to realize a disposable income equal to that of his family almost from the day he finds a job. Unfortunately, life does not freeze at this point. Since the earnings from such jobs often do not keep up with the demands on them, our suddenly free adolescent can look forward to the not-too-distant day when his own son or daughter will, for a brief and not-too-shining moment, likewise have things "better" than he. He would do well to consider the consequences.

To make this point about affluence and against deprivation theories of crime, I have had to exaggerate the importance of economic factors. It helps the parents if they have money and the child doesn't, but poverty of the parents is not a large factor in crime causation,[7] and the eventual poverty of the offender seems to be explained by the same factors that explain his criminality: people untrained to get along with others, to delay the pursuit of pleasure, or to avoid force and fraud simply do not do very well in the labor market. For this reason, delinquency predicts socioeconomic status better than socioeconomic status predicts delinquency.[8]

Parents with Criminal Records

There is good reason to expect, and the data confirm, that these delinquents do not do very well as parents either. In fact, a recent, well-designed, and careful study reports that "the fact that delinquency is transmitted from one generation to the next is indisputable."[9] The extent of this transmission is revealed by the fact that in this same study less than 5 percent of the families accounted for almost half of the criminal convictions in the entire sample. (In my view, this finding is potentially much more important for the theory of crime, and for public policy, than the considerably better known finding of Wolfgang and his colleagues that something like 6 percent of *individual* offenders account for about half of all criminal acts.[10]) In order to achieve such concentration of crime in a small number of families, it is necessary that *the parents and the brothers and sisters* of offenders also be unusually likely to commit criminal acts.

Why should the children of offenders be unusually vulnerable to crime? If we had the complete answer to this question, we would be much further down the road to understanding crime than we are. But if we don't know for sure, we do have important clues. Recall that our affection-monitor-recognize-punish model assumes that criminal behavior is not something the parents have to work to produce; it is something they have to work to avoid. Such behavior is part of the child's native equipment, and will remain unless something is done about it. Consistent with this view, parents with criminal records do *not* encourage criminality in their children and are in fact as "censorious" toward their criminality as are parents with no record of criminal involvement.[11] Of course, not "wanting" criminal behavior in one's children, and being "upset" when it occurs, do not necessarily imply that great effort has been expended to prevent it. And if criminal behavior is oriented toward short-term payoffs — which it is — and if child-rearing is oriented to long-term payoffs — which it is — there is little reason to expect the parents in question to be particularly interested in child-rearing.

And indeed "supervision" of the child in such families is "lax" or "in-adquate" or "poor." Punishment tends to be "cheap," i.e., short-term — yelling and screaming, slapping and hitting — with little or no follow-up. These factors do not, however, completely account for the concentration of criminality in a small portion of families. (Part of the reason, presumably, is that these factors are very difficult to measure adequately.) I suspect the reason is that the most subtle of the elements of child-rearing is not included in these analyses. This is the element of "recognition" of deviant behavior. According to the Oregon Social Learning Center research, many parents do not even recognize *criminal* behavior in their children. For example, when the child steals outside the home, the parent discounts reports that he has done so on the grounds that they are unproved and cannot therefore be used to justify punishment.

Given that recognition is necessary to the entire child-rearing model, it is unfortunate that so little systematic thought and research have gone into the question of what parents should and should not recognize as deviant behavior if they are to prevent criminality. Part of the reason for this neglect may be traced to "policy" concerns. The libertarian streak in all of us understands that by denying connections between forms of deviant behavior we can undercut efforts to reduce more serious forms (e.g., crime) by attacking less serious forms (e.g., drugs, alcohol abuse, delinquency). We therefore deny such connections and dismiss out of hand research and theory that attempt to establish their existence.

Parents concerned about their children cannot affort this luxury. In fact, parents successful in crime prevention seem inclined to err in the direction of over-control, to see seeds of trouble in laziness, unreliability, disrespect for adults, and lack of concern for property. (A thorough catalog of parental concerns among those successful in rearing their children as non-delinquents would probably read like The Protestant Ethic or Middle Class Values — which tells us a great deal about why academics tend to be embarrassed by the entire subject of crime and the family.) Unsuccessful parents, in contrast, are considerably more tolerant, inclined to see little if anything wrong with their children's behavior until it is too late. As a consequence, it may be true that "people in prison are more willing to accept the idiosyncracies of others."[12] It may also be true that, when they are not in prison, they are more willing to accept the "idiosyncracies" of their own children. If this kind of tolerance in parents tends to go with intolerable behavior in children, it may be exactly what is meant by those concerned with "moral decay." Little wonder those concerned with "moral decay" tend to feel embattled when they see the thrust of social policy moving in the direction of decriminalization and diversion on the one side, and the defense of "diversity" of lifestyles and values on the other.

Children in Large Families

One of the most consistent findings of delinquency research is that the larger the number of children in the family, the greater the likelihood that each of them will be delinquent. This finding is perfectly explicable from our child rearing model. Affection for the individual child may be unaffected by numbers, and parents with large families may be as able as anyone else to recognize deviant behavior, but monitoring and punishment are another matter. The greater the number of children in the family, the greater the strain on parental resources of time and energy. For this reason, the child in the large family is likely to spend more time with other children and less time with adults. Like the peers discussed earlier, other children are not as likely as adults to be effective trainers. They have less investment in the outcome, are more likely to be tolerant of deviant behavior, and do not have the power to enforce their edicts. One often sees a child demanding that parents punish a brother or sister. The brother or sister quickly learns to shift attention to the behavior of the accuser. Whatever the outcome of these particular contests, the parent is clearly dependent on the reports of surrogate monitors. If many parents are unwilling to act on deviant behavior they directly observe, fewer still will act on the testimony of children, especially when the behavior reported occurred some time earlier and has thus earned the foregiveness that comes with (even brief periods of) time.

If the analysis of these three confirmed correlates of criminality (adolescent employment, criminality of parents, and size of family) is sufficient to establish the plausibility of child-rearing explanations, we can now attempt to apply it to some of the more problematic issues in the connection between the family and crime.

The Single-Parent Family

Such family measures as the percentage of the population divorced, the percentage of households headed by women, and the percentage of unattached individuals in the community are among the most powerful predictors of crime rates. Consistent with these findings, in most (but not all) studies that directly compare children living with both biological parents with children living in "broken" or reconstituted homes, the children from intact homes have lower rates of crime. These differences amply justify concern about current trends in divorce and illegitimacy rates. The likelihood that the biological parents of a particular child will marry and stay together throughout the period of child rearing is lower today than at any time in the past.

If the fact of a difference between single- and two-parent families is reasonably well established, the mechanisms by which it is produced are not adequately understood. It was once common in the delinquency literature to distinguish between homes broken by divorce and those broken by death. This distinction recognized the difficulty of separating the effects of the people involved in divorce from the effects of divorce itself. Indeed, it is common to find that involuntarily broken homes are less conducive to delinquency than homes in which the parent was a party to the decision to separate.

With the continued popularity of marriage, a possible complication enters the picture. The missing biological parent (in the overwhelming majority of cases, the father) is often replaced at some point by a stepparent. Is the child better or worse off as a result of the presence of an "unrelated" adult in the house?

The model we are using suggests that, all else equal, one parent is sufficient. We could substitute "mother" or "father" for "parents" without any obvious loss in child rearing ability. Husbands and wives tend to be sufficiently alike on such things as values, attitudes, and skills that for many purposes they may be treated as a unit. For that matter, our scheme does not even require that the adult involved in training the child be his or her guardian, let alone a biological parent. Proper training can be accomplished outside the confines of the two-parent home.

But all else is rarely equal. The single parent (usually a woman) must devote a good deal to support and maintenance activities that are at least to some extent shared in the two-parent family. Further, she must do so in the absence of psychological or social support. As a result, she is less able to devote time to monitoring and punishment, and is more likely to be involved in negative, abusive contacts with her children.

Remarriage is by no means a complete solution to these problems. Stepparents are often decent people, but they are not superhuman: many report that they have no "parental feelings" toward their stepchildren, and they are unusually likely to be involved in cases of child abuse.[13] The other side of the coin is the affection of the child for the parent. Such affection is conducive to nondelinquency in its own right, and clearly eases the task of child rearing. It is for obvious reasons less likely to be felt toward the new parent in a reconstituted family than toward a biological parent who has been there from the beginning.

The Working Mother

The tremendous increase in the number of women in the labor force has several implications for the crime rate. Most analysts agree that this change has greatly contributed to the instability of marriage, a fact whose consequences for crime we have just discussed. Traditionally, however, the major concern with the working mother has been with the direct effect on child rearing. An early study of this topic showed that the children of women who work, especially the children of those who work "occasionally" or "sporadically," were more likely to be delinquent.[14] This same study also showed that the effect on delinquency of the mother's working was *completely* accounted for by the quality of supervision provided by the mother. (Such complete explanations of one "factor" by another are extremely rare in social science.) When the mother was able to provide (arrange?) supervision for the child, her employment had no effect on the likelihood of delinquency. In fact, in this particular study, the children of regularly employed women were least likely to be delinquent when supervision was taken into account. This does not mean, however, that the employment of the mother had no effect. It did have an effect, at least among those in relatively deprived circumstances: the children of employed women were more likely to be delinquent.

More recent research reports that a mother's employment has a small effect, which it is unable to explain. The advantage of the housewife over the employed mother in child-rearing remains when supervision and other characteristics of the mother, the family, and the child are taken into account.[15] One possible implication of this explanatory failure is that the effects of employment influence children in ways not measurable except through their delinquency. This conclusion is at odds with the conclusion we just reached (where "supervision" accounts for all of the effects of employment). It reminds us that our scheme does not allow us to separate the enduring effects of child "rearing" from the temporary effects of child "control," something we should be able to do if we are to devise effective programs for delinquency prevention.

Another consequence of women's working is that it contributes to the "destruction of the nest," where no one is home for large portions of the day. The unoccupied house *may be* less attractive to adolescent members of the family; it *is* more attractive to strangers interested only in its contents. Research shows that the absence of guardians in the home is a good predictor of residential burglary.[16]

Child Abuse and Delinquency

As far as I can determine, the gross correlates of child abuse are identical to the gross correlates of delinquency. Reports to the effect that large portions of delinquents have been abused as children are also common. The first fact suggests that child abuse and criminality have common causes; the second, that abuse causes criminality. These hypotheses are not necessarily mutually exclusive, and it seems reasonable to suppose that there is a large grain of truth in both of them. However, since "abuse" and "punishment" have elements in common, it is important that we take seriously the distinction between them. Otherwise, it will appear that punishment is conducive to delinquency. If so, our argument would be in serious trouble, to say the least.

One way to reconcile the abuse/delinquency results is to recognize that abuse does not occur in a vacuum. It is more likely the less the parent cares for the child and the fewer the resources the parent is able to devote to child-rearing. Recall that delinquency is also more likely under these circumstances. But before delinquency is possible, there exists the potentially delinquent child. This child has not yet been introduced properly. He or she is more likely to be "demanding, stubborn, negativistic,"[17] "aggressive," and "troublesome."[18] When the uncaring or overburdened parent faces such behavior, he is unlikely to see it as his own creation. But if our analysis is correct, it is—at least to some extent. If so, the abuse that follows should not be confused with "correction."

The Family in Secular Society

Privately promoting conservative, tribal values through child rearing is seen by most parents as simply one of the tasks of life, made easy or difficult by the luck of the draw in the nursery, by the devotion of others in the community to the same task, and by their ability to shield the child from contrary messages. With regard to the latter, there can be no doubt that the message of the media is often contrary, celebrating the very behavior parents attempt to teach their children to avoid. Gwynn Nettler has pointed out that "no moral community doubts [the] effectiveness" of the mass media in fostering corrosive attitudes among its members, and as a result, "censorship is a normal feature of...attempts to maintain moral difference."[19] By this test, few families qualify as moral communities, since few restrict their children's access to television, movies, books, or magazines in any systematic way. (According to some reports *everybody* watches television.)

This inconsistency between the values and the behavior of parents may stem from their feeling that they are simply no match for the media. It may also stem from the view that behavior is not much affected by images, whether good or evil. Our child-rearing scheme is consistent with the latter view (see notes 2 and 4). It suggests that the media's portrayal of a broad range of human experience is more likely to have a direct effect on the comfort and morale of parents than on the behavior of their children. But this leads to the possibility that the long-term effects of the media are to demoralize those whose task is to limit the range of experience of others. (Good, broadly informed people, it is often noted, are not necessarily effective parents.)

In any event, the impact of the media is very hard to assess. It seems reasonable to guess that children whose parents restrict access to the media are unlikely to be delinquent. I suspect, however, that it would be difficult to show that this particular restriction was responsible for the difference. Almost by definition, such families are already unusually sensitive to the moral implications of behavior. They are therefore already likely to have trained their children to be morally distinct from children in danger of delinquency. (Again, we must distinguish between the delicate issues that apply to basically socialized children and the crude issues that apply to children at the border between law-abiding behavior and crime. Parents concerned about the finer aspects of child-rearing are unlikely to have to visit their children in institutions.)

Improving Child-Rearing

The decline of the family, routinely reported by college students home to pick up money, clean clothes, and cheap advice from their parents, is real enough. The extended family that was so effective in controlling everyone's behavior remains only in vestigial form, and the nuclear family that replaced it does not have the stability and continuity it once had.[20] One response is merely to ascribe these facts to global processes of evolution over which government has no control. Another is to celebrate or bemoan the decline of the family on the grounds that it is essential to the perpetuation of current social and economic arrangements. From the perspective of crime policy, celebration does not seem to be in order. What, then, can be done to help the family?

Our analysis divides this question into two parts: Can parents or potential parents be better trained in the technology of child-rearing? Can they be induced to apply what they know?

In principle, education in *minimal* child-rearing does not pose particularly difficult problems. The techniques cannot be that complex: they are, after all, reasonably well applied by most parents. In principle, the best time to teach such techniques is when we have the attention of all those who are about to use them.

Straightforward application of these principles would produce child-rearing classes in high school. What would be taught in such classes? It is time to recall the previous reference to the metaphysic of our age. As things now stand, we could not expect the schools to intellectualize the child-rearing question without getting it, according to our lights, wrong—without preaching toleration for natural tendencies, without demeaning the practices of successful parents in the eyes of their own children.

What should be taught in such classes? It is time to recall previous reference to the ignorance of criminologists in child-rearing matters. As things now stand, we could not expect much in the way of consensus among experts in the field. And if we found it, we would have reason to be suspicious of its research base.

Still, I think the matter should be pursued. Research identification of child-rearing practices that separate the families of delinquents from those of nondelinquents should be possible. And promotion of these practices by the school is not as unlikely as previous discussion may suggest. The school, after all, is run by adults whose values and practices seem very close to those of successful parents; furthermore the school is already deeply involved in child-rearing. If the school and the family are now at odds on the principles of child-rearing, they are not at odds on child-rearing practice. In fact, at first glance the school seems to have advantages over the family. Teachers care about the behavior of children, if only because disruption makes their lives more difficult. By the standards of the family, school monitoring of behavior is highly efficient. As a class, teachers are probably more expert than parents in recognizing deviant (and predicting delinquent) behavior. Finally, the school has, and uses, a variety of means for punishing misbehavior. The fatal flaw in this otherwise ideal system is that the school can punish only those students who see education as important to them. If the student does not like school he or she can, in effect or in fact, quit. In this case, the school's child-rearing system too breaks down, and not surprisingly, "attitude toward school" becomes a major predictor of delinquency. But the failure of the school in dealing with some children should not obscure the fact that it does very well with others; more particularly, it should not obscure the basic compatibility between the school and the family on the child-rearing issue.

Beyond efficiency in child-rearing is the more difficult problem of commitment to the task. There may be no point in training parents to do a better job if the outcome has little significance for them. Historically, the incentives for doing a good job have included the honor of the family, security for oneself, and self-reliance for one's children. Today the major incentive appears to be some form of conspicuous display of one's accomplishments. (A doctor-son is nice to have, as is a Cadillac.) For those who cannot hope for such success, and who have little to fear from failure, the rewards of child-rearing may not be worth the effort.

All proposals in this area come down to efforts to increase the care and concern of family members for each other. Put this way, they seem like a good idea. But in fact such attempts require the state to increase the severity of its sanctions (or to extend them to those responsible for the child), to reduce its own responsibility for family members, or to make more difficult the creation and dissolution of families. In this light, proposals to increase the efficiency of the family as a child-rearing institution are not so attractive. Furthermore, on the basis of presently available information, there can be little assurance that such programs would be effective.

For the moment, then, it seems the best we can do is to encourage research on good child-rearing practices and the conditions favorable to them, with little or no expectation that the results will be of immediate practical benefit. The absence of such benefits should not concern us overly much; after all, the pursuit of immediate benefits is what causes all the trouble for delinquents.

Footnotes

[1]My discussion of the Oregon Social Learning Center work is based on G.R. Patterson, "Children Who Steal," in Travis Hirschi and Michael Gottfredson, *Understanding Crime* ((Beverly Hills: Sage Publications, 1980), pp. 73-90. As Patterson notes, the conclusion that punishment is necessary derives from "a series of studies" in the social learning tradition. These studies have found that *successful* teaching of social behavior does not reduce antisocial behavior. As a result, it appears the teacher must focus directly on the behavior he or she wishes to reduce. Since one cannot hope to reduce unwanted behavior by rewarding it, the "lack of transfer" finding has profound implications for the entire social learning tradition. To the everlasting credit of scholars in this tradition, they are a major source of the evidence against their original point of view.

[2]An excellent, extended discussion of the theory and practice of socialization may be found in Werner Stark, *The Social Bond* (New York: Fordham University Press, 1978). Stark's thesis, directly opposed to what he calls "the unconscious metaphysic of the age," is that "the principles of civilized and cultured conduct must be pressed on the developing individual, not merely presented to him."

[3]Patterson, pp. 88-89. Patterson's list of "parenting skills" contains seven items: "(a) notice what the child is doing; (b) monitor it over long periods; (c) model social skill behavior; (d) clearly state house rules; (e) consistently provide sane punishments...; (f) provide reinforcement for conformity; and (g) negotiate disagreements so that conflicts..do not escalate" (p. 81). I have reduced and modified this list in a manner consistent with Patterson's discussion and, I believe, consistent with the results of research on the family correlates of delinquency. Thus, for example, the strongest family correlates identified by the Gluecks were *affection* of the parents for the child, *supervision* of the child by the parents, and *discipline* of the child by the parents. Another factor emphasized by the Gluecks' data, cohesiveness of the family ("pride" in family), I interpret as equivalent to "affection," as another source of the willingness to supervise (monitor) and discipline (punish) the child (see Sheldon and Eleanor Glueck, *Unraveling Juvenile Delinquency.* Cambridge: Harvard University Press, 1950). In short, most of the components of the simplified model find support in research beyond that conducted by Patterson and his colleagues. As mentioned in the text, I see the "parenting skills" not included in the model as dealing with "fine-tuning" issues not directly relevant to delinquency, or even as potentially misleading bits of advice. For example, I doubt that it does that much good for the parent to "model" appropriate behavior. (This view gives some of the fun back to adults, but its origins are not solely in class or self interest. See note 2, and Travis Hirschi, *Causes of Delinquency* [Berkeley: University of California Press, 1969], pp. 94-97, 145-152.)

[4]According to Gary Jensen, one of the *best* predictors of drug use in a large suburban high school was the size of the student's weekly allowance.

[5]The relation between weak families and high criminality holds across cultures. Jackson Toby has shown that measures of family control differentiate offenders from nonoffenders in such diverse settings as Philadelphia, Stockholm, Tokyo, and Ghana. See his "Delinquency in Cross-Cultural Perspective," in LaMar T. Empey, *Juvenile Justice: The Progressive Legacy and Current Reforms* (Charlottesville: University Press of Virginia, 1979), pp. 105-149. For a summary of the literature on this topic, see Gwynn Nettler, *Explaining Crime* (New York: McGraw-Hill, 1978).

[6]D.J. West and D.P. Farrington, *The Delinquent Way of Life* (London: Heinemann, 1977).

[7]Much research has examined the relation between the socioeconomic status of the family and the criminality of the child. The "results" of this research are controversial. Some see a relation in the data; others see little or no relation. Even if we accept the idea that an inverse relation between socioeconomic status of the family and the criminality of the child has been established, we do not have to conclude that this relation reflects the impact of "poverty" on crime. Poverty suggests deprivation or need. As such, the term itself embodies a theory of crime that sees the offender as being forced into crime by honest needs that cannot be otherwise satisfied. Since, as mentioned, offenders do not appear to be deprived of food, drink, sex, drugs, jobs, excitement, or freedom, some other interpretation of the relation (e.g., less effective child-rearing) would seem to be required.

[8]This statement should probably read: criminality in adolescence predicts socioeconomic status in adulthood better than parental socioeconomic status predicts criminality (at whatever age such criminality occurs). But it would also be true were it to read: criminality predicts *employment* better than employment predicts criminality. In other words, if we (temporarily) control employment, we continue to have differences in delinquency, and we eventually have predictable differences in employment as well. For example, the bulk of the

Gluecks' large sample of delinquents and nondelinquents, identified before World War II, eventually ended up in the armed forces. (For psychiatric and moral reasons, the delinquents were less likely to be elibigle for such employment.) Differences in delinquency persisted: the delinquents were much more likely to be "brought up on charges" — two-thirds as opposed to one-fifth; the delinquents did not advance in rank as far as the nondelinquents; and the delinquents were more likely to be dishonorably discharged. See Sheldon Glueck and Eleanor Glueck, *Delinquents and Nondelinquents in Perspective* (Cambridge: Harvard University Press, 1968), Chapter XIII. In contrast, if we control employment, and employ some and not others, we find (1) no effect on subsequent delinquency; (2) a very small effect in the "right" direction; (3) a small effect in the "wrong" direction. (The latter finding is the rule in nonexperimental studies comparing employed adolescents with "other" adolescents of the same age. See Farrington and West, 1977; Glueck and Glueck, 1968, p. 191; and Hirschi, 1969, p. 188.) For an experimental study of the effects of employment, see Richard A. Berk, Kenneth J. Lenihan, and Peter H. Rossi, "Crime and Poverty: Some Experimental Evidence from Ex-Offenders," *American Sociological Review* 45 (1980): 766-786.

[9]West and Farrington, p. 109.

[10]Marvin Wolfgang et. al., *Delinquency in a Birth Cohort* (Chicago: University of Chicago Press, 1972).

[11]West and Farrington, p. 116.

[12]Draft registration resister Benjamin Sasway, quoted by the *Arizona Daily Star,* September 1, 1982. In standard contradiction, Sasway also says that the "only difference" between people in prison and those on the outside "is that these people have got caught." Although I am willing to grant that, in some contexts and with respect to some forms of behavior, offenders may be relatively tolerant, I realize that in most respects they are unusually intolerant.

[13]Robert L. Burgess, "Family Violence," pp. 91-101 in Hirschi and Gottfredson, *Understanding Crime.* Burgess discusses a good many of the correlates of child abuse beyond the two mentioned here, and I am indebted to his article beyond the extent suggested by this and subsequent references to it.

[14]Glueck and Glueck.

[15]See Hirschi, 1969, pp. 237-239, and F. Ivan Nye, *Family Relationships and Delinquent Behavior* (New York: Wiley, 1958).

[16]Lawrence E. Cohen and David Cantor, "Residential Burglary in the United States," *Journal of Research in Crime and Delinquency* 18 (1981): 113-127. Cohen and Cantor show that "less occupied households" are more likely to be burglarized. "More occupied" households were those in which at least one person did not go to school or work for more than 15 hours a week.

[17]Burgess, p. 98.

[18]West and Farrington, pp. 154-155.

[19]Gwynn Nettler, *Explaining Crime* (New York: McGraw-Hill, 1978), p. 341.

[20]Edward Shorter, *The Making of the Modern Family* (New York: Basic Books, 1977).

7

How Do Gangs Get Organized?

John M. Hagedorn

What started out as more or less of a social club in the late 1950s has grown into a powerful, well-organized, and violent street gang with chapters not only in Chicago, but also in many cities all over the Midwest.

Terrence McCarthy, *Chicago Police Dept.*

Q. How well organized do you consider your group?

A. Really, we not really organized in a sense. We are good friends. We are together. When a couple us get high, we just spend our last dollars. We'll just think of something to do and get us some more money. Like to hustling, stuff like that. Ain't really organized.

James, *Black Gangster, Disciples*

Why is it important to know how gangs are structured? Today's dominant law enforcement perspective understands the gang basically as a criminal conspiracy. According to this view, a gang has many misled followers on the "fringe," but its leaders are a "hard core" of sociopaths or career criminals. With this perspective, it is easy to believe that gangs may evolve into "organized crime" or turn into structured "branches" of metropolitan "supergangs." The job of law enforcement, then, is simply to jail the "hard core career criminals" to get them away from the more salvageable "fringe."

One minor problem is the gangs we studied in Milwaukee don't really seem to fit this stereotype. Milwaukee gangs don't look anything like the pictures often painted of them by law enforcement. But what is a gang?

Many studies spend considerable time discussing the definition of a gang.[1] Defining a gang has more than a little importance today. Since gangs are targets for vigorous law enforcement efforts, the current definition of a gang needs logically to reinforce a gang's criminal and violent image. At least one observer (Zatz, 1987) has charged that the criminal image of Chicano gangs has been promoted by law enforcement mainly to justify applications for federal grants to support special gang units.

Needle and Stapleton (1983) note widespread confusion in definitions. After reviewing past attempts, they decide that "contemporary usage" of the term by police departments will be their operational definition. This "contemporary usage" is basically borrowed from the works of criminologists Walter Miller (1975) and Malcolm Klein (1971). Miller has been most influential in criminalizing the current definition of gangs. His major monograph, "Violence by Youth Gangs and Youth Groups as a Crime Problem in Major American Cities" surveys officials in twelve U.S. cities concerning their definition of a gang. Miller (1975, 9) tells us those surveyed "reserved the use of the term 'gang' for associational units which were both more formalized and more seriously criminal than the more common type of street group." Miller then summarizes his respondents' views and accepts their definition of a gang as:

> a group of recurrently associating individuals with identifiable leadership and internal organization, identifying with or claiming control over territory in the community, and engaging either individually or collectively in violent or other forms of illegal behavior.

What we need to note here is that "gang" is differentiated from a "group" mainly by characteristics that are operationally important to law enforcement. But is this the only way one can define a gang? Community residents, parents, other youth, and the gang members themselves may have a very different way of understanding a gang. In fact Miller's definition is a radical departure from past sociological conceptions. Indeed, while Miller insists U.S. Gang activity has not changed much in sixty years, he paradoxically approves of a major change in image and formal definition.

Klein takes Miller's position to its logical conclusion. Beginning his book with a discussion of definitions, he points out that criminal justice agencies and the mass media "use the term gang more to meet their own ends than to achieve disinterested enlightenment" (1971, 7). However, Klein decides in the end a gang should be defined basically by the perceptions of others and fundamentally by the perception of law enforcement officials. For Klein, a gang is:

> any denotable adolescent group of youngsters who: (a) are generally perceived as a distinct aggregation by others in their neighborhood; (b) recognize themselves as a denotable group (almost invariably with a group name) and (c) have been involved in a sufficient number of delinquent incidents to call forth a consistent negative response from neighborhood residents and/or enforcement agencies (1971, 13).

In the final analysis, for Klein, a gang is any group of youth police call a gang. Needle and Stapleton quote Miller and Klein at length. They finally decide Klein's definition is best since, in Klein's own words, it "is nothing more than a confirmation of contemporary lay usage of the term."

While it is certainly important for law enforcement agencies to define "crime problems" and fashion policies appropriate to deal with them, to accept the law enforcement definition as fully descriptive of gangs is another matter. Criminologists leave little room for critical analysis when they ask what a gang is, then tell us how those concerned with law enforcement define "gangs," and finally turn around and say, since this definition is "contemporary usage," we should adopt it too.

The definitions of Klein, Miller, and others are quite different from other contemporary definitions and perspectives on gangs. Richard Cloward and Lloyd Ohlin, for example, although they thought gangs delinquent by definition, also defined them more broadly as part of "delinquent subcultures" spawned by three different types of poor communities. The well-integrated, stable slum with a criminal opportunity structure resulted in criminal gangs. A disintegrated, unstable slum whose residents could not find organized criminal opportunity resulted in fighting gangs. And badly disorganized slums, where nothing but demoralization could be found, led to despair and to drug-using gangs.

While Cloward and Ohlin's typology has major empirical problems their framework is quite different than Klein's or Miller's. Cloward and Ohlin define gangs within a perspective which tries to understand the influence of certain types of poor communities on the development of gangs. This perspective is more in step with classical sociological theories.

Back to Thrasher, One More Time

When Miller and Klein insist on defining gangs mainly by characteristics operationally significant for law enforcement, they stand in even sharper contrast to the work of Frederick Thrasher. As mentioned previously, for Thrasher, gang youth were neither more nor less criminal than other youth in their disorganized communities, a point supported by some recent research.[2] For Thrasher, and later Suttles and Moore, three aspects of gangs and their structure stand out: variation within a community, process of formation, and age divisions. It is these three characteristics that combine to define a gang.

For Thrasher, above all a gang is unique. "It may vary as to membership, type of leaders, mode of organization, interests and activities, and finally as to its status in the community" (1963, 36). Organizationally, Thrasher describes diffuse types, solidified types, conventionalized and criminal types, and even "the secret society." Thrasher found 1,313 different gangs in 1920s Chicago. Moore begins her descriptions of "Three Barrio Gangs" by saying: "Each of the gangs considered here is unique, reflecting the varying factors of the ethnic context of life in Mexican Los Angeles, the institutional structure, and the economic structure" (1978, 55). For Thrasher and Moore, there is no general type of gang, but gangs with collective histories reflecting the communities where they grew up. Suttles' Ph.D. dissertation is devoted to understanding the corner groups as a part of a specific local community, the Addams area in Chicago. For Suttles, the gang is so loosely organized it is seen by its members as no more than "a series of individual histories" or the "happy coincidence" of individual association (1968, 175-77).

Rather than define gangs in terms of their structure or how they are perceived by police, Thrasher defines gangs in terms of the process in which they are formed and their specific activities. His full definition can be sharply contrasted to Klein's and Miller's:

> The gang is an interstitial group originally formed spontaneously, and then integrated through conflict. It is characterized by the following types of behavior: meeting face to face, milling, movement through space as a unit, conflict, and planning. The result of this collective behavior is the development of tradition, unreflective internal structure, esprit de corps, solidarity, morale, group awareness, and attachment to a local territory (1963, 46).

To understand a gang, for Thrasher, Moore, and Suttles, one needs to understand not only specific communities, but the specific processes the gang undergoes in formation. Miller and Klein, while claiming violent and law-breaking conduct is typical of all gangs, make no mention of specific communities or internal process. Following Klein and Miller, most gang research today pays little attention to the wide differences in gang behavior or to how and why gangs are formed. Instead, researchers concentrate on the occasional violent and criminal acts of some gang members. Research is reduced to formulas for figuring out how to identify a gang member, how to prevent others from joining gangs, and how to deter present members from maintaining their gang loyalties. Gangs themselves become nothing more than their media and police stereotype.

Finally, for Thrasher, Suttles, and Moore, gangs are age-graded, not monolithic entities. Rather than a bureaucratic gang, we have a sort of coalition of age-graded groups. Moore has been tracking the history of formal age-graded "klikas" of three Chicano gangs back to the 1940s. Suttles analyzed each of his Addams area gangs in terms of its different age groups. Thrasher, in quoting a field worker, clearly describes the process of the formation of age-graded groups: "A new crop of youngsters in a district plays together and the older groups passes on. . . . One may see as many as four different age groups. . . ." (1963, 59).

Rather than picture the gang as a "core" of violent offenders and a "fringe" of less criminally involved youth, gangs for Thrasher, Suttles and Moore are divided by age, with considerable variation within each age group of friends. To analyze a gang, one must analyze each age-graded group, not merely look at the gang as a criminal structure with older "leaders" on the top and younger "fringe" on the bottom.

Some police departments want to picture the gang in the familiar bureaucratic pyramidal shape. Like a police department, the gang is seen as having a "Chief" on top and "lieutenants" commanding troops, who are on the bottom of the pyramid.[3]

If this is how the beat patrolman or social worker is taught to understand the structure of a gang, we need not wonder what kind of policies they will adopt.[4]

What Do Milwaukee Gangs Look Like?

Q. What's 2-7 right now? Where are they?

A. Well, OK, it's still some, but they're like the younger brothers and sisters. And they're so young, they're like twelve and thirteen and fourteen. It's like they still want to carry on that little stuff.

Q. Probably doing things that you did back then.

A. Right!

Doris, 2-7 Syndicates

Milwaukee's gangs come in a variety of forms and shapes, but none that look like a pyramid. They are all age-graded, with the gang beginning as a group of friends and youth roughly the same age. As the group ages, a new age-graded grouping forms from neighbors, acquaintances, and relatives.

We interviewed young people from nineteen founding groups that formed almost all of the major gangs which continue to function in Milwaukee. Members from six gangs reported three age-graded groups had formed within their gang by spring 1986, and seven reported two distinct groups. One gang, the Hillside Boys, who formed in a large Milwaukee housing project, reported four new groups and a history dating back to the 1960s and perhaps earlier.

Q. Did you start the Hillside Boys, or was it already there when you joined or what?

A. I think it was already there, 'cause it was like the older fellas that handed it down to us, you know. It was already there, so we just held the name.

Q. The Hillside Warriors, were they the group that was before?

A. Yeah. Them the guys who was there before us. And that's like handed down to us, like if we need backup, if we couldn't handle something, we just give them a call, and they would help us. We like first got running in 1980.

Clay, Hillside Boys

The Hillside Boys were the only black gang that reported groups with a history dating back before the 1970s. Punk Alley, the sole white gang interviewed, reported two previous age groups (one named "Teenage Wasteland") which formed beginning in 1973. Every other gang in our study was started by the "founding" group whose members we interviewed.

Each age-graded group has its own internal structure. Far from the stereotyped view of a gang with a "hard core" of criminally-minded leaders on top and a broad "fringe" network of impressionable kids, each age group develops its own sub groups.

> **Q.** When you joined with the Deacons, how many people would you estimate there were?
>
> **A.** Mainly it's about fifty tough Deacons who always beat and wouldn't turn around and run. But then there's other Deacons that wanna be Deacons, that just bum around with us and get high. It was always just like a "main group" and then there's the "wanna be's."
>
> **Q.** What's the difference between a "wanna be" and a true Deacon?
>
> **A.** "Wanna be's" are people you can't trust to watch your back. Real Deacons are the people that fight. I'm here man, any time you need me.
>
> Marcus, 1-9s

Each age-group has its own "main group," its leaders, and its "wanna be's," to use Marcus' apt phrase. Milwaukee gangs are in fact a combination or coalition of age-graded groups, each with their own "main groups" and "wanna bes." The makeup of each of these age groups varies between gangs and over time within each gang. A "wanna be" this week may be in the "main group" next week.

Becoming a member of a Milwaukee gang is usually an informal process, often related to some act showing courage or commitment. Because the gang is a semi-secret group, trust is necessary to become a "real member." Seven of those we interviewed answered that initiation rites included an act of some sort of "fighting," and two said the new member had to "rip off" something in order to become a member. All others (36) said either that there was no initiation procedure or that it varied with circumstance. For the originals who founded the gang, there did not appear to be any initiation rites whatsoever.

> **Q.** Is there an initiation?
>
> **A.** It all depends all right. Like for me, for me to go join (all it would take would be) saying I'll be in it. But if it's somebody that just came out in the street, they have to prove themselves. Like steal with one of us or something. You know, show that he's "down."
>
> Bob, Vicelords

> **Q.** Is there an initiation?
>
> **A.** Not really. There would be a time extended to yourself, to prove yourself like.
>
> **Q.** Probation, huh?
>
> **A.** More or less. Not to prove yourself to be a tough person, but to prove your trust, you know? Can you be trusted? Are you gonna go, you know, get just information and go talk to the other side. Stuff like that. Nothing like, OK, we wanna see how bad you are — go rob the next corner store you see. Nothing like that.

Q. So what happens once you've passed probation?

A. Then you're trusted and everything. You know, just become one of the fellas, and that's what you are.

Edwardo, *Latin Kings*

The transition between "juniors" and "seniors" or between different age groups also takes place in a variety of ways. For some gangs, there is no clear transition: it just happens as the group ages. For other gangs this process is formalized with, for example, "JKs" (Junior Kings) or "Peewee Cobras," representing specific age groups and having rituals for transition to the "seniors."

Q. How do you graduate from junior to senior?

A. You could be a LK (senior) at age 14. You have to prove yourself that you're down, that you can do your stuff right, you don't talk in front of nobody if you're going to do some stuff, so you don't get caught for it. Most of the people that be like bragging to girls, and right away, it gets around the street, and the cops already know. So everybody looks at the people that keep their mouths shut, they're down for their nation and all that stuff, they move them up.

Edwardo, *Latin Kings*

The age of the "originals," or founding members, when the gangs started supports this age-group interpretation of gang organization. Of the forty-four interviews of original gang founders, thirty-four were between thirteen and seventeen years old when the gang began. Milwaukee gangs began mainly with similarly aged middle-school youth in the early 1980s. Only four of the gangs were reported as forming before 1980.

Gang leadership varies as well between different gangs. Sixteen of the young people interviewed reported they were primarily responsible for the formation of their gang. Eleven are or were the recognized "leaders" of the gang. One-third of all those interviewed said reputation or ability to fight was the main criterion for a leader. A few (8) said someone was the leader because they knew most about gangs, usually meaning they knew rules and regulations from Chicago gangs. Some even disputed there ever was a leader:

Q. Was there a leader when you came together? A leader of Hillside?

A. No. Hillside is like, you know, you do what you want to do. Something like that. But if you need some help, you always got some backup. That's all.

Clay, *Hillside Boys*

Q. Was there a leader?

A. Nope. Not as far as I was concerned. If there was one, I didn't listen to him.

Chuck, *Vicelords*

For most age groups, however, there was a leader or leaders who had the most respect from his or her peers.

Q. Did you have a leader when it started out?

A. Well, when we first started out, it was like the most visible. Which, that was me and one of my buddies. And, you know, since we was the ones mostly doing all the fighting, we was like elected the leaders.

Q. What do you mean by "most visible?"

A. Well, say like when they come down in our neighborhood, we'd be the first ones to jump at 'em, you know, while everybody else—once we got fighting, everybody else would get into it, you know.

Tony, *Four Corner Hustlers*

Q. Why was RB the leader?

A. He knew the most, and he knew people in Chicago. Being from Chicago, you have connections there. And he was daring. Daring, dangerous, and not afraid. And that's what it takes to become a leader.

Dante, *Latin Kings*

For many groups, "titles" for the leader are nonexistent. In the past, "titles" were often taken from gang social workers who endeavored to re-direct the gang's delinquent energies by helping it become positively organized (Suttles 1968, 176-77). In Milwaukee, where there are titles, they are borrowed most often from the "literature" of Chicago gangs. "Elites," "Lords," "Kings," and other titles mimic Chicago gang names and customs. Seven of those interviewed reported a system of "ranks" or a semi-formal hierarchy. Specialized functions of "treasurer" or "war counselor" were reported by two gangs, but most of those interviewed emphasized the informal nature of the structure in each age group and in the gang.

Seventeen of forty-seven interviewed reported they paid dues while twenty-seven claimed there were no dues in the gang. Interestingly, of the fifteen interviewed who thought their gang was well organized, only seven reported they also paid dues, suggesting "well-organized" for many might mean something other than a structured organization. For all those who claimed they paid dues, the amount was less than five dollars per week.

Q. You got dues?

A. Oh yeah.

Q. Everyone always pay?

A. Not always. And it's like . . . we had it like everybody pay two dollars a week, and we get up two hundred to three hundred dollars and we buy weed. And we have parties to make the money back and certain persons go to jail and we bail him out.

When we asked how things had changed since the gangs began, we received a wide variety of answers. Most responses were related to "getting older" (3), "more hustling" (5), "more fear of jail" (4), "more members" (5), or "more guns" (4). Only one person said gangs today were "more organized" and only three said things were the same.

The Activities of a Gang

What does a gang do everyday? Crime occupies only a small portion of the daily existence of a gang, a point made throughout the academic literature. When we look at what one does while he or she is in a gang, we have to differentiate between ages. Clearly, a fifteen-year-old does different things each day than does a twenty-one-year-old. Following Whyte, we also want to look at routines, the daily life of a gang member. How do Milwaukee's gang founders describe what they did everyday when they were sixteen to eighteen and Milwaukee gang activity was at its height? Nearly everyone we interviewed (thirty-four of forty) was in agreement about the main activity of gangs—partying and hanging out. Only four responded "fighting," one "ripping off," and one "going places."

> Q. When you were together, what did you do most?
>
> A. Well, in the summertime, we'd come loiter on the corners, you know, and not anything wild. It's just we use to hang there and get everybody together so we can go drink some beer and play basketball on the Clarke playground.
>
> David, 2-7s

> A. On Fridays we'd all meet up on Reservoir Park. Sit down, get high, talk. See if anybody know any good, you know, good ways to make any money. That was it.
>
> Ben, *Vicelords*

> A. Getting high. Getting high, and the higher you got the more devilish things got on your mind. If we could work we would, but whenever we got off work and got paid we would always come back there and do what we had to do, you know, let each other know we was OK.
>
> Dan, *Castlefolks*

When the founding group was in its mid-teens, aside from hanging out, the gang was structured around fighting. We saw earlier how corner groups came in conflict with one another. David explains the structure of the 2-7s, strongly disavowing a military-like organization:

> Q. Did you have ranks?
>
> A. It wasn't an organization, it was a gang. We was organized enough that if one throw down, all throw down, you know, fight.

As the gangs expanded, as we've noted, they became involved with conflicts with other corner groups. Constant fighting occurs at a particular stage in the evolution of a gang. It helps shape the structure of the gang and lasts through the mid-teenage years. Gang structure, for these teenagers, enabled them to fight other gangs and not much more, a point emphasized by Suttles (1968, 181). One 2-7 told us:

> Q. How well organized do you consider your gang?

A. It wasn't organized until a fight came upon, and everybody wanted to fight! That's the only time it was organized, when a fight came. And, when everybody was getting high and most of the people who didn't have money was getting high free! That was the only organized time if you ask me.

Another form of conflict pits the gangs against authorities, especially the police. We should not underemphasize the significance of how authorities define and treat gangs. Hostility between police and other authorities and gang members plays a crucial role in how the gang is formed and how its members see themselves and acquire a delinquent or deviant identity. We'd like to illustrate this process with an edited interview with David, one of the leaders of the 2-7 gang. David explains, more clearly than most, how conflict with authorities affects gang formation and how the gang member feels the impact of police harassment and labeling. The interviewer is Hagedorn.[5]

David's Story

Q. Explain how the 2-7s started.

A. We began as just the Cameo Boys. That's how it started off. One day they had a competition for drill teams at the Uptown Theater, near your house. And the Time Boys was there. We had a grudge against them and they had a grudge against us from school. And we had it out with the Time Boys and that's when the gang started.

Q. How did you get the name, Cameo Boys?

A. Because we idolized the Cameos. Its a group called Cameo, so we just took the name "Cameo Boys" (laughter).

Q. After the fight, how did the Cameo Boys get so popular? What happened next?

A. By the time gangs got so known that everybody thought, "Hey, this is cool" to be in a gang. And plus they saw we had so much reputation. Someone might see you with this girl and that girl and really think you were cool.

Q. Was there a leader?

A. Well, everybody looked up to me and Dan. But the way I look at it, I never was the leader, even though everybody called me that because of the publicity that I had. When I got waived to adult court and all those newspaper articles appeared calling me the leader, everyone just thought I was. But the reason I actually became the leader was because of the policemen. They called me the leader first and they just spread it around. But that was because I stood up more than everyone else. We had a fight. There was about fifty people coming to fight. All my buddies ran, but I just stood there. I figured I just got to take that little whipping and whatever. Because I was always bold. I never considered myself as a leader and no one else considered me as a leader. But after that fight the police called me a leader so I guess I was. But I can go out right now today and go to the younger generation and I can go call the shots over them because they think I'm the leader. But the older organization would look at me like, "Is you crazy? You ain't no leader to me."

Q. Let's talk about the police a little. How did they react when you started getting a reputation?

A. They just started arresting as many people as they can so they can move up as quick as possible. You know, they don't want to listen to you. And if you are on probation you might as well forget it because you not going to make it through probation in Milwaukee. They are going to make sure you get revoked and go to jail. OK, just say a person with no record at all, you know nothing, got caught for being out after curfew (Milwaukee has an eleven o'clock juvenile curfew). He gets labeled down whatever neighborhood he get caught in. If he was in the 1-9s neighborhood, he's going to be a 1-9. And if he was in the 2-7s, he's a 2-7, and on and on. And they'll take his picture and post it up on this board and say, "Hmm, that's another gang member. Watch out for him. We're going to label him as this and we're going to give him a record. We're going to make sure that we get paid. And we're going to keep this little commotion going." The gang squad is the biggest gang.

Q. Frankie from the 1-9s told me how they got named by the police because they got arrested on 19th street.

A. They put ideas in your head. You know they actually yelled out from the loudspeaker in the police car in my neighborhood that I was the "leader of the 2-7s" and everybody heard. At the time I liked that. I was young. And you know I knew I was going to get a lot of props (support). And so, I just start saying I was the leader you know. And I started getting lots of props. And so they really put stuff in your head, instead of helping you.

Q. Do you remember any turning point when shit got a whole lot worse? Between the kids or from the police or anything? Was there anything that marked a change?

A. I can't really say. I got arrested for a lot of shit. Bullshit, you know, like curfew tickets. They used to arrest me like this: I was washing my clothes at the laundromat on 26th and Center in our neighborhood. And I was washing my clothes and the cops came in and said if you're here in another fifteen minutes when we come back, we're going to arrest you. I didn't leave, so they arrested me. Left my clothes in the dryer and everything. And I'm like, "Man how can you guys arrest me?" "Because we told you we going to get you every time you smart mouth us. We're going to get you." And they arrested me for loitering. But you know I was so young a man, I used to just tear the tickets up when they give them and throw them away. I never did go to court for them.

Q. Give me a rating on the Gang Squad. One to five. One they are doing a great job, five is total bullshit.

A. Five.

Q. Why is it I could've guessed that score? OK, now here I'm going to give you a job. The Chief of Police walks right in that door and he says you are going to run the Gang Squad. He's going to give you the job, Captain of the Gang Squad. All right, what do you have them doing?

A. Well, I don't want them out there harassing the gangs, you know, stirring up more and more. I want them to be out there, at least be like a counselor to them, you know. Get out there and talk to them. Don't get out there and start all types of things, driving on the sidewalk, just stopping them just to get their names. All that, making them look like criminals, even though they haven't done nothing. But suppose a bus passed and your school teacher was on that bus and she sees you getting stopped by the police. What is she going to think? She don't know they just want to stop you just to fuck with you. She probably thinks you're getting arrested because her bus is going to keep on going. She ain't going to see what else happened. You know, that fucks with a person too, man, just getting stopped for no reason.

Are there "Fighting Gangs," "Criminal Gangs," and "Drug-using Gangs"?

Not all theorists share the classical age-graded view of gang structure. Cloward and Ohlin, in postulating different "types" of gangs based on types of communities but disregarding age, have confused many empirical researchers (Hardman, 1967). Spergel's (1964) attempts to fit gangs of his "eastern city" into these types is only the most notable example of the harm done by Cloward and Ohlin's typology. Recent studies of gangs in the Midwest have also at times dogmatically followed the Cloward and Ohlin typology. The Evanston study, for example, seemed surprised to have found that some gangs have "split into an older group . . . and a younger group" (Rosenbaum, 17). Despite this observation, the study did not try to analyze Evanston gangs in terms of age divisions. Evanston gangs were described, Cloward and Ohlin style, as divided into "fighting street gangs" and "money-making gangs" (21), again a typology that can be meaningful only for law enforcement.

To understand most gangs as coalitions of age-graded groups clears up some of the confusion of Cloward and Ohlin's ideal types. All gangs we studied in Milwaukee were "fighting gangs," but the fighting period was generally when the gang members were "juniors" or in their early teens. As the gang matured, their interests turned more to fundamental problems of survival.

One gang we found in our Milwaukee interviews at first did appear to be a prototype of the Cloward and Ohlin "criminal gang":

Q. When you were all together with the fellas. What did you do most of the time?

A. Plot on stealing something to make some money if we hadn't already stole it. Yeah. It was like all the other gangs was out there fighting amongst each other, but the Vicelords worked downtown at the money. They fighting. We making money.

Q. Did you try to recruit other people?

A. No

Q. Why not?

A. We didn't need to share no more money with nobody.

Chuck, Vicelords

Further interviews, however, with other members disputed Chuck's emphasis on money-making. The others interviewed pointed out that the escapades Chuck was referring to took place during a very short period of time when the Vicelords regularly went to downtown Milwaukee and "ripped off" stores, snatched purses, and went on a crime spree. While this was undoubtedly the most exciting and memorable period for the Vicelords, it was a comparatively short time in the history of the gang.

Rather than a formal "type" of gang, based in a particular kind of community, we have a specific gang concentrating for a specific period of time on one kind of activity. Chuck and his friends stopped their criminal activities soon after police seriously turned their attentions to the Vicelords' antics. The gang dissolved after the Youth Diversion Project referred all the active members to jobs during 1984.

Milwaukee gangs vary, not only among themselves, but also between age groups within each gang, within the age groups, and over time. Rather than seeing the Vicelords as a "criminal gang" for once and always, we should see their criminal activities as one phase of a varied life of one age group in the gang.

Hustling, Drugs, and Survival

Q. How important was the gang to you during the time you were most into it?

A. I feel it was real important, 'cause you know when I was in the gang, it was about hustling. That's all we did was hustle at the time of the gang. We really didn't do a lot of fighting, but when we had fights it was about the hustling. I used to have new clothes every day, money in my pocket every day. I felt gangs was important to me at the time.

Corner life can be exciting, the drama of conflict with other gangs and with the authorities adds to their appeal to many young people. But life on the corner also means the need to have some money, especially as one gets older. With few jobs available, "hustling" is how a gang member might put a few dollars in his pocket. "Hustling" means surviving any way one can, "getting over" on someone, making a buck just to make it day by day. Because of the lack of good jobs, the hustling mentality has grown particularly among young males, and everything, including work, begins to be seen as a "hustle."

The need to hustle is accepted as legitimate, as necessary to survive. Don tries to "neutralize" the "wrongness" of stealing:

Q. Do you think stealing is wrong?

A. Yeah, you know something, I feel that stealing is wrong, but you know, stealing to try to either help yourself or your parents or something is OK, but it's not right. I wouldn't say it's right, it's, you know, OK if you're trying to help somebody. But if you're just trying to steal just to steal something, then I figure, you know, it's all the way wrong. If you taking something from the rich and giving it to the poor, then you know you're doing a good deed. But you're still doing something wrong.

As the gang members age, the need to support themselves becomes most important. One twenty-two year old rationalizes how he sees the gang and stealing:.

Q. Do you consider doing something like robbing. You consider it wrong?

A. No. I consider it like this here. At the time, ain't no jobs, and I'm not starving for nobody, you understand? I feel that if I gotta starve, I'd rather take than starve. Hey, if you gotta eat, and keep some clothes on your back, and take care of your bills, I don't think stealing is wrong. Less they gonna give you a job, that's all. And then, you know, I see if you got anything you need, you don't gotta steal, but if you ain't got it, you need to steal. That's how the organization came in effect. It stopped me from stealing. It was like, they gave me their support when I was feeling pretty bad myself.

Q. What does being in an organization mean to you?

A. Well, organizations is like, you don't gotta worry about starving. You can always go to your nation and ask and get. You've got support when you need it. You ain't gotta worry about nobody snatching your mama's purse.

"Hustling" by definition is unplanned, spontaneous money-making any way you can.

Q. I got a job for you, a full-time job. I'm going to let you run the Gang Squad and you can be Captain tomorrow and they're all saluting you. What are you going to tell them to do differently than they are doing now?

A. I'd try to understand really more or less where they come from. What makes them commit these crimes? Why do they do it? What makes them do it? How do they do it. I was reading the paper one time that they (the police) was wondering how (the gangs) get together to just go out and steal. It's not more or less planned. You don't plan that. You just all get together, you all have a little money, and you all talk about getting some more money. And you get high, and we play basketball and they say we want to get some money. We get away from there, split up, everybody going their own way. Check in later on in the night. It's more or less spontaneous, not just planned.

Selling drugs, especially marijuana, is a common hustle within the gangs. It is an easy way to make money and has "enjoyable" fringe benefits. Thirty of those interviewed reported their gang sold regularly, and eleven said the gang sold now and then. One person said her gang never sold illegal drugs, but an admitted cocaine problem that resulted in her imprisonment casts some doubt on her contention. Eight of those interviewed reported they presently sold drugs regularly, and twenty-one said they sold now and then. Only two persons interviewed, however, could be called "dealers," obtaining quantities of drugs for others to sell. Fourteen said they did not sell anymore. While four persons said they got their supplies from someone else in the gang, most (20) reported that the main suppliers were not in gangs, but contacts known on the street.

> You want to know where the drugs come from? Sure, we got a dealer (in the gang), but look at this block. There's a dealer here, there, there, there. and that just on one block.
>
> Diego, *Latin Kings*

As gang members age, the sales of drugs and other petty crime becomes one means of securing their survival. As one of the Black Gangster Disciples put it: "It's all about survival now." But it is not much more than survival. Drug sales for most gang members are just another low-paying job—one that might guarantee "survival," but not much else.[6]

Organized Crime and Milwaukee Gangs

What are the consequences of "hustling," drug sales, and other criminal ventures of older gang members? Does the gang inevitably mature into an organized criminal form? This is a serious question since we do have some precedent for gangs turning to organized crime. Thrasher described the process in some of his 1,313 gangs as they took up careers in organized crime, but they were clearly a small minority of all gangs. More recently, Moore (1978) has described the growth of Mexican "state-raised youth" (prisoners who have spent their entire lives in correctional facilities) forming organized crime networks within California prisons and barrios. She points out, however, that while the three gangs she studied all use heroin, they are not part of this "Mexican Mafia" nor could possibly be considered "organized crime."

The "super-gangs" in Chicago are widely considered to have organized a vast network of drug sales. While non-law enforcement research is lacking concerning today's Chicago gangs, we can reasonably believe that many of the founding groups of those gangs have stayed together and followed career paths of organized crime. To generalize, however, about all gangs in Chicago, even those of the same name, and consider them all "soldiers" in a vast drug empire, probably takes the issue too far.

When we look at Milwaukee, certain other factors stand out in suggesting organized drug sales may not be an easy path of development. In Chicago, gangs carved out turf in large high-rise housing projects, where a small organized group could control drug sales and reap enormous profits by simply controlling the housing project elevators by armed force. No such housing projects exist in Milwaukee.

Milwaukee gang drug sales, despite the clear intentions of some "entrepreneurs," have largely remained at an individual, "street" level. One Milwaukee gang founder had a clear notion of why Milwaukee gangs would not turn into organized crime:

> Q. Are the gangs here like Chicago? Do you think things are going to go that way here?
>
> A. No. Too much free enterprise. Ain't no brother gonna mess up no free enterprise. See in the neighborhood I know well, within two blocks about four people selling dope.

Indeed, those gang members whom we interviewed and we knew were considered "major dealers" hardly led a life of luxury. The ladder up the criminal opportunity structure is not readily available to many within the gangs. One gang we interviewed described a drug house they had set up to organize their distribution of drugs. The house was a "drive-in" where buyers drove their car up to the corner, a "waiter" or "waitress" came out and took the order and the gang filled it in a jiffy. But the house only lasted a few months and the gang discontinued organized drug sales. Why did they stop when they were making money? The reason the gang members gave was simple: It was too much of a hassle. This gang was not cut out to become an organized criminal venture. The police did not really bother their sales, but the organization necessary to pull off an on-going drug house was too much for this gang, whose members were concerned with "making it" day by day. While many of the adult members of this gang still sell cocaine and marijuana, it is done, as in most other gangs, individually and sporadically.

This is not to deny the possibility that some gangs or individuals may follow a career path in large scale drug sales. The existence of a leadership tradition and the formation of gangs based on Chicago style "nations," not neighborhoods may reinforce tendencies for some gang leaders to pursue careers in organized drug sales. The organized crime model is tempting, if difficult. The lack of full-time jobs certainly heightens the probability that some unemployed gang members will try to organize and expand drug sales into a major venture.

Law enforcement and community agencies need to differentiate between the very common street sale of marijuana that is nearly universal within the gang, and those "entrepreneurs" who wish to transform the gang into a network for drug sales. Given the variety of factors operating, the growth of Milwaukee's street gangs into organized crime at this time is far from inevitable and unlikely to be widespread.

Conclusion: The Formation Process of Milwaukee's Gangs

Rather than define gangs by describing a generic organizational structure, or define them by the occasional violent acts of some of their members, we have chosen to follow Thrasher and others whose focus is on age divisions, the wide

variations between and within gangs in the context of a specific community, and
the formation process. This formation process can be summarized in five stages:

1. Milwaukee gangs typically began as groups of thirteen- to sixteen-
   year-old friends hanging out together and forming a social network
   for one another. This social network usually condones use of
   marijuana, alcohol and various delinquent acts.

2. The group conflicts with other similar groups and begins to form an
   identity in opposition to a rival group. The gang is usually named after
   the place where its members hang out. Within the group, some persons
   assume a degree of leadership, generally because of fighting ability.

3. Conflict with police, school officials, and other authorities over fighting
   and other delinquent acts helps shape a delinquent and deviant identity
   about and within the group.

4. As the group of friends ages, a new younger group of friends emerges
   and emulates the original or older group. The younger age group has
   its own "structure" and "leaders" and relates to the older age group
   in a variety of formal and/or informal ways.

5. The older group, as its members reach age eighteen or so, turns from
   constant fighting and getting arrested to more adult concerns of
   survival.

The law enforcement paradigm defines gangs in a narrow and unchanging
manner, which neglects the process of development which different age groups
within gangs undergo and ignore or undervalue variations of all sorts. Gangs are
not seen as young people struggling to adapt, often destructively, to a specific
economic and social environment. Rather, gangs are treated as a major criminal
problem and their members dehumanized as no more than aspiring "career
criminals." Where data exists to support these stereotypes, it often consists of
generalizations in the media from the acts of a few to all "hard core" gang members.
The fact that gangs today are overwhelmingly minority and most police departments
overwhelmingly white, allows for racism to contribute to these stereotypes and
results in even greater hostility on the street.

Footnotes

[1] Geis (1965, 1) even gives us a lesson in etymology. The word "gang" came from early English usage
of a word for "journey," often a sea journey, thus the "gang" of a ship. It acquired a derogatory
usage with Chaucer, using "gonge" as a synonym for "privy." He compared "fool women" with
a "common gonge." Shakespeare continued this usage, noting in "The Merry Wives of Windsor,"
"there's a knot, a gang, a pack, a conspiracy against me." See also Arnold (1966) for an attempt
to redefine "a gang," and Miller's rather lengthy discussion (1976).

[2] Zatz (1987), in a well-researched paper comparing characteristics of juvenile gang members to non-
gang members referred to the Arizona Division of Corrections, finds that juvenile gang members

are not referred to juvenile authorities for violent crimes any more frequently than similar non-gang youth. Suttles (1968, 205-20) and Spergel (1964) support Thrasher. See Kornhauser (1968, 59-61) for a theoretical review of this point.

[3] Perhaps some gangs have organized in the bureaucratic format. Campbell reports female New York gang members telling her that their gangs are organized in a "pyramidal" fashion that is a reflection, according to Campbell, of "corporate America" (1984, 240).

[4] Consider this description received from correctional sources in Beloit, Wisconsin (letter to author). "Criminal justice professionals have come to recognize street gang activities as a never ending problem. Today's gangs are organized along a military style, and are highly mobile. The gangs are highly successful in their dealings of narcotics, trafficking, extortion, intimidation, assault, and murder. Recruitment is in full force throughout the nation."

[5] We decided to edit this interview for readability. David's answers explaining how the gang formed and the impact of labeling were spread out through nearly a hundred pages of transcript. Editing seemed the best way to present David's story. In most cases we have quoted the actual answers from the transcripts and merely combined them with quotes from other answers later in the interview. All other quotes from gang respondents are word for word unless otherwise cited.

[6] Glasgow sums up our findings precisely in his important book *The Black Underclass*. He is describing the relationship of underclass males to drug sales: The drug-seller role "somewhat resembled their relation to other economic systems, principally the legitimate job world. The drug trade was reputedly able to provide 'long bread,' good money, but only for a few. The typical . . . (black male) . . . could not gain access to the controlling positions or to the big sums collected daily. For him, even if he became a pusher the drug system would never be a major source of income. As usual, he held options at the bottom of the pole, either as a user or one able to be manipulated by outsiders. In respect to drug use, his major concern was finding a way to ease the pain of daily living, to get a 'hum' and a little 'high,' without losing control, which would be antithetical to ghetto functioning" (Glasgow 1980, 96).

References

Arnold, William R. 1965. "The Concept of Gang," *The Sociological Quarterly* 7:1, 59-75.
Cloward, Richard and Lloyd Ohlin. 1960. *Delinquency and Opportunity.* Glencoe, IL: Free Press.
Geis, Gilbert. 1965. "Juvenile Gangs," Washington, DC: President's Committee on Juvenile Delinquency and Youth Crime.
Glasgow, Douglas G. 1981. *The Black Underclass.* New York: Vintage.
Hardman, Dale G. 1967. "Historical Perspectives on Gang Research," *Journal of Research in Crime and Delinquency* 4:1, 5-27.
Klein, Malcolm. 1971. *Street Gangs and Street Workers.* Englewood Cliffs, NJ: Prentice Hall.
Miller, Walter. 1975. "Violence by Youth Gangs and Youth Groups as a Crime Problem in Major American Cities," Washington, DC: U.S. Department of Justice.
Miller, Walter. 1976. "Youth Gangs in the Urban Crisis Era," in *Delinquency, Crime and Society*, edited by James F. Short, 91-122. Chicago: University of Chicago.
Moore, Joan W., Robert Garcia, Carlos Garcia, Luis Cerda and Frank Valencia. 1978. *Homeboys.* Philadelphia: Temple University Press.
Needle, Jerome A. and William Vaughan Stapleton. 1983. *Police Handling of Youth Gangs.* Washington, DC: American Justice Institute.
Rosenbaum, Dennis P. and Jane A. Grant. 1983. "Gang and Youth Problems in Evanston: Research Findings and Policy Options," Illinois Center for Urban Affairs and Policy Research, Northwestern University.
Spergel, Irving A. 1964. *Racketville Slumtown Haulberg.* Chicago: University of Chicago.

Suttles, Gerald D. 1959. "Territoriality, Identity, and Conduct: A Study of an Inner-City Slum with Special Reference to Street Corner Groups." Unpublished Ph.D. dissertation, Champaign: University of Illinois.

Thrasher, Frederick. 1963. *The Gang*. (Abridged edition; orig. 1927) Chicago: University of Chicago.

Whyte, William Foote. 1943. *Street Corner Society*. Chicago: University of Chicago.

Zatz, Marjorie S. 1987. "Chicano Youth Gangs and Crime: The Creation of a Moral Panic," forthcoming, *Contemporary Crises*.

Section III

JUVENILES IN THE SYSTEM

A substantial amount of attention has been given to the operational units of the juvenile justice and the criminal justice system, which include the police, courts, and correctional agencies. Police officers are the gate keepers to the juvenile justice system. The police officer has the power to determine if a juvenile will be arrested, booked, detained, and perhaps processed. The officer may also decide to "adjust" the complaint, divert the offender, or informally handle the juvenile in other ways, depending on the community resources available.

Similarly, once a youth is referred to court officials, there is substantial discretion in the decision making process. Court officials determine the official charges, make decisions regarding release if the youth was detained, and ultimately decide if the youth is to be placed on probation or incarcerated in an institution.

Richard Lundman, Richard Sykes and John Clark, in "Police Control of Juveniles: A Replication," have replicated the classic 1970 Black and Reiss study on juveniles and the police. The authors examined levels of police activity, seriousness of juvenile deviance, arrest rates and issues related to the decision to arrest. It is important to note the finding that the great bulk of police encounters with juveniles were related to matters of minor significance. Few juveniles were arrested and the decision to arrest depended largely on citizen preference and the seriousness of the offense. Black juveniles, when compared to white juveniles were more often arrested, but primarily because black complainants lobbied for police action. The issue of respect was also examined and those who are unusually respectful or unusually disrespectful had a high probability of being arrested. While the study tended to minimize issues of discrimination, the amount of discretion available to the police cannot be overlooked. Seriousness of offense is important, but demeanor is also important in the police-juvenile encounter.

Bruce Bullington, James Sprowls, Daniel Katkin and Mark Phillips argue, in "A Critique of Diversionary Juvenile Justice," that the road to hell is often paved with good intentions. Diversion programs, for the authors, represent serious problems for the juvenile justice system because of ambiguity in program definitions, impracticable goals and potential denial of due process. The harsh attack also includes arguments that diversion might well work against the lower-class and minority youth who, according to the authors, might be seen as especially suitable for the variety of proposed diversion programs. They have raised, in a different era, the same issues raised by Tannenbaum more than 45 years ago. Their contention that today's reforms become tomorrow's abuses is not groundless. One need only examine the overwhelming complex bureaucracies which have developed over the past 85 years in the "child saving" business to understand why the authors are concerned.

The third article in this section, "An Observational Study of a Juvenile Court," is an excellent overview of the juvenile court in operation and problems related to researching this institution. While a great deal has been written on the philosophical and legal basis for the juvenile court, we know surprisingly little about its day-to-day operation. The kind of detailed research frequently conducted on the decision-making process in adult courts is difficult to carry out for the juvenile hearing process. Much of the difficulty lies in the fact that the juvenile court is shrouded in a veil of secrecy designed to protect the juvenile's identity and avoid the public stigma or label of being treated as a criminal. This veil of secrecy not only protects the juvenile but also shields the juvenile court from close scrutiny. James Walter and Susan Ostrander provide the reader with a detailed account of the decision-making process in a large metropolitan juvenile court. The authors findings are clear and their observations on the potential denial of Constitutional rights are insightful. Overall, one has a clear impression that things are not always as they should be in this complex bureaucracy that has as its major responsibility the rehabilitation of the youthful offender.

In the last article in this section, Victor Streib considers the practice of "Imposing the Death Penalty on Children." Streib notes that since colonial times 281 people have been executed for crimes committed while they were under 18. He also describes the 33 cases of juveniles on death as of March 31, 1987 and outlines the social and legal arguments for abolishing the death penalty for juveniles.

8

Police Control of Juveniles
A Replication

Richard J. Lundman, Richard E. Sykes
and John P. Clark

In 1970, Donald Black and Albert J. Reiss, Jr. presented a series of eight propositions which they suggested provided "the beginning of an empirical portrait of the policing of juveniles" (Black and Reiss, 1970:76). The propositions were as follows:

1. Most police encounters with juveniles arise in direct response to citizens who take the initiative to mobilize the police to action.
2. The great bulk of police encounters with juveniles pertain to matters of minor legal significance.
3. The probability of sanction by arrest is very low for juveniles who have encounters with the police.
4. The probability of arrest increases with the legal seriousness of alleged juvenile offenses, as that legal seriousness is defined in criminal law for adults.
5. Police sanctioning of juveniles strongly reflects the manifest preferences of citizen complainants in field encounters.
6. The arrest rate for Negro juveniles is higher than that for white juveniles, but evidence that the police behaviorally orient themselves to race as such is absent.

Richard J. Lundman, Richard E. Sykes, John P. Clark, "Police Control of Juveniles: A Replication," pp. 158-168 in *Juveniles in Justice: A Book of Readings,* edited by H. Ted Rubin. Copyright © 1978 by the National Council on Crime and Delinquency. Reprinted by permission of Sage Publications, Inc.

7. The presence of situational evidence linking a juvenile to a deviant act is an important factor in the probability of arrest.
8. The probability of arrest is higher for juveniles who are unusually respectful toward the police and for those who are unusually disrespectful.

Black and Reiss also noted that these propositions adumbrate a general theory of social control.

The central aim of the present study, therefore, is to examine the extent to which the Black and Reiss findings hold for police-juvenile encounters occurring in a large midwestern city, 1970-71.

Method

During a fifteen-month period beginning in June 1970, we conducted a participant-as-observer study of police-citizen encounters in a midwestern city of more than 500,000 located in a SMSA [Standard Metropolitan Statistical Area] of over 2,000,000. A group of seven observers, trained over three months, traveled with police on a random-time sample basis, using portable electronic coding equipment and an interaction process code. Without prior notice, observers appeared at a precinct station to ride in a randomly selected patrol car for a full shift. Which car they were to ride in was not known to the police in advance.

The data base consists of 2,835 *potential* police-citizen contacts. When such contacts involved police-citizen interaction, they were defined as encounters (n = 1,978 involving about 9,000 citizens), and the interaction was simultaneously and sequentially content analyzed and coded using the portable equipment. Among the situational factors coded were whether the encounter was initiated by the police or the citizen, the purpose of the call, the kind of space in which the activity occurred, and whether there was conflict between citizens when the officers arrived. The nature of the interaction was measured by a variety of action and interaction codes pertaining to civility and incivility, giving and following orders, and displays of anger; and codes relating to specific kinds of violence, aggressive threats, or acts. The specific outcome of the encounter was also coded. Demographic data were collected from visual and audial observation and coded for complainant, victim, alleged violator, participants, and bystanders. Interobserver reliability was calculated utilizing Scott's II (Scott, 1955; Krippendorf, 1970), and the coefficient for codes reported herein ranged between .70 and .80.

To isolate police-juvenile encounters from other activities, the calls selected for analysis in this study met the following two criteria: (1) An alleged violator was present, and (2) the alleged violator was under eighteen years of age. Of the 1,978 encounters, 200 or approximately 10 percent met these criteria.

Analysis and Results

In Order to facilitate comparison of our findings with those of Black and Reiss, we will follow the format established in the earlier paper. Consequently, we will compare our results with the earlier findings in the following areas: (1) detection of juvenile deviance, (2) seriousness of juvenile deviance, (3) arrest rates, (4) legal seriousness and arrest, (5) citizen preference and arrest, (6) race and arrest, (7) evidence and arrest, and (8) demeanor and arrest.

Detection of Juvenile Deviance

Of the 281 encounters observed by Black and Reiss, 72 percent were citizen initiated and 28 percent were initiated by the police while in patrol. Excluding traffic violations, the proportions become 78 percent and 22 percent, respectively. As a consequence, Black and Reiss concluded that most deviant acts by juveniles are detected by citizens rather than the police.

Of the 200 encounters we observed, 52 percent were *police* initiated and 48 percent were initiated by citizens. Excluding traffic violations, the proportions become 34 percent and 66 percent respectively. What accounts for these differences is that the police department of the city we studied maintained a monthly traffic ticket quota system for patrol officers, thereby forcing patrol officers to become more proactive.[1]

It is necessary, therefore, to modify Black's and Reiss's conclusion since departmental policy, as well as the moral standards of the citizens, (Black and Reiss, 1970:66), determines the detection of juvenile deviance. This modification is as follows: *(1) Police have the capacity to change the ratios of police-and citizen-initated encounters by becoming more proactive; (2) therefore, the ratios of police- and citizen-initiated encounters are dependent upon departmental policy.*

Seriousness of Juvenile Deviance

The Black and Reiss data reveal that only a minority of police-juvenile transactions involved alleged felonies. For both black and white juveniles, nearly two-thirds of the encounters observed involved nothing more serious than juvenile rowdiness. They note, however, that, compared to white juveniles, there was a greater tendency for black juveniles to be involved in alleged felonies. Finally, they note that their data do not contain evidence of

---

[1]For a discussion of the traffic quota system in operation, see Lundman (1979).

differential police selection by reference to race.

Our data are essentially supportive of these findings. First, only a minority of the juveniles we observed were involved in alleged felony encounters. Although more of our encounters revolved around alleged felonies than those observed by Black and Reiss, it remains that the great bulk of police encounters with juveniles pertain to matters of minor legal significance.

Second, our data are also supportive of the earlier finding that black juveniles are more frequently involved in alleged felony encounters than white juveniles. Specifically, our data, as compared to those of Black and Reiss, show an even greater rate of involvement of minority juveniles in alleged felony transactions. This is the case for both citizen- and police-initiated encounters, but the differences between the two data bases is especially clear when one examines citizen-initiated encounters.

Finally, there is also support for the earlier observation that there is no evidence of police selection of juveniles for involvement in encounters by reference to race. Based upon our data, it is clear that involvement of minority juveniles is much more frequent in citizen- than police-initiated encounters. Although these data do not speak directly to the issue of racial discrimination by the police, it does appear that Black's and Reiss's conclusion of an absence of evidence of discrimination is warranted.

Because of the essentially supportive nature of our data, it appears appropriate to suggest two subpropositions descriptive of the seriousness of juvenile deviance. They are *(1) As compared to white juveniles, black juveniles are more frequently involved in alleged felony encounters; and (2) the greater involvement of black juveniles in alleged felony encounters does not appear to be attributable to police discrimination.*

Arrest Rates

Of the encounters observed by Black and Reiss, only 15 percent ended in arrest. They note that the remaining 85 percent of the cases typically are not included in official delinquency statistics. And, since many juvenile offenses are never detected by citizens (see Williams and Gold, 1972), and of those which are detected, only a minority are reported to the police (Ennis, 1967), it is clear that police statistics significantly underestimate the total volume of juvenile deviance.

Of the 200 encounters we observed, only 16 percent ended in arrest. The juveniles involved in the 84 percent of the encounters which ended without an arrest were, in effect, diverted from the juvenile justice system. Therefore, it seems reasonable to note: *Police diversion of juveniles from the juvenile justice system is a common practice.*

Legal Seriousness and Arrest

Black and Reiss note that since only 15 percent of the encounters they observed ended in arrest, a "high level of selectivity enters into the arrest of juveniles" (1970:68). As a consequence, they undertake an extended analysis of the factors which influence police exercise of discretion.

The first of the variables they examined in relation to arrest was the legal seriousness of the alleged offense. They found that nearly three-fourths of the alleged felony encounters ended in an arrest, as compared to less than 15 percent of the rowdiness encounters and none of the noncriminal dispute encounters. They concluded that the probability of arrest increases with the legal seriousness of the alleged offense.

Our replication data are supportive of this conclusion. Thus, all of the alleged felony encounters we observed ended in an attempted or actual arrest, as compared to less than 5 percent of the rowdiness encounters and none of the noncriminal dispute encounters. Thus, the Black and Reiss conclusion that legal seriousness is among the factors which influence police exercise of arrest discretion is supported.

Citizen Preference and Arrest

A second set of factors examined by Black and Reiss was the relationship between the presence of citizen complainants and police exercise of arrest discretion. Black and Reiss reasoned that citizen complainants exert an important influence on police officers by their mere presence. Moreover, they reasoned that certain complainants may prefer arrest and that this preference increases the probability that the encounter will end in arrest.

Their data were supportive of both observations. Thus, encounters where only a suspect was present ended in arrest less frequently than encounters where a suspect and complainant were both present. And, in those encounters where it was possible to determine citizen preference, it was clear that when complainants preferred arrest, the probability of arrest was significantly greater than when complainants preferred an informal disposition.

Our data confirm these earlier findings. Thus, encounters where a suspect and complainant were both present ended more frequently in arrest than encounters where only a suspect was present. And, in those encounters where it was possible to determine citizen preference, the officers we observed complied with citizen preferences in every situation in which preference was made manifest. As a consequence, there is no reason to modify the basic Black and Reiss conclusion that police exercise of arrest discretion is influenced by complainant preferences.

It does appear reasonable, however, to add to this conclusion. As Black and Reiss indicate (1970:72), these data suggest that citizens, rather than the police, determine the total volume of official delinquency. In addition to citizens' exercise of discretion in the context of calling the police about a delinquent act they have witnessed, in their roles as complainants, citizens influence arrest rates by their willingness to remain at the scene of an offense until the police arrive and by making their dispositional preferences manifest. We would add the following subproposition: *Citizens, therefore, largely determine official delinquency rates.*

Race and Arrest

A number of studies both before and after the Black and Reiss study have considered the relationship between race and arrest. Piliavin and Briar (1964), for example, reported that with offense held constant, black juveniles were arrested more frequently than white juveniles. Wilson (1968) reached an essentially similar conclusion for the eastern city he examined. In one sense, then, the Black and Reiss conclusion of an absence of evidence of discrimination in the context of arrests stands as something of an exception when compared to other studies.

Black and Reiss base their conclusion on a number of interrelated observations. They note, first, that encounters involving black suspects more frequently contained (black) complainants than encounters involving white suspects. Second, they note that black complainants more frequently lobby for arrest of black suspects than white complainants involved in encounters with white suspects. Finally, they note that the police officers they observed complied more frequently with the arrest preferences of black complainants. Put simply, it is their argument that black complainants account for the higher rate of arrest of black juveniles.

Our data are supportive of these observations. Thus, in the encounters we observed, more of the black suspect than white suspect encounters involved complainants. Moreover, it was also the case that more black than white complainants lobbied for formal police action. Finally, police compliance with the arrest preferences of black complainants was also perfect. For these reasons, we concur with the Black and Reiss conclusion that there is no evidence that the police are behaviorally oriented to the race of juvenile subjects. *Instead it would appear that the higher rate of arrest for black juveniles is attributable to black complainants who lobby for formal police action.*

Situational Evidence and Arrest

Black and Reiss note that another variable that should affect the probability of arrest is the nature of the evidence present in the situation. They examined the impact of evidence on arrest decision;... encounters wherein a citizen linked a juvenile to an offense ended in arrest most frequently. Police-witness encounters occupied an intermediate position, while only one of the no-evidence encounters ended in an arrest. As a consequence, Black and Reiss emphasize the importance of situational evidence in police arrest decisions.

Our data, with the exception of no-evidence encounters, are essentially similar. Citizen testimony encounters ended in arrest more frequently than police witness encounters. Therefore, our data are supportive of the emphasis given the importance of situational evidence.

Our data, however, do not support the finding of a low rate of arrest in no-evidence encounters. Specifically, white suspect, no-evidence encounters ended in arrest more frequently than comparable citizen testimony or police witness encounters. Additional analysis revealed an explanation: A minority of the white suspects involved in these encounters were unusually respectful or disrespectful in their interactions with the police.

As a consequence, it appears necessary to offer the following by way of clarification: *In no-evidence encounters, the demeanor of the juvenile is the most important determinant of whether or not formal action is taken.*

Demeanor and Arrest

A number of studies both before (Piliavin and Briar, 1964) and after (Lundman, 1974) the one being replicated here have considered the relationships between citizen demeanor and police arrest decisions. And, as in the case with the Black and Reiss study, most have discovered that the probability of arrest increases with level of disrespect. Once again, though, Black and Reiss are unique in reporting higher rates of arrest for unusually respectful juveniles.

Our data are supportive of *both* observations. Thus, black and white juveniles who were antagonistic were arrested more frequently than juveniles who were civil. However, for white juveniles, the bipolar pattern reported by Black and Reiss holds for our data also. Thus, white suspects who were very deferential in their interaction with the police were also arrested more frequently than antagonistic juveniles. The small number of very deferential black suspects precludes meaningful comparison.

We would also agree with the explanation by Black and Reiss of this phenomenon. As the data from both studies make clear, the majority of police encounters with juveniles are civil. Only a minority of these juveniles are antagonistic in their interaction with the police and an even smaller group are very deferential. In one sense, deferential juvenils are suspicious because their demeanor is so clearly different from that of their colleagues. In another sense, their extreme deference is illogical or inappropriate given the circumstances in which it is expressed. Therefore: *The higher rate of arrest of very deferential juveniles may be explainable by reference to the suspicions their demeanor arouses among police patrol officers.* We agree with Black and Reiss however, that "a good deal more research is needed pertaining to the relations between situational etiquette and sanctioning" (1970:75).

Overview

We have in this paper replicated the research of Donald Black and Albert J. Reiss in the area of police control of juveniles. Based upon comparative data separated by four years and many miles, we found, in general, that our data were supportive of their earlier conclusions. We have, however, also offered a number of subpropositions, clarifications, and extensions of their basic findings. They, along with the propositions advanced by Black and Reiss and supported by us, can be summarized as follows:

1. Most police encounters with juveniles arise in direct response to citizens who take the initiative to mobilize the police to action.
   a. However, police have the capacity to change the ratios of police- and citizen-initiated encounters by becoming more pro-active.
   b. Therefore, the ratios of police- and citizen-initiated encounters are dependent upon departmental policy.
2. The great bulk of police encounters with juveniles pertain to matters of minor legal significance.
   a. As compared to white juveniles, black juveniles are more frequently involved in alleged felony encounters.
   b. The greater involvement of black juveniles in alleged felony encounters does not appear to be attributable to police dis-discrimination.
3. The probability of sanction by arrest is very low for juveniles who have encounters with the police.
   a. Police diversion of juveniles from the juvenile justice system is a common practice.
4. The probability of arrest increases with the legal seriousness of alleged juvenile offenses, as that legal seriousness is defined in criminal law for adults.
5. Police sanctioning of juveniles strongly reflects the manifest preferences of citizen complainants in field encounters.
   a. Citizens, therefore, largely determine official delinquency rates.
6. The arrest rate for Negro juveniles is higher than that for white juveniles, but evidence that the police behaviorally orient themselves to race as such is absent.
   a. Instead, it would appear that the higher arrest rate of black

115

juveniles is attributable to the more frequent presence of black complainants who lobby for formal police action.
7. The presence of situational evidence linking a juvenile to a deviant act is an important factor in the probability of arrest.
    a. In encounters where there is no evidence linking a juvenile to an offense, the demeanor of the juvenile is the most important determinant of whether or not formal action is taken.
8. The probability of arrest is higher for juveniles who are unusually respectful toward the police and for those who are unusually disrespectful.
    a. The higher rate of arrest of very deferential juveniles may be explainable by reference to the suspicions their demeanor arouses among police patrol officers.

References

Black, D., and A.J. Reiss, Jr. 1970, "Police Control of Juveniles." *American Sociological Review* 35 (February): 63-77.

Ellis, P. 1967, *"Crime, Victims, and the Police."* Trans-Action (June): 36-44.

Krippendorf, K. 1970, "Bivariate Agreement Coefficients for Reliability of Data." In *Sociological Methodology,* Ernest Borgotta and George Bornsted, eds. San Francisco: Josey-Bass.

Lundman, R.J. 1974, "Routine Police Arrest Practices: A Commonweal Perspective." *Social Problems* (Fall): 127-141.

———— 1979, "Police Work with Traffic Law Violators." In *Police Behavior: A Sociological Perspective,* Richard J. Lundman, ed. Chicago: Rand McNally.

Piliavin, I., and S. Briar 1964, "Police Encounters with Juveniles." *American Journal of Sociology* (September): 206-214.

Scott, W.A. 1955, "Reliability of Content Analysis: The Case of Nominal Scale Coding." *Public Opinion Quarterly* (Fall): 321-325.

Williams, J.R., and M. Gold 1972, "From Delinquent Behavior to Official Delinquency." *Social Problems* (Fall): 209-229.

Wilson, J.Q. 1968, "The Police and the Delinquent in Two Cities." In *Controlling Delinquents,* Stanton Wheeler, ed. New York: John Wiley.

9

A Critique of Diversionary Juvenile Justice

Bruce Bullington, James Sprowls,
Daniel Katkin and Mark Phillips

The atmosphere of juvenile justice systems today is charged with talk of diversion.[1] Professionals are planning diversionary programs and worrying about the feasibility of implementation.[2] Books, monographs, and articles are being rushed into publication.[3] Research projects are being funded.[4] Diversion is widely advertised as a panacea not only for delinquency but also for the inequities and imperfections of the juvenile justice system.[5] The National Advisory Commission on Criminal Justice Standards and Goals, for example, was sufficiently convinced about the worth of diversionary programs to suggest that the rate of delinquency cases coming to court should be reduced by 70 percent between 1973 and 1983.[6]

Several considerations underlie this "faddish" interest in diversion: (1) widespread dissatisfaction with the inequities and failures of traditional strategies for the treatment and prevention of delinquency; (2) recurring observations that the well-established practice of informal, unofficial diversion has great social utility; and (3) continuing concern for the effective and humane resolution of the problems of troubled children. While agreeing that these motives combine to create a compelling justi-

Bruce Bullington, James Sprowls, Daniel Katkin, and Mark Phillips, "A Critique of Diversionary Juvenile Justice," *Crime and Delinquency,* Vol. 24, Number 1 (January 1978), pp. 59-71. Copyright © 1978 by Sage Publications, Inc. Reprinted by permission of Sage Publications, Inc.

fication for reform, our purpose in this paper is to argue *against* the wide-spread development of diversionary programs. We believe that these programs are impracticable, that they are fraught with potential for inequity and abuse, and that they involve implicit renunciation of the civil libertarian values articulated in Supreme Court decisions such as *In re Gault*.[7] Before developing these objections it will be useful to explore in detail the reasons behind the contemporary interest in diversion.

Rationale for Diversion

Dissatisfaction with Present System

During the past twenty years the juvenile justice system has been subjected to scathing denunciations by journalists, scholars, judges, politicians, administrators, and concerned citizens.[8] For example, so reputable an authority as Dean Roscoe Pound described the juvenile court as a tribunal more awesome in its abuse of power than the star chamber.[9] Between 1965 and 1971 the constitutionality of juvenile court procedures received four major challenges: One three occasions the Supreme Court found that the rights of children were being violated.[10] In *Kent v. U.S.* the Court observed:

> Some juvenile courts...lack the personnel, facilities and techniques to perform adequately as representatives of the State in a *parens patriae* capacity, at least with respect to children charged with law violation. There is evidence, in fact, that there may be grounds for concern that the child receives the worst of both worlds: That he gets neither the protections afforded adults nor the solicitous care and regenerative treatment postulated for children.[11]

Mixed with criticism of the juvenile courts is widespread dissatisfaction with the quality of treatment programs available for adjudicated delinquents. In *In re Gault* the Supreme Court went so far as to suggest that the term *reform school* is little more than a euphemism for prison:

> However euphemistic the title, a "receiving home" or an "industrial school" for juveniles is an institution of confinement in which the child is incarcerated for a greater or lesser time. His world becomes "a building with white-washed walls, regimented routine and institutional laws...." Instead of mother and father and sisters and brothers and friends and classmates, his world is peopled by guards, custodians, state employees, and "delinquents" confined with him for anything from waywardness to rape and homicide.[12]

Christian Science Monitor editor Howard James and Philadelphia Judge Lisa Richette, to cite only two examples, have argued that institutions for delinquents are among the least humane in the nation.[13] Numerous investigative reporters are loudly voicing the same view.[14] Senator Birch Bayh contends:

> Too many young people are thrown into custodial institutions...[which are characterized by] punishment, isolation, neglect, and abuse... [including] harassment, affront to human dignity, and the gross denial of human rights.[15]

A picture of the formal structures of juvenile justice has begun to emerge which paints them not as agencies for the protection of children but rather as agencies from which children need to be protected. This picture has been reinforced by growing acceptance of propositions derived from labeling theory[16] — namely, that the imposition of stigmatizing labels such as "delinquent" may propagate deviant self-concepts and exacerbate patterns of lawbreaking behavior. The National Advisory Commission on Criminal Justice Standards and Goals observed:

> People...tend to become what they are told they are. The stigma of involvement with the criminal justice system, even if only in the informal processes of juvenile justice, isolates persons from lawful society and may make further training or employment difficult.[17]

To the extent that this is true, the juvenile justice system may be characterized not merely as "unfair," "inadequate," or "unresponsive," but also as a cause of delinquency. Even such an established figure as Milton Luger, head of the delinquency division of the Law Enforcement Assistance Administration and formerly director of juvenile correction for New York State and chairman of the National Association of State Juvenile Delinquency Program Administrators, has conceded:

> With the exception of a relatively few youths it [would be] better for all concerned if young delinquents were not detected, apprehended, or institutionalized. Too many of them get worse in our care.[18]

Criticism such as this, public dismay about the high cost of institutional services,[19] and increasingly militant minority groups — whose members are disproportionately likely to be singled out for delinquent labels and treatment[20] — have driven juvenile justice professionals to search for alternatives. That diversion has emerged as an attractive alternative is due, in part, to recurring observations that many misbehaving youngsters are already diverted from the formal mechanisms of juvenile justice with apparently beneficial results.

Diversion: The Rule

To appreciate the extent to which diversion already exists, one must recognize the pervasiveness of what might be considered delinquent behavior. Delinquency studies using self-reports of previous behavior indicate that almost 90 percent of all young people commit offenses for which they could be adjudicated delinquent.[21] Obviously, most of these youngsters never come to the attention of the police. In Pennsylvania, for example, it is estimated that there are 1.4 million children whose behavior would sustain a finding of delinquency[22]; yet, in 1971, only 92,000 were taken into custody by agents of any of the state's more than 4,000 police jurisdictions.[23] That doesn't mean that the other 1.3 million were actively diverted; most, quite likely, were never detected by anyone. In many other cases, the delinquencies were noticed by parents, neighbors, shopkeepers, teachers, social workers, and even policemen—who decided not to invoke the formal processes of law.[24] That is true diversion.

Diversion of youngsters from the formal processes of adjudication continues in police-juvenile interaction:

> Of 92,000 children against whom proceedings were initiated by the police in Pennsylvania in 1971, 47,000 (52 percent) were released without further referral. It is conceivable, but improbable, that the police decided that more than half of their juvenile arrests were made without cause. It is more likely that police divert known juvenile offenders as frequently as they detain them.[25]

This diversionary process does not stop with the police. In many states, statutes specifically authorize pretrial hearings at which probation officers attempt "informal adjustment" of cases.[26] In Pennsylvania, only one-third of the cases sent by the police to juvenile court result in findings of delinquency or neglect.[27] Some of the other 30,000 cases are resolved on the basis of factual innocence; most, however, appear to be instances of diversion.[28]

Even among the 15,000 formally adjudicated Pennsylvania youngsters, only about one-fourth are institutionalized.[29] If this is not a form of true diversion, it is at least an example of a closely related concept: "minimization of penetration."[30]

It can be argued, then, that juvenile justice systems are already in the business of diverting young offenders from formal adjudication and institutional treatment. The recent interest in expanded systems of diversionary justice seems to be motivated by three beliefs: (1) Diverted youngsters are less likely than institutionalized juveniles to persist in delinquent careers[31]; (2) the benefits of current diversionary practices are disproportionately likely to be bestowed upon white or affluent youths[32]; and (3) social services from community agencies are purchased by many of the offenders now diverted from the juvenile justice system; these should be augmented and publicly subsidized to meet the needs of a new class of diverted youngsters.[33]

With the possible exception of differential treatment based upon race and income, little evidence is available to support these beliefs.[34] Nevertheless, advocates of diversionary programs contend with certainty that families and social service agencies are currently providing advocacy and other services to large numbers of young offenders and that those offenders and the larger community benefit from the arrangement.[35]

In short, dissatisfaction with the formal mechanisms of juvenile justice *combined* with uninformed interest in traditional informal practices has produced this enthusiasm for diversion.

Diversion and Parens Patriae Justice

The widespread popularity of diversionary programs is due to the fact that they offer the appearance of significant reform without any major modification of values. The extension of "benign," "helping," community-based services to a larger population of youngsters is altogether compatible with the traditional parens patriae values of juvenile justice — namely, that treatment for juveniles should be therapeutic and nonpunitive and that procedures should be informal and nonstigmatizing.

These values have dominated the juvenile justice system since the turn of the century when zealous reformers created children's courts to "divert" young offenders from the stigmatizing and punitive processes of the criminal justice system.[36] Most planners and practitioners involved in developing diversionary programs subscribe to these values, whose attractiveness derives from the fact that they seek to introduce humanitarian aims and social scientific principles into the law, and whose power derives from the fact that they have broad constituencies among liberals, social scientists, and helping professionals. Diversionary programs appear to aid in "reforming" institutions without so much as suggesting a need to reassess objectives.

The Argument Against Diversion

Three related concerns underlie our opposition to diversionary programs: (1) The concept of diversion is dangerously ambiguous; (2) the goals of these programs may be unattainable; and (3) diversionary efforts may be incompatible with concepts of due process and fundamental fairness.

Definitional Ambiguity

In general usage the word *diversion* has two meanings. We may speak of diversion *from* something or of diversion *to* something. Diversion of youngsters from the juvenile justice system implies that the system will be limited in scope and authority. This makes sense in light of the persistent criticism that the processes of juvenile justice are unfair, stigmatizing, and dysfunctional.[37] But to achieve diversion from the juvenile justice system, no new "programs" are necessary. Increasing the number of programs for juvenile offenders is incompatible with the idea of diversion from the system: New programs, however we label them, are certainly a part of the overall system for responding to delinquency, and sending youngsters to those programs cannot fairly be characterized as keeping them out of the system. Diversion from the system—true diversion, as it is sometimes called—suggests that resources for the treatment of deviant youngsters ought to be reduced. If there are fewer programs, there will be room for fewer youngsters, and more will have to be diverted.[38] From this perspective, the phrase *diversionary program* is a contradiction. When new programs are proposed it can only be because it is hoped that youngsters will be diverted *to* them, thus remaining within the overall system.

At present, the term *diversion* is used, somewhat self-servingly, as if its two meanings were entirely compatible. Thus, critics of the juvenile justice system describe it as dehumanizing, argue that its caseload should be reduced, and call for diversion *to* new programs. In the name of diverting youngsters from the system, communities are asked to make additional resources available so that new treatment modalities can be created for youngsters who might otherwise be left alone.

The confusion between diverting children *from* the system and diverting them to new parts of it might be pardonable if it were clear that these new programs would provide humane, nonstigmatizing, helpful treatment for young offenders who had been fairly and equitably determined to need it. However, the evidence that new diversionary efforts will be more equitable or more effective than the traditional programs of juvenile courts, probation departments, and reform schools is not there.

Impracticable Goals

Advocates of diversionary programs are committed to the notion that services provided outside the aegis of the formal mechanisms of the juvenile justice system will be superior. They argue that these new programs will be less stigmatizing than traditional treatment and will provide services similar to those currently received by youngsters now informally diverted out of the system. Neither argument is persuasive.

There is no reason to believe that the labels imposed by Youth Services Bureaus and other instruments of diversion will be nonstigmatizing. The term *delinquent,* it should be remembered, was coined by turn-of-the-century reformers who wished to spare youngsters the stigma of criminality. It did not take long for popular language to catch up with this professional euphemism; Americans have known for a long time that delinquent is a nice way of saying "young hoodlum." Of course, it is possible to shift euphemisms again, but to believe that the public will not catch on and that the new terms (*child in need of supervision,* or *person in need of services*) will not convey stigma is naive. True diversion from the juvenile justice system might save children from the negative impact of stigmatizing labels; creating new labels by new programs will have little effect on the labeling process or on the secondary deviance labeling is thought to engender.[39]

Advocates of diversionary programs argue that youngsters currently adjudicated delinquent would benefit from the types of informal, supportive services available to youngsters who are currently being diverted. Indeed, it can be argued that adjudicated delinquents are a population discriminated against and deprived because they lack the resources to *purchase* the humane, effective support services available to middle- and upper-class children. It is hoped that if informal, community-based services are made available to more young offenders, fewer youths will be adjudicated. While the argument is attractive, there is little evidence to support its assumptions. Do affluent youngsters and their families actually purchase the types of services that will be provided through diversionary programs? Have such services been effective in preventing the eventual adjudication of offenders purchasing them? We do not know.

Furthermore, the argument that the present system of informal diversion can be effectively expanded through diversion programs is based upon the assumption that informal processes can be duplicated as part of a formal system. Is there any reason to believe that publicly supported programs, staffed by professionals or civil service employees, can actually function in the same manner as parents and others who are currently involved in informal diversion? Parents are permitted—perhaps even expected—to conceal their youngsters' actions in order to protect the children's interests; public employees cannot do that without seriously compromising themselves. Parents are expected to advocate their children's interests unfalteringly; formal programs will always be under some pressure to protect the community by identifying youngsters who seem to be failing. Professionals' concern with maintaining a program may interfere with their willingness to engage in advocacy on behalf of potentially dangerous youngsters whose trouble-making behavior might compromise that program's recidivism statistics. Advocates in the informal system are free of those types of constraints. To believe that services which are effective as part of an informal process of diversion can be bureaucratized with no loss of effectiveness is simply naive.

Formalized Diversion and Due Process

The nature of diversionary programs is that they involve disposition without adjudication. Services are to be provided outside the justice system without the stigmatizing processes of judicial or even quasi-judicial decision making. Those "stigmatizing" procedures, however, are also the core of a legal system which seeks to protect innocent people from unwanted intrusions into their lives. The history of the juvenile court testifies to the dangers of dispensing with procedural regularity in order to facilitate helpful treatment.

Juvenile courts, dominated by the parens patriae philosophy of justice, have always conceived of themselves as seeking to provide children in trouble with the type of care and custody they might receive at the hands of "wise" parents. Procedures have always been informal because it was thought to be obvious that the relationship between a parent and child — even an erring child — cannot be regulated by the same rules that apply in adult adjudication. Due process safeguards were generally considered unnecessary and potentially harmful: unnecessary because due process is a safeguard against unfair punishment and juvenile courts were never intended to be punitive; harmful because legalistic rules might interfere with the therapeutic process. As one appellate court put it:

> The natural parent needs no [due] process [of law] to temporarily deprive his child of liberty by confining it in its own home, to save it and to shield it from the consequences of persistence in a career of waywardness, nor is the state, when compelled, as *parens patriae,* to take the place of the father for the same purpose required to adopt... [due] process as a means of placing its hands upon the child to lead it into one of its courts.[40]

Such decisions freed the nation's juvenile courts from traditional due process restraint and set the stage for an experiment in informal justice. Lawyers, juries, Fifth Amendment rights, and traditional standards of notice and proof were excluded from delinquency hearings so that attention could focus on issues of treatment rather than on questions about factual and legal guilt.[41] Unfortunately, this "experimental" system has not fared well. It has been characterized by inequity, abuse, and unfairness. Consider, for example, the case of fifteen-year-old Gerald Gault, whose adjudication of delinquency for an alleged obscene telephone call made constitutional history. Gerald's trial took place without any notice of the specific charges against him ever having been given either to him or to his parents. The family was never advised of a right to counsel. The woman to whom the obscene call had allegedly been made was not present in court and could not be cross-examined. Gerald was interrogated by the judges without having been advised of the privilege against self-incrimination. An adult guilty of the same offense could have received a maximum punishment of two months' imprisonment or a fine of up to fifty dollars; Gault, however, was committed for treatment at a state industrial school for a period to extend until he was "cured" or until his twenty-first birthday, whichever came first.

Appalled by such cavalier deprivations of liberty, the United States Supreme Court ruled that any youngster charged with a delinquent act which could result in deprivation of liberty must be accorded "the essentials of due process and fair treatment."[42] The *Gault* decision has been hailed as a victory for civil libertarian values. Professionals in the juvenile system, who generally see themselves as liberal, are typically willing to admit that an unchecked system of parens patriae justice is potentially dangerous, and that *Gault* was a necessary corrective. Yet the concept of diversion, which permits intervention into children's lives with no formal process, has been enthusiastically embraced.

The juvenile justice system has come full circle. The juvenile court, once the informal mechanism of diversion from the stigmatizing and punitive processes of criminal justice, is now the legalistic tribunal from which children are to be diverted. The informal practices of parens patriae justice are being abandoned in juvenile courts only to be re-created in innovative diversion programs. Reformers in the field of juvenile justice do not seem to have learned much from history: They do not yet recognize the basic incompatibility of informality and justice, nor do they recognize that benign intentions are inadequate safeguards of individual liberties.

Summary and Conclusion

The idea that institutional confinement serves to rehabilitate deviants has lost much of its credibility in recent years. In juvenile justice, mental health, and even in adult correction,[43] one finds increasing support for the view that institutions serve the interests neither of society nor of its "deviants." Opposition to the warehousing of human beings in prisons, mental hospitals, and reform schools has become so widespread that it may no longer be fanciful to suggest that the demise of large state institutions is at hand.

It is incumbent upon would-be reformers to develop alternatives to institutionalization which will avoid (or at least minimize) the inequity and waste which have too often characterized current practices. While critics of juvenile justice have been convincingly articulate in documenting the brutality, futility, and injustice of existing programs for the care and custody of delinquents, they have been imprecise and unconvincing in attempts to formulate alternatives. Indeed, a central theme in this paper is that diversionary programs currently in vogue are potentially as abusive as the programs they seek to reform. Innovations being advertised as alternatives to incarceration may prove to be merely alternative forms of incarceration. It is essential that the professional literature stop describing the idea of diversion in optimistic generalities and begin to address itself to serious and difficult questions about the concept's practicability.

Who Is to Be Served?

While all of the talk today suggests that clients in diversionary programs will be youngsters who would otherwise penetrate deeply into the system, the practice may not follow these good intentions. Police officials, probation officers, and courts may use innovative diversionary programs for youngsters who might otherwise have been institutionalized, but they may also use them for youngsters who might otherwise have been ignored or released to the custody of their families. Unless safeguards are built into the system, diversionary programs intended to narrow the domain of the juvenile justice system and promote less restrictive alternatives may result in the official and semi-official processing of larger numbers of young people than ever before. Research on existing "experimental" programs ought to focus on the question of where clients come from: Are they in fact youngsters who would otherwise have been incarcerated or are they often youngsters who might have been left alone? To prevent the possibility of an unintended expansion of the juvenile justice system's confinement capacity, it may prove necessary to close institutional facilities at the same time as opening new programs; otherwise, we will be left with both.

Procedural Safeguards

Current discussion of diversion indicates that none of the recently won rights of juveniles will be applicable in diversionary headings. One can anticipate hearing familiar justifications for the denial of notice, counsel, cross-examination, and other constitutional rights in informal, treatment-oriented diversion hearings.

The reputedly therapeutic, nonpunitive nature of diversionary programs should not be permitted to serve as an excuse for the abridgement of fundamental constitutional freedoms. Placing properly adjudicated delinquents in these programs may be a commendable alternative to incarceration, but it would be a serious step backward to permit diversionary placements without legal safeguards which assure that the community has a sound basis for any intervention at all. It will be a sad irony, indeed, if the Supreme Court is compelled to observe, some twenty or thirty years hence: "However euphemistic this title, a diversionary program or community treatment facility for juveniles is an agency for the deprivation of liberty...." Research on existing diversionary programs ought to assess the extent to which "voluntary" participation is actually a result of plea bargaining away constitutional rights to minimize the chances of institutional confinement.

The Stigma

As long as institutional confinement is a commonly invoked sanction, lesser sanctions can be expected to be less stigmatizing. In the event that diversionary programs become widespread, with a concomitant reduction in the use of institutions, diverted younsters may come to be seen as the "most deviant," and participation in diversionary programs may carry a considerable stigma.[44] There is little reason to expect that current efforts will be any more successful than the efforts of the juvenile court reformers who coined the term *delinquent* to avoid the stigma of criminal classification.

Impact on the Poor and on Minorities

The criminal justice and social work professions share a long-standing bias against lower-class and minority lifestyles and social institutions.[45] The capacity of the black family, in particular, to function as a vehicle for socialization and social control is repeatedly questioned by these professions.[46] Diversionary programs are advertised as promoting interactions such as might be found in middle-class white families. Thus, such programs may come to be seen by judges and probation officers as particularly appropriate for youngsters from lower-class and minority cultures. There is no reason to believe that minority group and poor children will not continue to be overrepresented both in the populations of diverted youngsters and in the residual population of institutionalized juveniles.

One overwhelmingly clear lesson is to be learned from the history of juvenile justice in America: namely, that the path to hell is paved with good intentions. If this lesson is lost on the current generation of reformers, today's innovations may well become tomorrow's abuses. Reform of juvenile justice is necessary. It may have to involve bolder and more daring changes in our assumptions about juvenile justice than proponents of diversionary programs apparently perceive.

Footnotes

The term *diversion* is generally used to refer to the policy of processing youngsters accused of misbehavior away from the juvenile justice system's formal mechanisms of adjudication and institutional care. Donald R. Cressey and Robert A. McDermott, *Diversion from the Juvenile Justice System* (Washington, D.C.: National Institute of Law Enforcement and Criminal Justice, 1974), pp. 3-4, observe: "If 'true' diversion occurs, the juvenile is safely out of the official realm of the juvenile justice system and he is immune from incurring the delinquent label or any of its variations — predelinquent, delinquent tendencies, bad guy, hard core, unreachable. Further, when he walks out the door from the person diverting him, he is technically free to tell the diverter to go to hell. We found very little 'true' diversion in the communities studied." In the absence of "true" diversion, professionals have been developing diversionary programs which seek to process misbehaving youngsters away from juvenile courts, reform schools, and the stigmatizing labels associated with official delinquency. Diversionary programs, however, generally require some degree of participation in structured treatment of one type or another. We focus our attention in this paper on diversionary programs rather than on the pure, but generally unimplemented, concept of "true" diversion.

128   Bruce Bullington, James Sprowls, Daniel Katkin and Mark Phillips

[2]See, for example, Pennsylvania Department of Public Welfare, *Juvenile Justice: A Stance for Cooperation* (Harrisburg, Pa.: Pennsylvania Department of Public Welfare, December 1974).

[3]See, for example, the following books: Robert M. Carter and Malcolm W. Klein, *Back on the Street: The Diversion of Juvenile Offenders* (Englewood Cliffs, N.J.: Prentice-Hall, 1976); Daniel Katkin, Drew Hyman, and John Kramer, *Delinquency and the Juvenile Justice System* (North Scituate, Mass.: Duxbury Press, 1976). Monographs include: Cressey and McDermott, *Diversion from the Juvenile Justice Syste;* Raymond T. Nimmer, *Diversion: The Search for Alternative Forms of Prosecution* (Chicago: American Bar Foundation, 1974); Edwin M. Lemert, *Instead of Court: Diversion in Juvenile Justice* (Chevy Chase, Md.: National Institute of Mental Health, Center for Studies of Crime and Delinquency, 1971). See also the following articles: Thomas H. Kelley, Judy L. Schulman, and Kathleen Lynch, "Decentralized Intake and Diversion," *Juvenile Justice,* February 1976, pp. 3-11; Phillip Z. Cole, "Diversion and the Juvenile Court: Competition or Cooperation," *Juvenile Justice,* February 1976, pp. 33-37; Michael Wald, "State Intervention on Behalf of Neglected Children: A Search for Realistic Standards," *Stanford Law Review,* April 1975, pp. 985-1040; "A Symposium: Juveniles and the Law," *American Criminal Law Review,* Summer 1974, pp. 1-189; John Stratton, "Crisis Intervention Counseling and Police Diversion from the Juvenile Justice System: A Review of the Literature," *Juvenile Justice,* May 1974, pp. 44-53; Sanford J. Fox, "The Reform of Juvenile Justice: The Child's Right to Punishment," *Juvenile Justice,* August 1974, pp. 2-9.

[4]See, for example, Cressey and McDermott, *Diversion from the Juvenile Justice System.*

[5]See, for example, National Advisory Commission on Criminal Justice Standards and Goals, *A National Strategy to Reduce Crime* (Washington, D.C.: U.S. Govt. Printing Office, 1973, pp. 23-25.

[6]The commission recommended that juvenile status offenses be removed from the jurisdiction of juvenile courts and that the rate of nonstatus delinquency cases (those involving acts which would be crimes if committed by adults) be cut to half the 1973 rate. Ibid.

[7]In re Gault, 387 U.S. 1 (1967).

[8]See, for example, Howard James, *Children in Trouble: A National Scandal* (New York: McKay, 1970); Francis A. Allen, "Criminal Justice, Legal Values and the Rehabilitative Ideal," *Journal of Criminal Law, Criminology and Police Science,* September-October 1959, pp. 226-32; Orman Ketcham, "The Unfulfilled Promise of the American Juvenile Court," in *Justice for the Child,* M. Rosenheim, ed. (New York: Free Press, 1962); Lisa Richette, *The Throwaway Children* (Philadelphia: Lippincott, 1969).

[9]Roscoe Pound, "Foreword," *Social Treatment in Probation and Delinquency,* Pauline Young (New York: McGraw-Hill, 1937), p. xxvii.

[10]Kent v. United States, 383 U.S. 541 (1966); in Re Gault, 387 U.S. 1 (1967); In re Winship, 397 U.S. 358 (1970); McKeiver v. Pennsylvania, 403 U.S. 528 (1971) (finding against the right to a jury trial in juvenile court).

[11]Kent v. United States 383 U.S. 541, 555-6 (1966).

[12]In re Gault, 387 U.S. 1, 27 (1967).

[13]James, *Children in Trouble,* and Richette, *The Throwaway Children.*

[14]See, for example, the 1971 documentary by the National Broadcasting Corporation: *This Child is Rated X.*

[15]U.S., Congress, Senate, Committee on the Judiciary, Subcommittee to Investigate Juvenile Delinquency, 92d Cong., 1st sess., May 3-18, 1971.

[16]See Katkin, Hyman, and Kramer, *Delinquency and the Juvenile Justice System,* pp. 57-66.

[17]National Advisory Commission, *National Strategy to Reduce Crime,* p. 23.

[18]Quoted in James, *Children in Trouble,* p. 108.

[19]See Robert D. Vinter, George Downs, and John Hall, *Juvenile Corrections in the States:*

Residential Programs and Deinstitutionalization (Ann Arbor, Mich.: National Assessment of Juvenile Corrections, November 1975), pp. 20-29.

[20]See, for example, Melvin P. Sikes, *The Administration of Injustice* (New York: Harper & Row, 1975); and Irving Piliavin and Scott Brier, "Police Encounters with Juveniles," *American Journal of Sociology,* September 1964, pp. 206-14.

[21]See, for example, Martin Gold, *Delinquent Behavior in an American City* (Belmont, Calif.: Brooks/Cole, 1970); National Council on Crime and Delinquency Survey, *A Feasibility Study of Regional Juvenile Detention* (Hackensack, N.J.: NCCD, 1971).

[22]Katkin, Hyman, and Kramer, *Delinquency and the Juvenile Justice System,* p. 133.

[23]Ibid.

[24]Ibid., pp. 134, 175-79. See also Sophia Robinson, *Can Delinquency Be Measured?* (New York: Columbia University Press, 1936).

[25]Katkin, Hyman, and Kramer, *Delinquency and the Juvenile Justice System,* p. 135.

[26]See, for example, Pennsylvania Juvenile Act of 1972, Section 18.

[27]Katkin, Hyman, and Kramer, *Delinquency and the Juvenile Justice System,* p. 136.

[28]Ibid.

[29]Ibid., p. 137.

[30]This term is used by Cressey and McDermott, *Diversion from the Juvenile Justice System,* to describe programs which do not qualify as "true" diversion but which operate to minimize the use of formal sanctions.

[31]See Katkin, Hyman, and Kramer, *Delinquency and the Juvenile Justice System,* pp. 396-400.

[32]See, for example, Nathan Goldman, *The Differential Selection of Juveniles for Court Appearance* (New York: National Research and Information Center, NCCD, 1963).

[33]See, for example, Sherwood Norman, *The Youth Service Bureau: A Key to Delinquency Prevention (Paramus, N.J.: NCCD, 1972).*

[34]For a discussion of these issues, see Katkin, Hyman, and Kramer, *Diversion from the Juvenile Justice System,* pp. 167-85, 406-50. See also J.A. Seymour, The Current Status of Youth Services Bureaus (unpub. manuscript, University of Chicago Law School, Center for Studies in Criminal Justice).

[35]See, for example, George G. Killinger and Paul F. Cromwell, Jr., *Corrections in the Community* (St. Paul, Minn.: West, 1974), pp. 1-60.

[36]See Anthony Platt, "The Rise of the Child Saving Movement: A Study in Social Policy and Correctional Reform," *Annals of the American Academy of Political and Social Science,* January 1969.

[37]Ibid., pp. 1-4.

[38]This argument is well made by Kai T. Erikson, *Wayward Puritans* (New York: Wiley, 1966), pp. 13-18.

[39]See Edwin M. Schur, *Labeling Deviant Behavior* (New York: Harper & Row, 1971).

[40]Commonwealth v. Fisher, 213 Pa. 48, 53, 62, At. 198, 200 (1905).

[41]For an excellent discussion, see W.V. Stapleton and L.E. Teitelbaum, *In Defense of Youth* (New York: Russell Sage Foundation, 1972), pp. 1-55.

[42]In re Gault, 387 U.S. 1, 41 (1967).

[43]See, for example, the following discussions of the inadequacies and injustices of current institutional practices: Erving Goffman, *Asylums* (New York: Doubleday, 1961); David J. Rothman, *The Discovery of the Asylum* (Boston: Little, Brown, 1971); Nicholas N. Kittrie, *The Right to Be Different* (Baltimore, Md.: Johns Hopkins Press, 1971); Thomas S. Szasz, *Law, Liberty and Psychiatry: An Inquiry into the Social Uses of Mental Health Practices* (New York: Macmillan, 1963); Thomas S. Szasz, *The Manufacture of Madness* (New York: Harper & Row, 1970); American Friends Service Society, *Struggle for Justice* (New York: Hill & Wang, 1971).

⁴⁴See Kai T. Erickson, *Wayward Puritans,* p. 11.

⁴⁵For a critical discussion of this bias, see, for example, Eleanor Bunke Leacock, ed., *The Culture of Poverty: A Critique* (New York: Simon and Schuster, 1971); and Charles A. Valentine, *Culture and Poverty* (Chicago: University of Chicago Press, 1968).

⁴⁶Daniel P. Moynihan, *The Negro Family: The Case for National Action* (Washington, D.C.: U.S. Department of Labor, 1965) has probably had the greatest influence on recent policy in the field.

10

An Observational Study
of a Juvenile Court

James D. Walter and Susan A. Ostrander

The creation of a special justice system for juveniles is a rather recent development, with the first system usually credited as having been established in Cook County, Ill., in 1899. This new system was developed because it was felt that children suffered an injustice when they were treated as if they were fully functioning mature adults. Based upon the concept of "parens patriae," it was felt that youths would be harmed by facing the "rigidities, technicalities, and harshness" of adult criminal court proceedings; that going through a criminal trial and suffering criminal punishment would cause juveniles to be traumatized and stigmatized.[1] It was felt that the stigma would actually push the child further into a criminal career.

The rationale behind the creation of a separate juvenile justice system was therefore based on a sincere belief that an informal, paternalistic system would benefit the wayward youth and remove him from much of the trauma and stigma of criminal proceedings. Bullington et al. pointed out that due process safeguards were usually considered unnecessary and potentially harmful.[2] An appellate court in 1905 presented this viewpoint:

> The natural parent needs no (due) process (of law) to temporarily deprive his child of liberty by confining it in its own home, to save it and to shield it from the consequences of persistence in a career of wayward-

Walter, James D. and Ostrander, Susan A., "An Observational Study of a Juvenile Court." *Juvenile and Family Court Journal,* August 1982, Volume 33, Number 3, pp. 53-69.

ness, nor is the state, when compelled, as *parens patriae,* to take the place of the father for the same purpose required to adopt...(due) process as a means of placing its hands upon the child to lead it into one of its courts.[3]

This humane ideal soon came into question, as it came to be seen that the informal system was not operating the way the ideal suggested. By the 1950s, sociologists were wondering whether the juvenile court system was actually causing more difficulties than it solved. In 1966, the U.S. Supreme Court wrote in the *Kent* decision:

> There is evidence, in fact, that there may be grounds for concern that the child receives the worst of both worlds: that he gets neither the protection accorded to adults nor the solicitous care and regenerative treatment postulated for children.[4]

With this dissatisfaction came the realization that many juveniles were not being aided by the ''parens patriae'' system but actually suffering from the loss of the Constitutional safeguards.

The *Gault* decision in 1967 was the first juvenile court case which the Supreme Court decided on Constitutional grounds, ruling that being a minor did not remove due process protections of the 14th Amendment.

Hellum has said that a second revolution is occurring in the juvenile court system, with status offenders being routed out of the traditional system and delinquents being dealt with in a more punitive, legalistic manner:

> For delinquent offenders...especially those charged with felony violations, there is an emerging iron-fist, punitive approach that requires either remand to the regular criminal courts or juvenile court findings akin to adult corrections with the possibility of fine and set terms of imprisonment.[5]

So although juveniles still do not have all the Constitutional guarantees of adults, the tendency since *Gault* has been to provide more safeguards to juveniles. However, studies made after the *Gault* decision began discovering that the new rulings really were not bringing about major changes in the day-to-day operation of the juvenile court. For example, Lefstein examined three court systems and found that the courts were not complying with the new requirements; and even when the juveniles were informed of their rights, many were informed in such a manner to diminish their impact.[6]

More than a decade has passed since the *Gault* ruling and there is need to determine whether the findings of Lefstein are still operative or whether the trend toward increased legal protections is now positively affecting the operation of juvenile courts. That is, are the Constitutional safeguards upheld in court decisions now being granted to every youth the court deals with? Are attorneys operating effectively within the juvenile court system and providing their clients with the best service possible? Finally, if decisions are not being made on purely legal grounds, what are the factors which affect the decision-making process in juvenile courts? That is, what factors are related to juvenile court adjudications and dispositions?

In order to gain better understanding of the juvenile justice system, and to help answer the above questions, a study was conducted of a juvenile court in a large north central city. Volunteer observers recorded events at court sessions in an attempt to gain increased insight into the day-to-day operations of a juvenile court.

Background and Methodology

The study was contracted by a broad-based community action group which was concerned, among other issues, with alleged racial discrimination within the county's juvenile court. The group was composed of some 15 civic organizations. Over a 10-week period, some 40 volunteers from these community organizations attended juvenile court sessions to observe the proceedings. Each observer received 20-25 hours of training, which included familiarization with juvenile law; courtroom procedures, facilities and resources; and disposition alternatives; as well as training in the use of the observational questionnaire.

The sample on which data is based consisted of 627 juveniles. The sample of hearings to be observed was selected through an alphabetical rotation of judges and referees, with observers being assigned to as many courtrooms as there were observers available. The systematic nature of this process maximized the obtaining of a representative sample of all juveniles who appeared before juvenile court. The demographic characteristics of the sample obtained for this study was very similar to the entire population of juveniles that appeared before juvenile court during the observation period, according to the court's annual report. The similarities were in terms of residence (whether the youth lived in the city or in the suburbs), sex, types of charges and distribution of charges between males and females. Such evidence supports the representativeness of sample and enhances its generalizability.

A large number of "unknowns" were also noted during coding verification. Possible reasons for this vary by specific case but include factors such as observer and coding error, observers failing to mark the observation questionnaire and ambiguity in the proceedings. Observers were frequently unable to tell what happened or what rulings were made even though they took place directly in front of them. Research indicates that juveniles and parents have limited understanding of what happens in the juvenile court.[7] The difficulties of observers to comprehend the proceedings simply emphasize this difficulty of many youths and parents (who are untrained in court observation) to understand exactly what is happening in court.

The political context of this study has its history in the several years of negotiation preceding permission for observers to enter the courtroom. Juvenile hearings are closed in the state in which this study was conducted, and access was thus at the will of the judge. Once access to hearings was gained, limits were stringent. Observers were not allowed access to court records and were not allowed to converse with the juvenile, lawyers or anyone else inside or outside the courtroom. Judges would occasionally initiate discussion of the case with observers, but not on any systematic basis. Furthermore, the study was in constant danger of being halted. After the preliminary phase of data collection had been completed, whose primary purpose was to pretest the adequacy of the observation instrument, a three-month period of negotiation was necessary to convince judges again of the need to continue the study. The study was thus conducted under somewhat tense conditions with an inability to fill in with other means data that could not be readily collected by the rather rigid circumstances of observation. This, in addition to the above noted "normal" ambiguity of the courtroom, contributes to the large numbers of "missing data" evident in the tables presented here. Categories of information for which "unknowns" occurred in more than 25 percent of the cases are age of juvenile, area of residence, previous court record, identification of complainant, juvenile employment record and presentation of written report by probation officer. These are matters which do not come up in every hearing, and the observer thus was limited by the imposed method of data collection.

Findings

Type of Hearing

Of the 627 juveniles whose hearings were observed, 88 percent (517 juveniles) of these were official hearings (when an official complaint has been filed and 12 percent (70) were unofficial (when no official complaint has been filed — usually conducted by referees). Categories of types of hearings were as follows: adjudication 17 percent (98), adjudication and disposition 42 percent (240), continued adjudication 9 percent (50), continued adjudication and disposition 1 percent (8), adjudication and continued disposition 8 percent (45), disposition 9 percent (54), continued disposition 13 percent (72), preliminary hearing 0.7 percent (4) and continued preliminary hearing 1 percent (7).

Group hearings were observed in 20 percent (177) of the cases and individual hearings in 71 percent (444) of the cases. In a group hearing, two or more youths charged with the same complaint are heard together. More than two-thirds of the youths who appear in court had previous records. This is equally true of males and females, white and non-whites, suburban and city youths.

Prosecutors were present in contested adjudicatory delinquency hearings about half the time. When a judge was hearing the case as compared to a referee, a prosecutor was present for nearly three out of every four hearings.

Length of Hearings

The median number of minutes for the hearing was 15 minutes. Twelve percent (66) of the juveniles had hearings of five minutes or less and the same number had hearings of more than one hour, with the vast majority falling within these two extremes. The length of hearing was, as might be expected, significantly related to type of hearing.

Length of hearing also varied by type of charge. Hearings where the charge was delinquency were significantly longer than hearings where the charge was unruliness.[9] The length of hearing was found not to be affected to a significant degree by the presence of an attorney or prosecutor, or by the plea of the juvenile.

Demographic Characteristics

Of the youths whose hearings were observed, more than half were white and the remainder were non-white. Nearly three out of four were male and the remainder were female (females were most likely to appear for unruly behavior, males for delinquency). Of those 342 juveniles for whom age was noted in court, 5 percent were 12 years and under, 25 percent were 13 or 14, 43 percent were 15 or 16 and 27 percent were 17 or 18. Of those 393 youths for whom residence was known, more than two-thirds resided within the city and the remainder (32 percent) lived in suburban communities.

Rulings and Dispositions

In nearly half the cases which were brought before juvenile court, the ruling was delinquency. In one of four cases, there was a continuance. About one in 10 cases were declared unruly and nearly the same number of cases were dismissed.

The final stage in the hearing process is the disposition of the youth. The most frequent disposition in this juvenile court was probation, which occurred in nearly half of the cases. The next most frequent disposition was suspension of a sentence to be institutionalized with either the state youth commission (17 percent were sent to the state youth commission for the first time but had their placement suspended and 1 percent were returned to the state youth commission but had their placement suspended) or to the county development center (7 percent were sent to the county development center for the first time but had their placement suspended and 2 percent were returned to the county development center but had their placement suspended). After probation and suspended sentence the most common dispositions in order of frequency, were to return the youth to his parents, send the youth to the state youth commission or send the youth to the county development center.

In nearly one out of every three disposition hearings, the court official referred to some difficulty in finding suitable placement for the youth. Most often the reason for this difficulty was lack of financial resources on the part of the youth and family. In about one of five cases, the difficulty was due either to overcrowding or waiting lists at the preferred facility or agency, or a concern on the part of the court official that the youth's problem was not amenable to treatment by existing facilities.

The most difficult youths to place were those with a previous court record and those with a poor school performance and attendance record. Difficulty in placement was not related to the youth's race, sex, age or area of residence, nor did the type of complaint seem to make a difference.

Factors Related to Ruling and Disposition

Presence of Attorney

Of the youths observed, 32 percent (178) had an attorney. Whether a juvenile had an attorney was significantly associated with the sex of the youth with males being twice as likely to have attorneys (36 to 18 percent). Although girls were less likely to have attorneys, this was probably due to the fact that girls were more often charged with unruliness than with delinquency. Age was also a significant factor since only 5 percent of those juveniles 14 years and under had an attorney, while 24 percent of those 15 to 18 had one. Although older youths were found to be more likely to have attorneys than younger ones, it was found that this should not be explained by the seriousness of the charge since age was not found to be related to the type of charge against the youth.

The presence of an attorney was found to be related to the advisement of rights. When attorneys are present, youths are less likely to be advised of their rights. This probably is because the court officials assume that the attorneys will take on the responsibility. Whether youths were advised of their legal rights was only examined for adjudicatory hearings which were observed in their entirety. This was done since advisement could have occurred at the initial phase of a continued hearing when the observer was not present.

It was particularly disturbing to discover that when a youth had an attorney, court officials might omit the advising of rights—apparently assuming that the juvenile's attorney had carried out the task. This assumption is not consistent with the law, that is, the Supreme Court did not rule that court officials should assume that the youth's attorney will take over their duties. The Supreme Court specifically placed responsibility for advisement of rights on the juvenile court. Even if court officials believe that the youth's attorney has taken over this duty, the court at least has the legal obligation to check to be sure that attorneys have in fact informed their clients of all their Constitutional rights. Since the observations of this study occurred only within the courtroom setting, it was possible that court officials advised some juveniles of their rights outside the courtroom. Within the courtroom, however, some juvenile court officials were not in full compliance with required procedures.

The reliance on attorneys to carry out court duties is especially brought into question when the performances of the juveniles' attorneys are analyzed. As previously mentioned, the study by Lefstein which was conducted soon after the *Gault* decision discovered that the presence of an attorney did not appear to aid a juvenile in the ruling and disposition of his case and, in some cases, actually tended to harm the youth because many judges resented lawyers entering their courtroom and using adversary tactics.

Since this study was not designed to interview judges and determine the reasons of their actions, we cannot determine whether the juvenile court judges observed would report resentment of attorneys in their courtrooms, but the data does indicate that the effects of an attorney on juvenile court proceedings are still negligible.

Juvenile Court Officials

Judges were much more likely to deal harshly with juveniles than were referees (judges sent 21 percent of the youths appearing before them to public institutions while referees only sent 10 percent). It would seem that the factor most responsible for this finding would be the seriousness of the offenses which judges and referees hear. But even when type of offense is held constant, the referees are always either more lenient or else there is no difference between the two types of officials.

Type of Offense/Previous Record

When determining adjudication and disposition one would imagine that the type of offense and the juvenile's past delinquent history (as indicated by previous record) would be the most important factors considered. As expected, previous record was discovered to be significant in determining the court's decisions (e.g., 24 percent of those with a previous record are placed in public institutions, while only 6 percent of those who have no record are institutionalized).

In regard to type of offense, however, even though status offenders were somewhat less likely to be placed in public institutions than youths who committed other types of offenses, overall there was no statistically significant association between type of offense and disposition.

Thus it appears that factors other than type of offense have consequences for determining ruling and disposition. For instance, the youth's school performance and attendance appeared to be an important factor in influencing ruling and disposition.

Presentation of School Record

In 261 cases, the youth's school record was presented in court. School record was more likely to be presented in unruly cases (88 percent of cases) than in delinquency cases (74 percent of cases), probably because the unruly behavior was often likely to directly involve problems at school. School records were as likely to be presented at disposition hearings as at adjudicatory hearings, and as likely to be presented at hearings where the youth did not have a previous record as where the youth did.

About half the time, youths were reported in court as having a generally poor level of performance in school, with only about one in eight youths who appear in court having a generally good record at school. White and non-white youths who appeared in court did not differ significantly in their school performance record.

School performance was found to be significantly associated with the ruling of the court, as youths having poor school records were more likely to be ruled delinquent and were less likely to have their cases dismissed. School performance and attendance were also significantly associated with the disposition imposed. Court officials particularly placed emphasis on these two factors as indicators of whether a youth should be institutionalized (in either the state or county institution).

Race

One of the most surprising findings of the study concerned the lack of effect of race upon the disposition of cases. As previously stated, the study was originally contracted by a community action group which was concerned with reports of racial bias within the county's juvenile court system. The findings of the study, however, did not support the contention that non-white youths receive harsher treatment than white youths.[11] In nearly every type of offense there was no significant difference between white and non-white juveniles in either ruling or disposition.

While the study was not designed to examine events which transpired outside of the juvenile courtroom, it is possible to at least surmise why no racial discrimination was discovered by court observations even though some segments of the community had observed its existence. First, racial discrimination could have occurred prior to the youths appearing in court. If non-whites are more likely to be brought into court on lesser charges and less frequent delinquent actions, this might result in their receiving more lenient treatment than white youths who would have to be more hardened before they would end up in court. Second, an important factor in affecting court treatment of whites and non-whites might be place of residence. Suburban youths tended to be white, while non-white youths tended to reside in the city. It is likely that many of the suburban youths were handled within their own community until their delinquent activity became so frequent that the youths were finally sent down to the city for hearings, while many non-white youths were sent more directly to court since the court was located in their own area. Again, if this process took place, the white youth who finally ended up in juvenile court may have been defined as in need of more severe treatment and his perception could have offset any effects which racial discrimination may have had. Finally, the reason why race was not found to be a factor in determination of ruling and disposition might be because it truly was not a significant factor — that no racial discrimination took place, at least during the period that the court was under investigation. This explanation appears to have some credibility since judges and referees were aware that courtroom observers were present and were aware that one impetus for the project was a concern of charges that racial discrimination occurred in the county's juvenile court. It seems plausible that this knowledge could significantly affect the behavior of court officials. However, it must once again be emphasized that the study focused on transactions which took place within the courtroom and not upon social factors operating outside the courtroom or upon the motivations of juvenile court judges and referees.

Summary and Implications

It appears from this study that it is possible to take a highly individualized event like a juvenile court hearing and develop a means of discovering patterns of action and objectifying subjective procedures. The findings of this report are based on observation of hearings for 627 juveniles. Summary of the findings are as follows:

1. Most youths appearing in court had individual hearings, but one in five are heard in a group.
2. The length of hearing varied appropriately with the type of hearing. Combined adjudications and dispositions were longer than either alone, group hearings were longer than individual hearings

and delinquency hearings were longer than unruly ones.

3. One-third of the youths appearing in court had an attorney, with legal aid attorneys allowing non-white and city youths to be represented as frequently as white and suburban youths.

4. More than three out of four youths without presence of counsel were advised in court of their right to attorney and to remain silent. Three of four were advised of their right to awareness of consequences and to subpoena and cross-examine witnesses.

5. Whether a youth was brought to court for delinquency or unruly behavior (i.e., status offenses) was unrelated to the youth's race or area of residence. Females were more likely to be charged with unruly behavior, and males with delinquency.

6. More than two out of three juveniles who appeared in court had been there before. This was equally true of males and females, whites and non-whites, suburban or city youths.

7. In three out of four cases, the youth's school record was presented in court. About half the youths had a generally poor level of school performance and were reported as usually absent and/ or late for school. School record was an important factor in determining court ruling and disposition.

8. In nearly half the cases youths were adjudicated delinquent. A fourth of the time the cases were continued. One in 10 cases was dismissed, and about the same number were adjudicated unruly. With the exception of previous record and school record, court rulings appeared to be made on the basis of unique features of the case.

9. The most frequent court disposition was probation for nearly half the youths. One of three was referred to the state youth commission for placement in a public institution, but about half of these placements were suspended. One in five youths was returned to the parents, and about as many were referred to the county development center for placement in a public institution run by the county, although half of these referrals were suspended.

11. Factors influencing ruling and disposition most significantly were the type of official hearing the case (judges were more likely than referees to institutionalize juveniles), the existence of a previous record and school performance and attendance (juveniles with good school records were treated more leniently than juveniles with poor school records).

12. Factors which were not associated with ruling and disposition included the type of offense committed, sex, age, race and the presence or absence of an attorney.

The results of the observations help provide some insight into the operations of a juvenile court system. For instance, the findings demonstrate that the juvenile court under observation had not yet overcome some of the problems initially discovered by studies conducted soon after the *Gault* decision. Even though more than a decade has passed since the decision, the data indicates that juvenile court officials (at least in the jurisdiction investigated) were still not in full compliance with the *Gault* ruling. Even though some rights were being advised to a large majority of youths (i.e., the rights to counsel and to remain silent), the other Constitutional rights which juveniles posssess were not being advised to many juveniles (e.g., the rights to subpoena and cross-examination).

Greater attention needs to be given to this problem. The granting of Constitutional rights to juveniles is meaningless unless the juveniles are aware of them. Even when a youth has legal representation, the court must carry out its duties and inform the youth of his rights under the law and must also determine whether the youth understands those rights. Anything less than a total commitment to this duty is depriving the youth of due process of law. Originally, as discussed previously, juveniles were treated as adults, with adult protections of the law. The shift to a juvenile court system based on the paternalism of the *parens patriae* perspective was not a total success so the Supreme Court ruled in 1967 that the juvenile justice system must restore many of the Constitutional guarantees lost when the shift occurred. They stated:

> A proceeding where the issue is whether the child will be found to be "delinquent" and subjected to the loss of his liberty for years is comparable in seriousness to a felony prosecution. The juvenile needs the assistance of counsel to cope with the problems of law, to make skilled inquiry into the facts, to insist upon regularity of the proceedings, and to ascertain whether he has a defense and to prepare and submit it. The child requires the guiding hand of counsel at every step in the proceedings against him.[12]

The movement now seen in many states toward deinstitutionalization of status offenders is further evidence that the approach to juvenile justice is once again becoming more legalistic in nature (as opposed to paternalistic). The observations, however, discovered that the *parens patriae* perspective was still firmly entrenched in the court examined. This could most clearly be seen when examining the factors associated with ruling and disposition. While factors affecting the disposition of the case varied by particular case, those factors which appeared to have the greatest influence in determining whether a youth would be placed in a public institution were the existence of a previous record, the type of official (judge or referee) hearing the case, school performance and school attendance. The type of offense committed and the presence of an attorney was found to lack significant association with disposition and ruling.

The importance of a previous record would hold true whether the court followed a *parens patriae* or legalistic perspective but the importance of type of official and school record indicates the workings of a paternalistic system. As can be seen from the data presented in Table 8, youths receive harsher treatment from judges than from referees. Since this difference remained even when type of offense was held constant, the reasons for this difference can perhaps be best traced back to the conception which judges and referees hold of their roles in juvenile justice. Referees are not supposed to handle "serious" cases (although they frequently do), so they appear far less willing to impose "serious" dispositions (such as placement into state or county institutions).

In regard to the apparent ineffectiveness of attorneys in the juvenile court in obtaining positive rulings and dispositions for their clients, many court observers (while conducting observations for this study) commented that some attorneys (particularly private attorneys) were unfamiliar and unprepared in defending their clients in juvenile court. Every individual deserves competent, knowledgeable representation and it appears especially essential for youths to be provided with the best possible representation, but juveniles in the jurisdiction studied appeared to be not significantly better off (in terms of ruling and disposition) having legal assistance.

It is not to be concluded from this statement, however, that the solution to the problem is to deprive youth of counsel because they are ineffectual. Instead, it implies that law schools should carefully examine their training of lawyers in the field of juvenile justice. A basic assumption in jurisprudence is than an attorney's presence should result in the client gaining the best possible ruling and disposition. The effectiveness of an attorney in any courtroom setting should be measured on this basis. The results of this study imply the law schools have a strong need and obligation to promote and encourage law students to develop expertise in the field of juvenile justice, since the data demonstrates that the law profession is not being successful in providing youths with the best possible defense.

A factor which appears to be most related to court ruling is the youth's school record, as a youth with a good school record is less likely to be ruled delinquent or unruly and more likely to have the case dismissed. The fact that these indicators are given so much emphasis clearly demonstrates the differences in approach of juvenile and criminal court judges. While the work record of an adult who has been charged or convicted of a crime would usually not be a manifest factor in ruling or sentencing in a criminal court proceeding, in a juvenile court proceeding school records are considered vital.[13] This is undoubtedly because juvenile court judges and referees are not as concerned with what the youth has done (i.e., type of offense) as with the type of youth he is. This conception is held so strongly, in fact, that by law, a youth who has not even committed delinquent acts could still be removed from his home if such an action is deemed to be in the youth's best interest.

This concern with the juvenile as a total individual can be traced back to the historical development of the juvenile. Since the juvenile court was established upon the assumption that it is not in the best interest of the child to have a totally legalistic trial, non-legalistic factors such as school record and attendance play a major role in juvenile court proceedings — major in the sense that it is felt that factors such as school record are good indicators of the youth's character, future actions and potential for treatment. The correctness of the assumption that youths with poor school records need harsher treatment should be examined at greater length to see if school record is truly a good indicator of the need for severe treatment or whether the relationship between school record and delinquency is the result of a self-fulfilling prophesy — with those youths having poor school records being negatively labeled, harshly punished and pushed even further into a delinquent career as a result of the labeling process.[14] Court officials should carefully examine the assumptions they have been operating under in this regard and ask themselves whether failure at school should so strongly condemn youths before them or whether it might be more fruitful to examine other, more legalistic, indicators such as seriousness of offense when deciding which youths deserve to return home and which require institutionalization.

Footnotes

[1] *Parens patriae* is the belief that the state has the right and obligation to protect and direct those citizens who need such protection and direction, since the state is the ultimate father and protector of its citizenry.
In re Gault, 387 U.S. 1, 13 (1967).
[2] Bruce Bullington et al., "A Critique of Diversionary Juvenile Justice," *Crime and Delinquency* 24, no. 2 (1978): 68.
[3] *Commonwealth v. Fisher,* 53 A. 198, 200 (1905).
[4] *Kent v. United States,* 383 U.S. 541, 566 (1966).
[5] Frank Hellum, "Juvenile Justice: The Second Revolution," *Crime and Delinquency* 25, no. 3 (1979): 300.
[6] Norman Lefstein et al., "In Search of Juvenile Justice: *Gault* and Its Implementation," *Law and Society Review* 3, no. 4 (1969): 491-562.
[7] Paul D. Lipsett, "Juvenile Offender's Perceptions," *Crime and Delinquency* 14 (1968): 49.
Katherine Catton and Patricia Erikson, *The Juvenile's Perception of the Role of Defense Counsel in Juvenile Court — A Pilot Study* (Toronto, 1975), reported in Katherine Catton, "Children in the Courts: A Selected Empirical Review," *Revue Canadienne de Droit Familial* 1 (1978): 344.
[8] Forty cases were unknown. All of the following data includes only known cases.
[9] An unruly child includes any child who does not subject himself to the reasonable control of parents, teachers or guardians; who is an habitual truant from home or school; who acts in such a way as to injure or endanger the health or morals of self or others; who acts to

enter marriage relations without consent of parents, legal guardian or other legal authority; who is found in a disreputable place or associates with vagrant, vicious, criminal, notorious or immoral persons; who engages in an occupation prohibited by law, or is in a situation dangerous to life or limb or injurious to the health or morals of self or others; or who has violated other laws applicable only to a child (status offenses).

[10]"Heard and submitted" is a specific court ruling that can be made at the completion of an adjudication hearing. A period of up to six months is used to observe the youth's behavior before adjudication and/or disposition is made. It is used primarily with first offenders who commit minor delinquencies for the purpose of keeping them from becoming more deeply involved in the process of the juvenile court.

[11]Lawrence Cohen and James Kluegel, "Determinants of Juvenile Court Dispositions: Ascriptive and Achieved Factors in Two Metropolitan Courts," *American Sociological Review* 43 (April 1978): 162-176.

Cohen and Kluegel, in their examination of the impact of discriminatory factors on the severity of juvenile court dispositions, also discovered that there was little support for the contention that race directly affects disposition.

[12]*In re Gault.*

[13]Such factors as occupation and work record may serve a latent function of influencing court decision, particularly as indicators of social class and status.

[14]Although most of the literature on the relationship between schol performance/attendance and delinquency shows a strong relationship between the two, some researchers show that this relationship may not be a precise one. For example, Senna discovered that "poor academic achievement per se appears to explain less than 5 percent of the delinquency variance in suburbia." Polk found in this 1976 study that school performance was relevant only when there was also a high level of involvement in a teenage culture and that when such involvement was low, poor students had low delinquency rates. But none of these studies on the effect of school performance/attendance test whether this relationship means that those who do poorly in school are more in need of institutionalization than youths who do well in school, or that community programs will work for good students but not for poor ones. Research is necessary to test this assumption.

Joseph Senna et al., "Delinquent Behavior and Academic Investment Among Suburban Youth," *Adolescence 9,* no. 36 (1974): 481-494.

Kenneth Polk, "Schools and Delinquency Experience," *Criminal Justice and Behavior* 2, no. 4 (1975): 315-338.

11

Imposing the Death Penalty on Children

Victor L. Streib

A quite rare but nonetheless shocking dimension of the death penalty in our criminal justice system is the imposition of that ultimate sanction upon our children. Offenders under the age of 18 at the time of their crimes, generally defined under American law as children or juveniles, have been executed in our past and 33 of their brothers and sisters are currently residing on the death rows of 15 states.

This chapter explores this complex issue from both legal and empirical viewpoints. First the legal environment is described in order to understand how some adolescents come to such an ignominious end. Then the past practice of actual executions for juvenile offenses is analyzed, focusing upon the executing jurisdictions, the crimes, the offenders, and the victims. Next the present practice is examined, including all juvenile death sentences imposed since 1982 and all persons currently under juvenile death sentences. A trend away from the death penalty for juveniles is identified, and the final section sketches seven key criteria to be addressed in such a trend.

Legal Environment

Juveniles in Criminal Court

Even when offenders are under the chronological age limit for juvenile court, several means exist by which their cases could be processed in adult criminal court rather than in juvenile court. The consequences of this change of court are enormous. although juvenile court is limited to ordering probation or perhaps institutionalization until the child is age 21 (David, 1986), the criminal court

Victor Streib, "Imposing the death penalty on children," pp. 245-267 in *Challenging Capital Punishment* edited by Kenneth C. Haas and James A. Inciardi. Copyright 1988 by Sage Publications, Inc. Reprinted with permission of Sage Publications, Inc.

typically has the full range of criminal sentences available even for young teenage offenders, including long terms in prison and even the death penalty (Zimring, 1982).

Three primary means are available for placing a juvenile offender's case in adult criminal court. Some states expressly exclude certain offenses from juvenile court jurisdiction and place all of these designated offenses within criminal court jurisdiction regardless of the age of the offender (Fox, 1984: 8). In these instances the case against the child is always filed directly in adult court and never goes through the juvenile court procedure.

A second method by which the case might be filed directly in adult criminal court is illustrated by those few states that give the prosecuting attorney the discretion to file cases either in juvenile court or in adult criminal court (Davis, 1986: 2-22). The third means by which a person under the juvenile court age could nonetheless end up in adult criminal court is for the juvenile court to waive its original jurisdiction over the case and transfer the case to the adult criminal court (*Kent v. United States*, 1966).

No matter how the child's case gets to adult criminal court, once there the case proceeds essentially as it would for any adult. The child receives all the rights and protections of adult criminal defendants but also faces all or most of the adult criminal sentences. For the most serious offenses, such sentences may include the death penalty.

U.S. Supreme Court Rulings

The Court's attention to death penalty issues during the past 15 years is well-known and widely reported (Bedau, 1982), making a detailed presentation unnecessary here. *Gregg v. Georgia* (1976) launched the current era, holding that the death penalty does not violate per se the eighth amendment. Although the issue was not specifically before the Court in *Gregg*, in passing the Court approved of Georgia requirements that the jury consider the youthfulness of the offender (*Gregg v. Georgia*, 1976: 197).

In a companion case to *Gregg*, the Court also approved of the Texas statute, which provided that the sentencing jury "could further look to the age of the defendant" (*Jurek v. Texas*, 1976: 273) in deciding between life imprisonment and the death sentence. In 1978 the Court's decision in *Lockett v. Ohio* held that unlimited consideration of mitigating factors was constitutionally required, in part because the Court thought it important that a defendant's youthful age be considered in the sentencing decision.

A few years later the Supreme Court agreed to decide the specific issue of the constitutionality of the death penalty for an offense committed when the defendant was only 16 years old. In its final holding, however, the Court in *Eddings v. Oklahoma* (1982) avoided that constitutionality issue, and instead sent the case back for resentencing after full consideration of all mitigating factors per the *Lockett* holding. On the issue of the offender's youth, however, the Court did hold that "the chronological age of a minor is itself a relevant mitigating factor of great weight" (*Eddings v. Oklahoma*, 1982: 116).

The Supreme Court has agreed again to consider the constitutionality issue, but as of this writing has not decided the case (*Thompson v. Oklahoma*, 1987). The determination of the legality of capital punishment for juveniles is thus left to each individual jurisdiction. The only constitutional mandate is that each jurisdiction must permit consideration of the youth of the offender as a mitigating factor of great weight by the sentencing jury or judge.

Specific Statutory Provisions

Within the 50 states and the District of Columbia the statutory law seems fairly well settled. Of these 51 jurisdictions, 15 have no valid death penalty statutes. These 15 jurisdictions don't execute anyone, including juveniles. The other 36 states have apparently valid death penalty statutes.

Table 1 arrays the 36 death penalty states according to their establishment, by whatever means, of the minimum age of the offender at the time of the offense for eligibility for the death penalty. No minimum age whatsoever is established in ten of these states.

Of the 26 states that do establish a minimum age, 10 states use age 18 directly in their death penalty statutes. Seven states have established age 14 as the minimum either as a result of their juvenile court waiver statutes or through their exclusive or concurrent jurisdiction provisions. Although this does operate to establish a minimum age for the death penalty, it is more precisely a minimum age for any criminal court jurisdiction. The rest of these 26 states have minimum ages scattered from 10 to 17.

Table 1

Minimum Age of Offender Required by
36 Death Penalty Jurisdictions

Age at Offense	Jurisdiction	Total
18	California, Colorado, Connecticut, Illinois, Nebraska, New Jersey, New Mexico, Ohio, Oregon, and Tennessee	10
17	Georgia, New Hampshire, and Texas	3
16	Nevada	1
15	Louisiana and Virginia	2
14	Alabama, Arkansas, Idaho, Kentucky, Missouri, North Carolina, Pennsylvania, and Utah	8
13	Mississippi	1
12	Montana	1
10	Indiana	1
No minimum	Arizona, Delaware, Florida, Maryland, Oklahoma, South Carolina, South Dakota, Washington, and Wyoming	9
Total		36

Lower Court Cases

Eddings was decided by the U.S. Supreme Court on January 19, 1982, and has been relied upon by many lower courts since that time. As was discussed earlier, the Court in *Eddings* reaffirmed that youth of the offender is a mitigating factor of great weight that must be considered, but the Court avoided any direct holding on the constitutionality of the death penalty for juveniles. However, several lower courts have divined more from the *Eddings* holding than seems reasonable.

Cases such as *High v. Zant* (1983) and *State v. Battle* (1983) have cited *Eddings* as holding that the death penalty for juveniles is not unconstitutional. This proposition is, of course, precisely the issue presented to but not decided by the Supreme Court in *Eddings*. Most lower courts have agreed that *Eddings* did not settle the constitutionality issue but some then have gone on to decide that issue themselves. An illustrative case is *Trimble v. State* (1984) in which a Maryland court first noted that *Eddings* left the constitutionality question unanswered. Then the Maryland court went on to resolve the issue from reference to other Supreme Court cases. The *Trimble* court concluded that indicators of society's evolving standards of decency did not reject this punishment for Trimble and that it should take a case-by-case approach to future cases of the death penalty for juveniles.

A third approach to *Eddings* is exemplified by such cases as *Cannaday v. State* (1984). In *Cannaday*, the Mississippi Supreme Court noted that the U.S. Supreme Court had not found the death penalty for juveniles to be unconstitutional and so left the matter there without attempting its own constitutional analysis. The court reversed Attina Cannaday's death sentence on other grounds but expressly excluded the constitutionality issue as a basis for that reversal.

A final group of state court cases has placed strong emphasis upon the great mitigating weight to be given the defendant's youth, as is required by the *Eddings* case, and then found that mitigation to be so compelling that the death sentence must be reversed. A leading example is *State v. Valencia* (1982), in which the Arizona Supreme Court set aside the death penalty and ordered that 16-year-old Valencia be sentenced to life imprisonment. The *Valencia* court did not rule out the death penalty for all juveniles but left the clear impression that only the most extraordinary facts would justify a juvenile death penalty.

The lower court decisions, then, have gone in at least four directions. Some have erroneously assumed that *Eddings* decided the constitutionality issue for capital punishment of juveniles. Others have agreed that *Eddings* left that question undecided but then went on to decide the issue themselves, to the detriment of the young offenders before them. A third group has relegated the matter totally to their legislatures, finding no restrictions from *Eddings* or any other source. The last group has focussed upon the *Eddings* observation that youthfulness of the offender is to be given great weight as a mitigating factor and then usually have gone on to find that great weight to be a compelling reason in the case before them to reduce the juvenile's sentence from the death penalty to long-term imprisonment.

Questionable Constitutionality

Careful examination of the constitutional justifications for the death penalty for adults reveals their inapplicability to the death penalty for juveniles (Streib, 1986). The empirical evidence is overwhelming that the death penalty is not a greater general deterrent to murder than is long-term imprisonment (Bowers, 1984: 271335) but some continue to cling to their intuitive belief that it is (*Gregg v. Georgia*, 1976: 185-186). Even if they were correct in the case of adults, it would not be correct for juveniles.

From what we know about and adolescent psychology, teenagers have no meaningful concept of death and thus don't understand the threatened penalty (Corr and McNeil, 1986). To the degree to which they know that certain behavior could result in their death, they often seem attracted to it. Witness their persistent involvement in dangerous driving, ingestion of dangerous drugs, suicide attempts, and so on. It seems obvious that teenagers would be much more deterred by the threat of long-term imprisonment (no cars, no girlfriends, no parties) than by some fantasized perception of death.

The primary reason why our society strongly supports the death penalty in general is retribution, defined broadly as a sense of justice and the need for legal revenge against the offender (*Journal of Criminal Law and Criminology*, 1983). On this issue it seems generally agreed that "Crimes committed by youths may be just as harmful to victims as those committed by older persons, but they deserve less punishment because adolescents may have less capacity to control their conduct and to think in long-range terms than adults" (Twentieth Century Fund, 1978: 7).

The argument for the death penalty as the ultimate means of incapacitating juvenile offenders from committing future offenses asks for simply too much punishment for too little additional result. Juvenile murderers have one of the lowest recidivism rates of any type of offender and long-term imprisonment of them is more than adequate incapacitation (Vitello, 1976: 32-34).

The death penalty unequivocally rejects the alternative of rehabilitative efforts to reshape the offender into an acceptable member of society. This may be an acceptable decision when the offender is a 40-year-old, three-time loser who shows no desire or ability to change. However, the essential nature of teenagers is that they will grow and mature, almost always in directions more acceptable to society (*Workman v. Commonwealth*, 1968: 378). To unequivocally reject rehabilitation for teenagers is to deny the fundamental characteristics of that transitional stage of life.

As a result of increasing societal rejection of this penalty (Southern Coalition Report, 1986) and a general lack of justifications for it, the imposition of the death penalty upon juveniles is a prime example of an arbitrary, capricious, and freakish punishment. Juveniles commit about 1,500 intentional criminal homicides each year, about 9% of the total (Federal Bureau of Investigation, 1974-1984). Less than 0.5% of these juvenile homicides result in the juvenile death penalty being imposed.

Of the approximately 300 total death sentences imposed each year (U.S. Department of Justice, 1986), juveniles receive only about five of them. Moreover, no rational basis can be discerned for why these three to six juveniles were sentenced to death and the hundreds of other juvenile murderers were not.

Perhaps the only question remaining is the specific age at which the line should be drawn for the death penalty. Age 18 seems by far to be the obvious choice. Eighteen is the juvenile court age for 38 states (Davis, 1986) and is the most common age for majority for noncriminal purposes (Zimring, 1982). Eighteen is the age used in international treaties and by almost all other countries (Amnesty International, 1979).

It seems clear that a firm line must be drawn and not simply be left to an after-the-fact deliberation concerning the maturity of a particular teenager. This is the approach used in comparable areas of law. Chronological age, not mental maturity, is the sole determinant for voting, drinking alcoholic beverages, getting married, buying a house, and scores of other adult rights and privileges (Zimring, 1982). To deny the offender under age 18 all of these adult rights and privileges but to impose the harshest of adult punishments raises the most serious questions of constitutionality, fundamental fairness and justice.

Past Practice

At least 15,000 legal, nonmilitary executions have occurred in the United States since colonial times. Executions for crimes committed by a person under age 18 have accounted for only 281 or less than 2% of these total executions. These relatively few juvenile executions occurred from 1642 through 1986 for a variety of crimes and in a variety of jurisdictions (Streib, 1987).

The first satisfactorily documented juvenile execution occurred in 1642. In that year, 16-year-old Thomas Graunger was executed in Roxbury, Massachusetts, for the crime of bestiality (Teeters and Hedblom, 1967: 111). The last juvenile execution occurred on May 15, 1986, when Texas executed Jay Kelly Pinkerton for a murder he committed at age 17 (*New York Times*, 1986).

Table 2 categorizes these juvenile executions by the decade in which they occurred, beginning with 1900. During the nineteenth century the numbers per decade had increased steadily, totaling 91 for the century. Executions of juveniles as well as adults reached maximum frequency in the twentieth century. The number of juvenile executions per decade increased steadily to an all-time high of 53 in the 1940s but dropped off dramatically after that decade. Juvenile executions ended temporarily in 1964 and did not reappear until 21 years later.

A total of 36 jurisdictions have executed persons for crimes committed while they were under age 18, including 35 states and the federal government. Georgia is by far the leader with 41 juvenile executions, surprisingly over twice its nearest competitors. The second tier of states with a considerable number of juvenile executions includes not only the southern states of North Carolina, Texas and Virginia but also the northeastern industrial states of New York and Ohio. Florida and Texas, current leaders in adult executions in the 1980s (NAACP, 1987), historically are not among the top leaders in juvenile executions.

As mentioned earlier, 81% of these executions have been for crimes of murder and 15% for rape. The rape cases have been more of a modern phenomenon, with 84% (36 of 43) occurring since 1900.

Although murder cases constitute 81% of the total, of these 226 murder cases, 19 were instances of rape or attempted rape in which the offender also killed his victim. This means that cases involving sexual assault total 64, or 23% of the total 280 cases for which the crime is known (43 rapes, 2 attempted rapes and 19 rape/murders). A total of 35% (80 of 226) of the murder cases involved a robbery or burglary that resulted in a murder.

The other crimes are few in number but nonetheless surprising in some ways. Perhaps one's view is clouded by a 1980s perspective that limits the death penalty in essence to the worst forms of murder. It still seems odd that juveniles have been executed for crimes no more serious than arson, assault and battery, attempted rape, buggery, and robbery, none of which resulted in the taking of a human life or, in some of the cases, even any injury to any human being.

All 281 of these cases involved offenders who were less than 18 years old at the time of their crimes. The range of ages is somewhat surprising, running from a few days before the eighteenth birthday down to age 10.

Table 2

Total Executions and Juvenile Executions by Decade

Time Period	Total Executions	Juvenile Executions	Percentage
1900-1909	1,192	23	1.9
1910-1919	1,039	24	2.3
1920-1929	1,169	27	2.3
1930-1939	1,670	41	2.5
1940-1949	1,288	53	4.1
1950-1959	716	16	2.2
1960-1969	191	3	1.6
1970-1979	3	0	0
1980-present[a]	67	3	4.5
Total	7,335	190*	2.6 (average)

SOURCE: For all executions: W. Bowers, *Legal Homicide: Death as Punishment in America, 1864-1982* (1984) and NAACP Legal Defense and Educational Fund, *Death Row, U.S.A.* (1987).

[a] Current as of March 31, 1987

* An additional 91 juvenile executions occurred prior to 1900.

Well over half of these 281 offenders were age 17 at the time of their crimes. A total of 82% were ages 16 or 17. Executions of persons under age 14 at the time of their crimes have been quite rare with only 12 cases documented out of 15,000 executions in American history. Only one such case has occurred in this century. In fact, during this century 89% of all juvenile executions have been for crimes committed by persons age 16 or 17. Executions of younger juveniles was much more common prior to 1900 than in this century.

Of the 281 juveniles executed in American history, only nine have been females (Streib, 1985). The earliest case that could be documented occurred in 1786 (Sanders, 1970: 320) and execution of juvenile females ended in 1912 (Bowers, 1984: 515). However, two juvenile females are currently under a sentence of death, although they are appealing their cases.

The American experience with the death penalty has been one heavily infused with racial imbalance (Bowers, 1984: 67-102) and this truism seems to apply equally to the death penalty for juveniles. Executed white juveniles comprise only one-fourth of all executed juveniles.

Predictably, blacks constitute the overwhelming majority of these offenders, 69% of the total. And this is not simply an eighteenth and nineteenth century practice of executing slaves and poor blacks. The percentage of blacks has risen dramatically from 54% prior to 1900 to 76% after 1900. The percentage of whites fell from 36% prior to 1900 to 20% after 1900.

The race of the victim has always had an impact in death penalty cases and is an issue of current importance in death penalty law (*McCleskey v. Kemp*, 1986). In striking contrast to the fact that 69% of the executed offenders have been black, only 9% of their victims have been black. Overwhelmingly the victims have been white, 89% overall. For 90 cases the race of the victim could not be determined with satisfactory reliability but in most of those cases it seemed reasonable to assume that the victims were apparently white. Thus the 89% figure for white victims is somewhat conservative.

Considering all 276 victims for whom sex is known, 42% of the victims were female and 58% were male. The proportion of female victims has increased since 1900. Before then, only 35% of the victims were female. Since 1900 this proportion has increased to 46% female.

Present Practice

This 345-year experience of juvenile executions seems determined to continue for at least a little while longer. However, the practice is fading and may well disappear in the not-too-distant future.

Juvenile Death Sentences, 1982 to 1987

In the time period from January 1, 1982, through March 31, 1987, 16 states actually imposed death sentences for crimes committed by persons under age 18.

These juvenile death sentences were imposed in 38 separate instances upon a total of 34 different offenders. Four of these offenders received more than one death sentence for the same crime during this time period, an earlier death sentence having been reversed and then subsequently reimposed. Nevertheless, on 38 separate occasions a state trial court decided to sentence an offender to death for a crime he or she committed while under the age of 18.

The number of juvenile death sentences has declined significantly during this period. A total of 11 such sentences were imposed in 1982, 9 in 1983, 6 in 1984, 4 in 1985, 7 in 1986, and one during the first three months of 1987. Although the annual number of juvenile death sentences has fallen by at least 50%, the number of adult death sentences has remained fairly constant at a rate of 250 to 300 each year (U.S. Department of Justice, 1986).

During this five and one-quarter year time period, 36 states had apparently valid death penalty statutes. Of these states, 30 permitted imposition of the death penalty for crimes committed by persons under the age of 18. Only about half (16 states) actually imposed such a sentence. These 16 states represented a broad spectrum of the United States, ranging from New Jersey to Texas, and from Missouri to Florida.

The states in the south region dominated this juvenile death-sentencing practice as they did in adult death sentencing. Almost three-quarters of the juvenile death sentences were imposed in the South, and 11 of the 16 states (69%) that imposed juvenile death sentences were in the south. Texas is the leader with five sentences but all five offenders were age 17 at the time of their crimes. Texas law establishes age 17 as the juvenile court cutoff (Texas Family Code, 1986) and as the minimum age at crime for the death penalty (Texas Penal Code, 1986). Other states with several juvenile death sentences are Florida and Maryland with four each.

Of the 38 juvenile death sentences imposed, five (13%) were for crimes committed while the offender was only age 15. These exceptionally youthful offenders were sentenced across the country including Arkansas, Indiana, North Carolina, Oklahoma, and Pennsylvania. Perhaps surprisingly, all of these death sentences for crimes committed at age 15 have been imposed in the past two years. Nine death sentences were imposed for crimes committed while the offender was age 16, but the majority (24/38 or 63%) were age 17 at the time of their crimes.

The race of the offenders is somewhat surprising, with 23 (61%) being black and 15 (39%) being white. The overrepresentation of blacks is not a result particularly of the sentences in the south, where a somewhat lower proportion (16/28 or 57%) were black. Outside of the south region, 70% (7/10) were black. Death sentences for female juvenile offenders were quite rare, comprising only two (5%) of the 38 sentences. They occurred in Indiana and Mississippi. The girls were ages 15 and 16, respectively, at the times of their crimes.

Overall, 82% (37/45) of the victims were white, excluding the three victims for whom race is unknown. All multiple victim cases involved only white victims. The region of the country involved does seem to be important as to race of victim.

Analysis of the sex of the victims reveals another imbalance. For the 48 victims nationwide, 28 (58%) were female.

In summary, the 38 juvenile death sentences during these five and one-quarter years fit a rough pattern. The sentences were imposed primarily in the earlier years but in a wide variety of states. The offenders were likely to have been black males who were age 17 at the time of their crimes. They almost always killed a single victim, typically a white female.

Juveniles on Death Row, March 31, 1987

Of the 38 death sentences described in the preceding section, plus perhaps 50 or more imposed between 1972 and 1982, only 33 persons remain on death row for crimes committed while they were under age 18. Overall, 15 states are now holding such persons and apparently are ready, willing, and able to execute them.

During the time period from January 1, 1982, through March 31, 1987, the total death row population in the United States grew from 860 persons to 1,874 persons (NAACP, 1981, 1987). This is an increase of 118% in five and one-quarter years, and 1,874 is the greatest number of persons on death row in U.S. history. During this same period the number of persons on death row for crimes committed while they were under age 18 remained essentially the same, ranging from the low to high 30s. Table 3 presents some basic information about the 33 persons under a juvenile death sentence as of March 31, 1987.

The original death sentencing date for these 33 persons ranges over more than 11 years, from March 19, 1975 for Larry Jones in Mississippi (*Jones v. Thigpen*, 1983) to February 25, 1987, for William Lamb in Florida (Johnson, 1987). Their ages as of March 31, 1987, range from 17 (Ronald Ward in Arkansas, Paula Cooper in Indiana, and Sean Sellers in Oklahoma) to 30 (Larry Jones in Mississippi). Most of these 33 persons have been sentenced to death only once for their crimes as juveniles. However, four of them have received two such death sentences, and two have received three such death sentences. All of the latter categories were instances of being sentenced to death originally, having that sentence reversed on appeal, and then being sentenced to death again at a subsequent trial court sentencing hearing.

Only two of these 33 persons is under a sentence of death for a murder unconnected to another major felony. The other 31 persons committed their homicides in connection with another crime. Most commonly the other crime was rape, involved in 15 of the cases. The other commonly connected crime was robbery, involved in 13 of the cases. In addition were two cases involving kidnapping and one case involving burglary. Overall, in 94% (31/33) of the cases the capital homicide was proven by the state through a felony-murder prosecution, involving proof of the seriousness of the homicide primarily through proof of its connection with another serious felony.

Table 3

Persons Under Juvenile Death Sentences
as of November 1, 1986

State	Name	Age at Crime	Race	Crime
Alabama	Davis, Timothy	17	white	rape/murder
	Jackson, Carnel	16	black	rape/murder
	Lynn, Frederick	16	black	burglary/murder
Arkansas	Ward, Ronald	15	black	Rape/murder
Florida	LeCroy, Cleo	17	white	robbery/murder
	Livingston, Jesse	17	black	robbery/murder
	Magill, Paul	17	white	rape/murder
	Morgan, James	16	white	rape/murder
Georgia	Burger, Christopher	17	white	robbery/murder
	Buttrum, Janice	17	white	rape/murder
	Williams, Alexander	17	black	rape/murder
Indiana	Cooper, Paula	15	black	robbery/murder
	Patton, Keith	17	black	rape/murder
Kentucky	Stanford, Kevin	17	black	rape/murder
Louisiana	Comeaux, Adam	17	black	rape/murder
	Prejean, Dalton	17	black	murder
Maryland	Johnson, Lawrence	17	black	robbery/murder
	Trimble, James	17	white	rape/murder
Mississippi	Jones, Larry	17	black	robbery/murder
	Tokman, George	17	white	robbery/murder
Missouri	Lashley, Frederick	17	black	robbery/murder
	Wilkins, Heath A.	16	white	Robbery/murder
New Jersey	Bey, Marko	17	black	rape/murder
North Carolina	Brown, Leon	15	black	rape/murder
Oklahoma	Sellers, Sean	16	white	murder
	Thompson, Wayne	15	white	kidnap/murder
Pennsylvania	Aulisio, Joseph	15	white	kidnap/murder
	Hughes, Kevin	16	black	rape/murder
Texas	Cannon, Joseph	17	white	robbery/murder
	Carter, Robert	17	black	robbery/murder
	Garrett, Johnny	17	white	rape/murder
	Graham, Gary	17	black	robbery/murder

Overall, 26 (79%) of them received their death sentences from states in the southern region. However, a broad spectrum of jurisdictions currently have such persons on death row, ranging from the Northeast to the Midwest to the deep South. Florida with five and Texas with four have the greatest number, but three each are in Alabama and Georgia. Nationwide, persons under a juvenile death sentence account for less than 2% (33/1,874) of the total death row population (NAACP, 1987:1).

Black offenders are 55% (18/33) of the total. Compare this to the total death row population, of which only 41% are black (NAACP, 1987:1). This overrepresentation of blacks among those under juvenile death sentences seems distributed fairly evenly among the various regions of the country. The sex of these offenders is overwhelmingly male (31/33 or 94%).

There were a total of 41 victims of these 33 offenders. Seven cases involved multiple victims, but 26 cases (78%) involved only one victim. Of the 41 victims, 33 (80%) were white. The sex of the victims was female in 66% (27/41) of the cases overall.

In summary, the 33 persons now under a juvenile death sentence are alike in some ways but quite different in others. Although all were ages 15 to 17 at the time of their crimes, those crimes were committed from 1974 through 1986 and the ages of the offenders now range from 17 to 30. They have been under sentences of death from less than one year to over 12 years. The typical person now under a juvenile death sentence is a black male who was age 17 at the time of his crime. He was sentenced to death in the South for a murder connected to robbery or rape. He had only one victim, a white female. And, since he has been on death row over five years, his time is running out.

Criteria for Change

Whether or not the death penalty for juveniles will be banned as unacceptable in our society is largely to be determined by appraisal of "the evolving standards of decency that mark the progress of a maturing society" (*Trop v. Dulles*, 1958:101). Such progress is halting at best, and precision in determining the level of progress at any one time is extremely difficult. However, can it now be said that we have reached a maturation level at which we will reject the death penalty for juveniles?

During this accelerating change in societal acceptance of the juvenile death penalty, many individuals and groups are being asked to decide where they stand. Agencies as diverse as the U.S. Supreme Court, the Georgia State Legislature, leading political figures, and individual sentencing juries are considering making an exception for juveniles in their otherwise unwavering support for the death penalty. What are the key criteria that should be addressed in such considerations and decisions?

First, the choice of criminal punishment should be based both upon the harm inflicted and upon the criminal intent of the offender. It seems generally accepted that adolescents typically do not have an adult level of maturity and sophistication in their thought processes. Although they can intend behavior, it is unlikely they have thought about it deeply with insight and understanding. They fall short in the critical criterion of criminal intent and thus their punishment should be a little short of the punishment for a comparable adult's acts.

Second, retribution does not require the death penalty for juvenile crimes. Soaring anger at the misdeeds of children is always blunted somewhat, at least for reasonable persons, by the knowledge that children cannot be expected to behave as adults all of the time. The nonetheless strong if blunted need for retribution cannot be ignored but can be satisfied by long-term imprisonment. The death penalty is simply an excessive and overly emotional deference to this undeniable retributive feeling.

Third, deterrence is not enhanced by choosing the death penalty. The alternative sentence, long-term imprisonment, may be a punishment even more feared by adolescents. The only question left open in this regard is how long the imprisonment must be in order to provide satisfactory deterrence, a question answered in widely varying ways by different jurisdictions.

Fourth, it is unreasonable to totally disregard the goals of reform and rehabilitation for juvenile offenders. Behavior patterns change significantly as persons mature from adolescence to adulthood and into middle-age, usually to ways more acceptable to society. Imposing the death penalty for juvenile crimes completely disregards these universally accepted truisms about maturation. Long-term imprisonment holds out the possibility of such a destructive teenager becoming an acceptable adult at some time in the future.

Fifth, consider the message juveniles receive from juvenile death sentences. The crimes they have committed are almost always the killing of a person in order to solve some problem the juvenile perceives as otherwise unsolvable. Now they see the government struggling with a problem of its own, a person whose behavior is unacceptable to them. How does the government solve its problem? It kills the person who is causing the problem. It is most difficult to convince teenagers that they should not do something if they regularly see government officials doing it with the apparent blessings of adult society.

Sixth, abolition of the death penalty for juveniles is a common ground on which death penalty proponents and opponents can meet and agree. Opinion surveys have found that a majority would agree that at least this branch of the death penalty laws should be trimmed back (Southern Coalition, 1986). If everyone can reason together on this small issue, avenues of dialogue and understanding can be opened for more rational and constructive discussion of the death penalty for adults and for the appropriate application of criminal punishment in general.

Finally, if we discard the death penalty for juveniles what can be done about violent juvenile crime? For many, the willingness to acquiesce in the death penalty for juveniles stems from fear and outrage about violent juvenile crime. This fear and outrage is shared by all reasonable persons, whether for or against the death penalty. Two answers to this problem suggest themselves. The temporary solution is to impose long-term prison sentences on such violent juveniles. This will ensure that they are reasonably mature adults and have been subjected to whatever rehabilitative programs are available before they would ever again be free. And they would not be freed easily or by any means automatically even after many years in prison.

The long-term solution to violent juvenile crime cannot come from harsh criminal punishment, whether imprisonment or death. Our society must be willing to devote enormous resources to the search for causes and cures of violent juvenile crime, just as we have for the causes and cures of diseases such as cancer and polio. And, we must not demand a complete cure in a short time, since no one knows how long it will take.

Finally, we must beware of those who push for harsher punishment as the sole cure for violent crime. They are akin to the snake oil salesmen who loudly proclaim the curative effects of their foul tasting elixirs. Unfortunately, no one now has the cure for violent juvenile crime. However, it seems clear that the death penalty for juveniles has been given a long trial period and has been found wanting. Its societal costs are enormous, it tastes terribly foul, and it delays our search for a wise and just means of reducing violent juvenile crime.

References

Amnesty International. 1979. *The Death Penalty.* New York: Amnesty International.

Bedau, H.A. (ed). 1982. *The Death Penalty in America.* New York: Oxford University Press.

Bowers, W.J. 1984. *Legal Homicide: Death as Punishment in America, 1864-1982* Boston: Northeastern University Press.

Corr, C.A. and J.N. McNeil. (ed). 1986. *Adolescence and Death*, New York: Springer.

Davis, S.M. *The Rights of Juveniles* (2nd ed.), 1986. New York: Clark Boardman.

Federal Bureau of Investigation. 1975-1985. *Uniform Crime Reports.* Washington, DC: Government Printing Office.

Fox, S.J. *The Law of Juvenile Courts in a Nutshell* (3rd ed.), 1984. St. Paul, MN: West.

Johnson, P. "Convicted killer Lamb given the death penalty," 1987. *Florida Today* (Cocoa), Feb. 26, 1987, p. 1, col. 4.

Journal of Criminal Law and Criminology. "Capital punishment for minors: An eighth amendment analysis," 1983. Volume 74, 4:1471-1517.

NAACP Legal Defense and Educational Fund, Inc. *Death Row, U.S.A.* 1981. (December).

NAACP Legal Defense and Educational Fund, Inc. March, 1987. *Death Row, U.S.A.* New York Times. 1986, May 16, p. 11, col. 1.

Sanders, W. (ed.). *Juvenile Offenders for a Thousand Years*, 1970. Charlotte: University of North Carolina Press.

Southern Coalition Report on Jails and Prisons "SCJP poll results: Don't execute juveniles," 1986. Volume 13, 1 (Spring): 1.

Streib, V.L. "Females executed for crimes committed while under age eighteen," 1985. (Unpublished report available from author).

Streib, V.L. "The eighth amendment and capital punishment of juveniles," 1986. *Cleveland State Law Review* 34, 3:363-399.

Streib, V.L. *Death Penalty for Juveniles*, 1987. Bloomington: Indiana University Press.

Teeters, N.K. and J.H. Hedblom ". . . Hang By The Neck. . . ." 1967. Springfield, IL: Charles C. Thomas.

Texas Family Code Annotated, Section 54.02 (Vernon Supplement 1986).

Texas Penal Code Annotated, Section 807 (d) (Vernon Supplement 1986).

Twentieth Century Fund Task Force on Sentencing Policy Toward Young Offenders, 1978. Confronting Youth Crime.

U.S. Department of Justice. 1986. *Capital Punishment 1984*. Washington, DC: Government Printing Office.
Vitello, "Constitutional safeguards for juvenile transfer procedure: The ten years since *Kent v. United States*," 1976. *DePaul Law Review* 26:23.
Zimring, F.E. *The Changing Legal World of Adolescence*, 1982. New York: Free Press.

Cases

Cannaday v. State (1984) 455 So.2d 713 (Miss.)
Eddings v. Oklahoma (1982) 455 U.S. 104
Gregg v. Georgia (1976) 428 U.S. 153
High v. Zant (1983) 250 Ga. 693, 300 S.E.2d 654, certorari denied (1984) 104 S.Ct. 2669
Jones v. Thigpen (1983) 555 F.Supp. 870 (S.D. Miss.), reversed (1984) 741 F.2d 805 (5th Cir.), vacated (1986) 106 S.Ct. 1172
Jurek v. Texas (1976) 428 U.S. 262
Kent v. United States (1966) 383 U.S. 541
Lockett v. Ohio (1978) 438 U.S. 536
McCleskey v. Kemp (1987) 107 S.Ct. 1756
State v. Battle (1983) 661 S.W.2d 487 (Mo.) (en banc), certorari denied (1984) 104 S.Ct. 2325
State v. Valencia (1982) 132 Ariz. 248, 645 P.2d 239
Thompson v. Oklahoma (1986) 724 P.2d 780 (Okla.Cr.App.), certiorari granted (1987) 107 S.Ct. 1281
Trimble v. State (1984) 300 Md. 387, 478 A.2d 1143, certiorari denied (1985) 105 S.Ct. 1231
Trop v. Dulles (1958) 356 U.S. 86
Workman v. Commonwealth (1968) 429 S.W. 2d 374 (Ky.)

Section IV

THE JUVENILE IN
CONFINEMENT

The incarceration of juvenile offenders continues to be a thorny issue reflecting a history of neglect, an absence of planning, and a general refusal to examine goals for the juvenile justice system carefully. As a result, institutions for juveniles were subjected to harsh public criticism in the 1960s and a number of reforms were made. However, in spite of the reforms, juvenile institutions continue to be plagued with management problems. Compounding problems for the administrator is the possibility that today's youth have far more serious problems than youth in the previous generation. Those who argue this position point to the significant increases in drug and alcohol consumption among juveniles, earlier involvement in delinquency and serious criminality, and the alleged deterioration of the family.

Many juvenile facilities are facing serious shortages of space, and despite years of government mandates, many localities still have no separate facilities for juvenile offenders. In their search for creative, affordable, solutions to this problem, some jurisdictions have been utilizing the policy of house arrest. Richard Ball, C.Ronald Huff and J. Robert Lilly discuss these issues in "House Arrest and Juvenile Justice." They describe the use of the house arrest alternative, the conditions of house arrest, and the process by which young people are chosen for the house arrest alternative. Finally, they discuss the problem of deciding what constitutes a successful house arrest program. They conclude that while some house arrest programs do seem

161

more effective than others, the reasons for this success are not clear. While research on the topic is just beginning, it seems likely that the use of house arrest will continue so long as the system is strapped for resources.

Regardless of the position argued, the evidence seems to support the notion that incarceration for many juveniles enhances the potentials for additional and more serious problems. Michael G. Flaherty, writing for the Community Research Forum, has addressed one of the most critical problems in the incarceration of youth. His article, "An Assessment of the National Incidence of Juvenile Suicide in Adult Jails, Lockups, and Juvenile Detention Centers," calls our attention to one of the most tragic problems in juvenile justice—the incarceration of juveniles in jails, and the resultant suicide that occurs more often than most would like to admit. Flaherty argues that the policy of incarcerating children in adult jails and lockups may be contributing to the relatively high rate of suicide among those children. Study after study has outlined the tragic consequences for youth when incarcerated in jails and lockups, yet the practice continues.

Vicki Agee, in "Treatment of the Violent Incorrigible Adolescent," addresses a problem of growing concern—youth who do not respond to available treatment modalities. She has traced the development of the "aversive treatment evader" (ATE) through the life cycle. Through the presentation of a number of case histories, Agee documents the failure process as institutions fail to respond to the needs of the youth they attempt to treat. Her portrayal of the dumping process is indicative of the extent to which mental health professionals escape accountability for their ineffective and perhaps inappropriate treatment programs.

In the last article in this section, Clemens Bartollas, Stuart J. Miller and Simon Dinitz examine, "The Exploitation Matrix in a Juvenile Institution." Hidden from public view, juvenile institutions have many characteristics of adult prisons including sexual exploitation. The authors' discussion of power issues, homosexuality and the consequences of incarceration for a significant number of youth reminds us that these institutions have changed little over the decades. When former Supreme Court Justice Abe Fortas argued, in Kent v. United States, that "juveniles get the worst of both worlds" in the treatment process, he was writing about these kinds of institutions. The tragedy lies in the fact that youth who "graduate" from these institutions often move on to adult criminal careers.

12

House Arrest and Juvenile Justice

Richard A. Ball, Ronald Huff
and J. Robert Lilly

Placing juveniles on house arrest, as an alternative to the use of secure detention facilities, has evolved in response to concerns about (1) the harmful effects of confining juveniles in adult jails, (2) the dysfunctional aspects of isolating youths from their families and from the communities in which they live, (3) the over-crowding that exists in many adult jails and juvenile detention centers, and (4) the absence of suitable facilities in many areas of the nation. The history of juvenile justice in America is filled with policy debates — even social movements — concerning the confinement of juveniles in jails and other secure detention facilities. The preadjudicatory detention of juveniles in a secure facility, analogous to holding an adult in jail prior to trial, has been the subject of numerous task forces and commissions, which have concluded that tight restrictions should be placed on juvenile detention practices.

Jailing Juveniles: A Suicidal Policy?

The most severely criticized practice has been the use of adult jails to detain youths. A federal initiative to reduce this practice has won support, not only from child advocates, but from the National Association of Counties, the National League of Cities, and the National Sheriffs Association, among others (Rubin, 1985: 128). In addition to being concerned about the welfare of children locked up in such jails, these professional associations are also keenly aware of the problems involved in jailing juveniles—including inefficient use of jail space and the expanded personal liability they may face if a juvenile is victimized or commits suicide while in jail.

Nonetheless, approximately 500,000 youths are held in adult jails each year, about 60 of whom die before leaving jail (Rubin, 1985: 128). A recent national study found that the suicide rate for juveniles in adult jails is nearly five times greater than it is for juveniles in the general population, and nearly eight times greater than it is for juveniles held in separate juvenile detention centers (Community Research Center, 1980). This high suicide rate is a good illustration of how a well-intentioned policy can have unintended consequences. Federal policy mandating the separation of juveniles from adults "by sight and by sound" was intended to eliminate the assaults, rapes, and other abuses that had occurred as a result of the "commingling" of adults and juveniles in confinement. However, as is so often the case, the implementation of such policy reform often presents its own set of problems.

One of the authors has visited many adult jails, built in the late 1800s, where compliance with this federal policy means that when a juvenile is being held, he or she will be placed either in the basement of the jail or its top floor. This isolation, intended to separate and protect the youth from older, perhaps more "hardened," inmates, also makes it almost impossible to supervise these isolated youths in understaffed jails.[1] Since youths held in jail following their arrest may be filled with feelings of guilt, remorse, or even self-hatred, it is not difficult to appreciate why the risk of suicide is dramatically elevated. The isolated location of these youths within the jail precludes both effective supervision and any meaningful opportunity to discuss their problems. Also, such facilities typically offer little or no programming for either youths or adult inmates. For example, when asked what the juveniles do for recreation, a jailer told one of the authors, "Oh, we take them out to the [country] fairgrounds and let 'em run once in awhile" (Huff, 1980).

The Deinstitutionalization Movement

Although many areas of the nation still do not have separate detention facilities for juveniles (and many of those that *do* exist are inadequate), the focus of more recent reformers has shifted to advocacy for community-based *alternatives* to detention centers and jails. In the juvenile justice arena, this movement gained considerable momentum as a result of two pieces of federal legislation—the Omnibus Crime Control and Safe Streets Act of 1968[2] and the Juvenile Justice and Delinquency Prevention Act of 1974[3] (as amended in 1977)—both of which mandated the deinstitutionalization of status offenders. This means, in effect, that youths who are charged with, or who are found to have committed, "offenses" that would not be illegal acts if committed by an adult, shall not be confined in a secure detention or correctional facility (except, under certain conditions, for a period not to exceed 24 hours, or for having violated a valid court order).

The rationale for community-based alternatives to institutional confinement has at least some of its roots in a theoretical perspective commonly known as "labeling theory,"[4] which holds that the juvenile and adult justice systems, especially their correctional facilities, are themselves "criminogenic," or cause additional criminality and delinquency, by treating their "clients" as abnormal. According to this perspective, the stigma associated with these systems "marks" an individual in our society, thus reducing his or her chances of being accepted and leading a normal, noncriminal life.

Although the general validity of the labeling perspective has not been effectively demonstrated, it has great intuitive appeal and "face validity." Furthermore, the implications of labeling theory overlap significantly with the emphasis of those promoting the development of a "least restrictive alternatives" policy in the administration of juvenile justice. From the latter point of view, the least restrictive alternative should be used in each case, and secure detention should be reserved almost exclusively for those charged with or convicted of serious crimes, especially crimes against persons.

Consider, for example, the juvenile detention policy guidelines advocated by a joint task force of the Institute of Judicial Administration and the American Bar Association. Detention, the task force said in Standard 6.6, should be limited to juveniles who are fugitives from justice or who are charged with violent felonies where commitment to a secure institution is likely if the offense is proven, and where one of the following additional factors is present:

(1) the crime charged is a class one juvenile offense;

(2) the juvenile is an escape from an institution or other placement facility where he was sentenced following adjudication for criminal conduct; or

(3) there is a recent record of willful failure to appear at juvenile proceedings, and no measure short of detention will reasonably ensure his appearance at court (Institute for Judicial Administration—American Bar Association, 1980).

These IJA-ABA *Standards*, as well as those promulgated by the National Advisory Committee for Juvenile Justice and Delinquency Prevention (1980), reflect a "least restrictive alternatives" policy preference, developed in response to the overcrowding, neglect, and abuse in many of the nation's detention facilities and jails.

House Arrest: The Least Restrictive Alternative?

Just a few years after the catalytic Omnibus Crime Control Act of 1968, the nation's first house arrest program for juveniles was implemented in St. Louis.

Since that beginning, in 1971, many additional programs—known variously as house arrest, home detention, or home supervision—have evolved, and most have been patterned after the programmatic model developed in St. Louis.

How do these programs work? Who staffs them? How are they structured? What are the major goals of these programs? What policy issues do they address? How successful are they? What does *success* really mean? What is their comparative cost? Who is referred to them and what criteria do they use to screen potential candidates for house arrests? Do they threaten public safety by keeping in the community juveniles who belong behind bars? Do they represent a true alternative to secure detention or do they merely expand the "net" of social control by focusing on youths who normally would have been placed on regular probation with less intensive supervision? All of these questions, and others, must be addressed if we are to make responsible policy choices in the controversial area of juvenile correction. Fortunately, some valuable descriptive and evaluative information on such programs is available (see, for example, Keve and Zanick, 1972; Young and Pappenfort, 1977; Swank, 1979; Rubin, 1979, 1985). In the remainder of this chapter, we shall review what is known about house arrest programs for juveniles in the United States.

How do These Programs Operate and What are the Rules?

In Jefferson County (Louisville), Kentucky, house arrest is imposed on the youth and his or her parents or guardian. The probation officer is expected to discuss with the youth and family all conditions imposed by the court prior to their leaving court, to ensure that the youth and family have a contact at the agency 24 hours a day, and to check for compliance, "If the probation officer suspects for any reason that these conditions are not being adhered to" and "to inform the Court of any noncompliance" (Jefferson County Juvenile Probation Services, 1983).

The court order imposing house arrest specifies the conditions and exceptions concerning the youth's activities during the house arrest sanction, and makes clear that the youth is considered to be in detention status, just as if he or she were detained in the Youth Center, and that any violation of the order will result in a return to the Youth Center. The parents or guardian are expected to enforce the rules of house arrest; if they fail to do so and fail to notify the court concerning violations, they may be prosecuted for contempt of court or for contributing to the delinquency of a minor (Jefferson County Juvenile Probation Services, 1983).

The Jefferson County Juvenile Court may also impose home supervision, if a juvenile and his or her family are thought to be in need of additional support services during the adjudicatory process. Workers supervising youths placed in home supervision status have a maximum caseload of five and are expected to (1) execute a contract with the youth and the parent or guardian prior to their leaving court, (2) have at least one face-to-face *and* one telephone contact with the youth, and (3) have at least one face-to-face *or* one telephone contact with the parent or guardian each week. These contacts are intended to enable staff to identify problems, monitor the youth's adjustment, and provide needed services. If a youth violates the provisions of the agreement, a conference is held to determine whether to return the youth to court for noncompliance.

According to Swank (1979), the San Diego Home Supervision Program began in 1976 with a grant from the State Office of Criminal Justice Planning to the San Diego County Probation Department. Prior to the implementation of this program, whenever Juvenile Hall was overcrowded, minors had been released at detention hearings under house arrest and advised to stay at home until their next hearing. There was one major problem with this arrangement: The youths were not monitored to see if they were complying with the court's order. This situation changed dramatically on March 14, 1977, when the first two juveniles were referred to the Home Supervision Program, which assured judges that youths referred to the Program would either stay at home as required or be taken into custody.

Despite the warnings given to these first two youths, less than a week passed before one of them was arrested for smoking dope in his bedroom with his buddies. While being returned to Juvenile Hall, the youth reportedly commented, "I didn't think you'd be coming. I've never seen a probation officer so much" (Swank, 1979: 50). The staff was apprehensive that this initial program failure might cause the referring judge to lose confidence in the program. Actually, just the reverse occurred. The judge was impressed that the probation officers were enforcing the court's orders. That incident stimulated judicial confidence in the program's accountability and helped fuel its subsequent growth.

Rapid growth of these programs can, in fact, present significant problems, and the San Diego program is a good example. Consider the fact that San Diego County is approximately the size of the State of Connecticut. Then contemplate the fact that in the early days of the program, two probation officers were responsible for supervising youths throughout the County and that officers often carried caseloads of 30 or so at any one time (Swank, 1979)! Nonetheless, with the assistance of volunteers, the program was able to provide random monitoring 24 hours a day and 7 days a week.

On January 1, 1977, the Dixon Bill,[5] having been enacted by the California Assembly, officially became law. This law encouraged increased community treatment and the separation of status offenders from delinquents. It also required that all counties operate home supervision programs as one type of community alternative to the use of detention facilities. Further, the California Welfare and Institutions Code (Section 628.1) required the probation officer to release a minor from the detention center and place him or her on home supervision if the probation officer "believes 24-hour secure detention is not necessary in order to protect the minor or the person or property of another, or to ensure that the minor does not flee the jurisdiction of the court" (San Diego County Probation Department, 1986). Two goals are mandated for such home supervision programs in California: (1) to assure appearance at interviews and court hearings and (2) to assure that the

the minor obeys the conditions of release and commits no offenses pending disposition of the case.

Workers' salaries are essentially subsidized by the state and caseloads may not exceed 10. When possible, supervising officers are assigned to monitor youths in the same geographic area in which the officers reside. San Diego County's commitments, in return for these funds, are: (1) to maintain at least 80% of the minors in the community without returning them to custody, (2) to personally contact each minor at least once a day, and (3) to provide supervision for at least 800 minors who would otherwise be detained. Minors who do not comply with the terms of home supervision may be arrested by probation officers and returned to juvenile court for review and possible placement in secure detention.

All seven of the early house arrest programs evaluated by Young and Pappenfort (1977) were administered by juvenile court probation departments. In general, these programs were staffed by paraprofessionals known as "outreach workers," "community youth leaders," or "community release counselors." Each staff member typically had a caseload of five youths at any one time. All seven programs expected their youth workers to exercise daily supervision and to keep their charges "trouble free and available to the court" for their hearings.

Surveillance in these programs was accomplished primarily by daily personal contacts (at least one per day) with each youth, and daily telephone or personal contacts with the youths' parents, teachers, and (where applicable) employers. The youth workers who staffed these programs typically worked out of their automobiles and their own homes rather than at probation offices or court facilities. There was an effort to keep paperwork requirements to a minimum so the youth workers would have more time to be actively engaged in the supervision of their assigned cases. In fact, travel vouchers and handwritten daily activity logs often constituted the only significant paperwork required of these workers.

The youths placed in such programs typically had the program's rules of participation explained to them in the presence of their parents. These rules usually included:

(1) attending school;

(2) observing a specified curfew;

(3) notifying parents or work as to whereabouts at all times when not at home, school, or work;

(4) abstaining from drugs; and

(5) avoiding companions or places that "might lead to trouble."

In addition to these general guidelines, additional rules or conditions could usually be added as agreed upon by the parties involved. Written contracts setting forth these conditions were frequently used in these programs.

All seven programs were based on the rationale that close supervision would generally keep juveniles "trouble free and available to the court." Six of the seven programs also rested on another assumption: that this type of program would enable youth workers to provide needed services to youths and their families, thus increasing the probability of success. Some programs emphasized counseling and services more than others did, however, even going so far as to expect youth workers to try to achieve a "big brother" type of relationship with each youth supervised, sometimes combined with advocacy and involvement with the youths' parents. Youth workers in three of the seven programs organized weekly recreational or cultural activities for all youths placed in their respective programs.

Youth workers in these programs often coordinated their efforts to provide better services (for example, one worker "covering" or taking responsibility for another when necessary). In all seven programs, youths who did not adhere fully to program requirements could be taken to secure detention by program youth workers.

Who is Referred to House Arrest Programs and What Screening Criteria are Used?

It is interesting that not one of the seven programs evaluated by Young and Pappenfort (1977) was designed exclusively for status offenders. Two programs accepted only alleged delinquents, while the other five included both alleged delinquents and status offenders. Most (5) of the programs served 200-300 youths per year, while the other two accepted just over 1,000 youths in the fiscal year preceding the evaluation.

A recent study by one of the authors found that in the State of Ohio, juvenile court judges responding to a statewide survey reported that they consider three factors to be the most important in screening candidates for house arrest:

(1) the seriousness of the alleged offense;

(2) the youth's previous record; and

(3) the home environment.

A second "cluster" of factors, though less important, are also taken into consideration. These factors include protection of the child, protection of others, population or crowding in the detention facility, school adjustment, and time of day when the alleged offense occurred. Judges reported that the recommendations of court staff, especially probation officers, are very important in the decision to use house arrest (Huff, 1986).

In the seven programs assessed by Young and Pappenfort (1977), burglary was the most frequent delinquency charge filed against program participants. When charges filed against program participants were compared with those filed against youths in secure detention facilities, the two populations were similar, except for homicide, aggravated assault, and rape (relatively infrequent and rarely released to such alternative programs). Most delinquency charges filed against program participants were judged to be moderately serious.

What Does *Success* Mean in Such Programs and How Successful are They?

In attempting to assess program success, the key question is one of definition. What constitutes success? Should one consider it a success if a youth, while in home detention status, is not charged with any new *offenses* prior to adjudication? Or does success require that he or she complete the period of home detention without any violations of the home detention agreement? Or without having been returned to secure detention? Bear in mind that even if a youth violates the rules and is returned to secure detention, he or she is still available to the court, just as would have been the case had the youth been in the detention center the entire time. This question is somewhat similar to the distinction made between parole revocation for an alleged criminal *offense* versus revocation for a *technical violation* of parole conditions.

Depending on one's operational definition of success, the data reported by Young and Pappenfort (1977) indicate that home detention programs' "success rates" ranged from 71% to 98%. That is, if one defines success as having completed home detention *without incident* (the most restrictive possible definition of success), Young and Pappenfort's data indicate that the *least* successful programs in their sample were 71% successful. If, on the other hand, one adopts a more liberal definition of success (having completed home detention without any new alleged offenses), the *best* programs they evaluated attained a success rate of 98%. In addition, the San Diego program reports that it monitored 910 minors in Fiscal Year 1984 and had a "97%+" success rate (San Diego County Probation Department, 1986).

In all seven of the programs selected for Young and Pappenfort's (1977) national evaluation, the percentages of youths returned to secure detention for rules violations exceeded those returned for either alleged new offenses or for running away. This suggests that the quality of supervision in these programs was quite high. Also, because all of the youths returned to secure detention for rules violations did subsequently appear in court, one might argue that the preventive measures of returning them to detention should be viewed as a success (it may have prevented serious delinquency and the youth was still available to the court), rather than as a program failure. Indeed, return to secure detention is a planned option in all such programs.

It is noteworthy that those programs, designed exclusively for alleged delinquents, were as effective as those that accepted status offenders as well as delinquents (Young and Pappenfort, 1977), underscoring once more the fact that "offense categories" are often a poor proxy, for either past behavior or future risk. Indeed, the researchers concluded that additional youths could have been handled in home detention programs and other alternative programs, and that some courts were "unnecessarily timid" in referring youths to such programs (Young and Pappenfort, 1977: 31).

A recent Ohio study found that a sample of 2,708 youths released on house arrest in 1984, a total of 2,470, or 91%, successfully complied with the conditions imposed upon them during the period of conditional release and subsequently appeared for adjudication. In this study, technical violations again accounted for far more "failures" than did new allegations of offenses (Huff, 1986). Furthermore, 85% of the juvenile courts responding to the survey indicated that their experience with house arrest was either "good" or "very good," with none rating the results worse than "fair" (Huff, 1986).

Of course, not all youths placed on house arrest succeed. One who did not is described in an anecdote involving one of the most memorable (and humorous) apprehensions in the history of house arrest programs:

> A home supervision officer was chasing a violator who scaled a wall. When the officer also went over the wall, he realized he had stumbled into a nude swimming party. The quick thinking youth apparently shed his clothes and disguised himself as one of the guests. He was apprehended the following day (fully clothed and grinning ear-to-ear) [Swank, 1979: 51].

What is the Comparative Cost of these Programs?

According to Keve and Zanick (1972), the cost per child per day in the original (St. Louis) home detention program was $4.85, compared to $17.54 per child per day in the juvenile detention center. This approximate one-to-four cost advantage also characterized another early home detention program begun in Louisville, Kentucky, in 1975 (Rubin, 1979: 101). Huff's (1986) Ohio study of house arrest indicated that secure detention costs averaged $42.57 per day; nonsecure detention and other nonsecure placements cost an average of $280.07 per day; and that house arrest was the least expensive of these three categories at just $14.94 per day (about one-third the cost of secure detention).

Conclusion

In this chapter, we have considered the nature and evolution of house arrest programs for juveniles in the context of historical reform movements and the policy debates surrounding juvenile detention. The smoke from these fiery debates over what to do with "juvenile delinquents" has not yet cleared, with articulate proponents of "locking them up" squaring off against equally eloquent adversaries favoring policies that promote the use of "the least restrictive alternatives" and "community based corrections."

We have also presented an overview of what is known about house arrest programs nationally, based on available research findings. The corpus of this research, while encouraging the proponents of house arrest as a viable alternative to secure detention, leaves unanswered many questions that must be resolved if we are to develop sound public policy. Like much of the program evaluation literature, what we have reviewed tends to concentrate on *aggregate* findings and general descriptions. We are left with a blurry picture of generally successful programs, but we don't come away knowing *why* they work, fail to work, or work for some and not others. Very little of what has been published helps us understand the *differential* effects of these programs on different subgroups of participants, the political contexts in which house arrest programs operate, the views of the judiciary who refer youths and the workers who supervise them, and other important matters.

Editor's Note: Many of the issues raised in the conclusion of this chapter are subsequently addressed in the larger work from which this chapter was drawn.

Footnotes

[1] Such jails, many of them in rural counties, typically have neither sufficient staffing nor the equipment required for effective electronic monitoring inside the jail.
[2] Omnibus Crime Control and Safe Streets Act of 1968, Public Law No. 90-351, 82 Stat. 204 (codified as amended at 42 U.S.C. Section 3701, *et seq.*).
[3] Juvenile Justice and Delinquency Prevention Act of 1974, Public Law No. 93-415, 88 Stat. 1109 (1974).
[4] Although typically referred to as "labeling theory," this is really a theoretical *perspective*, rather than a systematic theory, since it does not incorporate any explanation of the subject's illegal behavior *prior* to his or her involvement in the justice system (the behavior that led to the arrest). If "labeling effects" explain subsequent law violations, what explains the original law violations? Labeling "theory" is essentially silent on this point.
[5] California Assembly Bill 3121, effective January 1, 1977.

References

American Bar Association/Institute of Judicial Administration Standards. 1980. New York: American Bar Association.
Community Research Center. 1980. An Assessment of the National Incidence of Juvenile Suicide in Adult Jails, Lockups, and Juvenile Detention Centers. Champaign, IL: Community Research Center.
Huff, C. Ronald. 1980. Field notes (interview in a rural jail), July.
Huff, C. Ronald. 1986. "Home detention as a policy alternative for Ohio's juvenile courts: A final report to the governor's office of criminal justice services." (unpublished)
Jefferson County, Kentucky. 1983. Juvenile Probation Services Policy and Procedures Manual, Sections 803.11 and 803.12.
Keve, Paul C. and Casimir S. Zanick. 1972. Final Report and Evaluation of the Home Detention Program, St. Louis, Missouri, September 30 (1971) to July 1 (1972). McLean, VA: Research Analysis Corp.
National Advisory Committee for Juvenile Justice and Delinquency Prevention Standards for the Administration of Juvenile Justice. 1980. Washington, DC: Government Printing Office.
Rubin, H. Ted. 1985. Juvenile Justice: Policy, Practice, and Law (2nd ed.). New York: Random House.
Rubin, H. Ted. 1979. Juvenile Justice: Policy, Practice, and Law. Santa Monica, CA: Goodyear.
San Diego County, California Probation Department. 1986. Personal correspondence (February).
Swank, William G. 1979. "Home supervision: Probation really works." *Federal Probation* (December): 50-52.
Young, Thomas M. and Donnell M. Pappenfort. 1977. Secure detention of juveniles and alternatives to its use. National Evaluation Program, Summary Report, Phase I. National Institute of Law Enforcement and Criminal Justice, LFAA. Washington, DC: Government Printing Office.

13

An Assessment of the National Incidence of Juvenile Suicide in Adult Jails, Lockups, and Juvenile Detention Centers

Community Research Forum

Introduction

In 1923, Fishman (1969:18, 83) visited 1500 American jails, and he noted that very young children were routinely imprisoned with adult inmates. Federal policy in the United States still permits children to be incarcerated in adult jails and lockups if they are kept separate from adult prisoners. Indeed, we estimate that more than 213,000 juveniles were held in adult jails during 1978 although only a very small minority of them were charged with felonies. Furthermore, from 1969 to 1979, there was an increase of 156 percent in the number of persons below the age of eighteen who were

Michael G. Flaherty, "An Assessment of the National Incidence of Juvenile Suicide in Adult Jails, Lockups, and Juvenile Detention Centers." This document was prepared by the Community Research Forum of The University of Illinois under grant no. 78-JS-AX-0046 awarded by the Office of Juvenile Justice and Delinquency Prevention, Law Enforcement Assistance Administration, United States Department of Justice. Points of view or opinions stated in this document are those of the Community Research Forum and do not necessarily represent the official position of the U.S. Department of Justice. Copyright © 1980 The Board of Trustees of the University of Illinois. Reprinted with permission.

arrested (U.S. Department of Justice, Federal Bureau of Investigation, 1969:115; 1979: 194). That figure implies an increasing tendency to place children in adult jails. This, despite the fact that the federal Juvenile Justice and Delinquency Prevention Act of 1974 clearly called for a reduction in the use of secure detention for youth (Public Law, 1974).

The separation of juvenile prisoners from adult inmates may reduce the incidence of child abuse, but it may also be conducive to juvenile suicide in adult jails. Past research demonstrates that facility and staff limitations of jails and lockups often result in children being held in isolation without supervision (U.S. General Accounting Office, 1976; Children's Defense Fund, 976:4; James, 1975:197; Sarri, 1974:30). These studies imply that placing children in adult jails, even when separated from adults, is both physically and emotionally damaging to those children. This is quite evident in the following comments by investigators from the Children's Defense Fund (1976:4).

> ...the conditions of most of the jails in which we found children are abysmal, subjecting them to cruel and unusual punishment through physical neglect and abuse. Solitary confinement or confinement in a dank basement or closet-like enclosure for the sole child in an adult jail removes him or her from other inmates, but also from the attention of caretakers and can have severe traumatic effects on an already troubled and frightened youngster.

Such observations suggest that one of the tragic consequences of this policy is the facilitation of juvenile suicide in adult jails, and there is much anecdotal data which supports this hypothesis (Juvenile Justice Digest, 1979: 10; Wooden, 1976:151; U.S. Senate Committee on the Judiciary, 1971:5116; Looking Glass, 1980:7-11). A higher rate of suicide among children held in adult jails and lockups, as compared to that of similar populations of children in secure juvenile detention facilities and the general youth population, would be a vivid indicator of the harmful impact of incarcerating juveniles in adult jails. Yet, there has been no systematic empirical documentation of these claims.

Suicide in Jails

Although the professional literature on suicide is simply enormous, very little of it is directly concerned with the occurrence of suicide in jails, and not even one reference could be located which specifically examines juvenile suicide in adult jails (Beall, 1969; Prentice, 1974). Nonetheless, much of the data on the problem of adult suicide in jails seems applicable to juvenile suicide in that same setting. Litman (1966:16) states that the risk of suicide is increased when a so-called "respectable" person is arrested for something shameful or when an inmate is rejected by loved ones. As one would expect, isolation within the jail setting has also been linked to suicide (Danto, 1973:619) as have both fear and stress among prisoners (Johnson, 1976:127; Gibbs, 1978a). Toch (1975:51) writes that embarrassment, guilt, and self-condemnation can coalesce to produce a fatal self-hate. Recalling the status integration theory of suicide, Irwin's (1970:39) description of incarceration is instructive:

> These experiences — arrest, trial, and conviction — threaten the struc-
> ture of his personal life in two separate ways. First, the disjointed exper-
> ience of being suddenly extracted from a relatively unfamiliar and seem-
> ingly chaotic one where the ordering of events is completely out of his
> control has a shattering impact upon his personality structure. One's
> identity, one's personality system, one's coherent thinking about him-
> self depend upon a relatively familiar, continuous, and predictable
> stream of events. In the Kafkaesque world of the booking room, the
> jail cell, the interrogation room, and the visiting room, the boundaries
> of the self collapse.
>
> While this collapse is occurring the prisoner's network of social rela-
> tionships is being torn apart.

Juveniles are rarely held for very long in adult jails, but suicides among adult inmates frequently occur soon after arrest. Heilig (1973:49) reports that eleven of seventeen suicides transpired during the first day following incarceration. Likewise, Fawcett and Marrs (1973:89) counted five of thirteen suicides within the first week of imprisonment. Most authorities agree that cutting or hanging are the most common methods for committing suicide in jail (Beigal and Russell, 1973:110; Danto, 1973a:8; Wilmotte and Plat-Mendlewicz, 1973:71). Finally, it is interesting to note, given our focus on juvenile suicide in jails, that Koller and Castanos (1969:858) discovered a strong relationship between parental deprivation and attempted suicide among adult prison populations.

Suicide Among Children

A number of general statements can be made concerning the incidence of suicidal behavior among youth. Females make many more suicide attempts than males, but males are successful much more frequently than are females (Shafii et al, 1979:229). In the same vein, non-whites commit suicide much less frequently than whites (Shafii et al, 1979:9; Toolan, 1962:719; Holinger, 1978:754). There is quite a lengthy catalogue of precipitating causes for suicidal conduct among children, but several are cited repeated-ly. Shaffer (1974:287) points out that, "The most commonly occurring situation before the suicide was one in which the child knew that his parents were to be told of some type of anti-social behavior or loss of face," and Mulock (1955:158) as well as Faigel (1966:188) refer to legal problems as a cause of juvenile suicide. Parental deprivation as a result of divorce, rejection, or death is another frequent cause of suicidal conduct among children (Cashion, 1970; Barter et al., 1968; Finch and Pozanski, 1971; Dorpat et al, 1965; Peck, 1968; 1970). In addition, individual isolation has often been listed as a major source of juvenile suicide (Bakwin, 1973; Jacobs, 1971; Teicher and Jacobs, 1966; Seiden, 1969). Finally, and perhaps related to the preceding variables, some authors simply mention psychological depression as the precipitant for suicide among youth (Bakwin, 1966; Gould, 1965; Schrut, 1964).

Hypotheses

We would expect to find feelings of isolation, humiliation, parental deprivation, and depression more widespread among youth imprisoned in adult jails than among youth in secure juvenile detention centers. This expectation is based upon the aforementioned federal policy of separating juveniles from adult prisoners (which often results in isolation for the sole child in an adult jail), as well as the chronic facility and staff limitations of adult jails. By the same token, those feelings are likely to be more prevalent among youth held in juvenile detention facilities than among children in the general population of the United States. In light of the foregoing, it is hypothesized that the rate of juvenile suicide in adult jails is higher than that of secure juvenile detention centers, and in turn, that the rate of suicide in juvenile detention facilities is higher than that among youth in the general population. Since we are interested in measuring the harmful effects of placing children in adult jails, suicidal conduct was chosen as the indicator for those effects because "self-inflicted injury is an act that typically requires medical attention," and for that reason, "it is more likely to be reflected in institutional records" than are other phenomena such as sexual or physical assaults (Gibbs, 1978b:23).

Sample

Our sample is drawn from the Criminal Justice Agency List which is a complete compilation of all institutions in America that are involved in any facet of the criminal justice process (U.S. Department of Commerce, 1978a). The sampling frame, therefore, consists of names, addresses, telephone numbers, and other information on 3,493 jails, 13, 383 lockups, and 372 juvenile detention centers.

Since the number of juvenile detention facilities is not large, all of those institutions were included in our sample. However, because financial considerations precluded the inclusion of all adult jails in our sample, we drew a twenty percent random sample of the jails which have an average daily population of fewer than 250 inmates, and a one hundred percent sample of jails which have an average daily population of 250 prisoners or more.

Subsequent to pretesting the instrument, 1158 questionnaires were mailed to 372 juvenile detention centers and 786 jails. After revising the instrument, 913 questionnaires were mailed to the lockups in our sample. Second and third mailings were followed by telephone calls to the non-responding institutions. We have received usable responses from 97.6% of the juvenile detention facilities, 83.3% of the jails, and 64.0% of the lockups in our sample for an overall response rate of 77.4%.

Findings

The Number of Juveniles in Adult Jails and Lockups

There is great variation in the estimates of the annual number of children who are held in adult jails and lockups. Perhaps the highest projection is that of Sarri (1974:5) who suggests that 500,000 juveniles are incarcerated in adult jails and lockups each year. In contrast, Poulin and his colleagues (1979:11) estimate that 120,000 children annually are held in jails only. Neither of these projections, however, is based on primary research. Rather, they are based on syntheses of secondary sources. Lowell and McNabb (1980:29) conducted a nationwide survey, and they project a one day count of 4,061 sentenced persons below the age of eighteen in jails. Unfortunately, apart from ignoring the many unsentenced juveniles in adult jails, their study had a response rate of only 51%, and they admit that their data seriously underestimate the parameters in large urban areas (Lowell and McNabb, 1980:27-28).

We have documented 383,328 children in secure juvenile detention centers during 1978. Given our response rate, we estimate the actual total to be approximately 392,662. We have documented 170,714 juveniles in adult jails. Again, given our response rate, we estimate the actual total to be 213,647. In addition, we have documented 11,592 juveniles in adult lockups. Once again, given our response rate, we estimate the actual number to be 266,261. That yields an overall estimate of 479,908 persons below the age of eighteen who are held for any length of time in an adult jail or lockup during 1978.

The Incidence of Juvenile Suicide

Table 1 presents the suicide rates for children in adult jails, lockups, and juvenile detention centers during 1978, and the suicide rate among youth in the general population of the United States during 1977. Information on the general population from 1977 is used because final mortality data for 1978 has not, as yet, been computed by the National Center on Health Statistics (U.S. Department of Health, Education, and Welfare, 1979). The number of suicides among children in the general population during 1977 is obtained from unpublished data at the National Center for Health Statistics (U.S. Department of Health, Education, and Welfare, 1980), and the number of children in the general population of the United States during 1977 is available in published form from the Bureau of Census (U.S. Department of Commerce, 1980).

Table 1

Suicide Rates for Children in Adult Jails, Lockups, and Juvenile Detention Centers during 1978, and Children in the General Population of the United States during 1977

Population	Number of Children	Number of Suicides	Number of Suicides per 100,000 Children
Children in Adult Jails during 1978	170,714	21	12.3
Children in Adult Lockups during 1978	11,568	1	8.6
Children in Juvenile Detention Centers during 1978	383,238	6	1.6
Children in the General Population of the United States during 1977*	49,008,000	1313	2.7

*The number of children in the general population of the United States during 1977 represents all persons between the ages of 5 and 17, while data for children in adult jails, lockups, and juvenile detention centers during 1978 represent persons below the age of 18.

The rate of suicide among juveniles in adult jails during 1978 is 12.3 per 100,000 which is 4.6 times larger than the suicide rate of 2.7 per 100,000

among youth in the general population during 1977. We find that the difference between those two suicide rates is statistically significant. *The rate of
suicide among juveniles in adult lockups is 8.6 per 100,000 which is more
than three times larger than the rate of 2.7 among children in the general
population,* and that difference is also statistically significant. Unexpected-
ly, the suicide rate among children in juvenile detention facilities is only 1.6
per 100,000, which is lower than that of the general population, but this
difference is not statistically significant. The suicide rate of juveniles in
adult jails is almost 7.7 times larger than that of juvenile detention centers,
and that difference is statistically significant. Similarly, the suicide
rate among juveniles in adult lockups is more than five times larger than
that of juvenile detention facilities, and that difference is also statistically
significant.

Discussion

There is support for our hypothesis that the rate of suicide among
children held in adult jails and lockups is significantly higher than that
among children in juvenile detention centers and children in the general
population of the United States. However, the data do not indicate that the
suicide rate among youth placed in juvenile detention facilities is greater
than that of children in the general population. Several comments are perti-
nent to these observations. First, bear in mind that even the confidential
admission of the occurrence of a juvenile suicide in an institutional setting is
deeply embarrassing. To the extent that our data are characterized by
response bias, such bias would, in all likelihood, contribute to an underestimate of the suicide rate in jails and lockups. Second, the data indicate
that the average length of stay for children in jails is approximately seven
days while the average length of stay in lockups is less than two days. In
contrast, the average length of stay in juvenile detention facilities is seventeen days, and the suicide rate for children in the general population is calculated for an entire year or 365 days. In other words, children in adult jails
and lockups kill themselves more frequently than do children in juvenile
detention facilities and children in the general population despite the fact
that children in jails and lockups have less time in which to commit suicide.
Third, one must also bear in mind that it is more difficult to commit suicide
in jails and lockups than it is in the general population simply because the
techniques at one's disposal are much more limited. Together, these considerations imply that the problem of juvenile suicide in adult jails and lockups may well be even more serious than is suggested by our data per se.
Fourth, the validity of our primary hypothesis is bolstered by the fact that
seventeen of the suicides occurred despite the fact that in these cases sight

and sound separation had been accomplished. Finally, the low rate of suicide among children in juvenile detention centers may be attributable to the greater supervision which is available at those facilities, and to the participation by juveniles in the ongoing youth activities at those facilities as opposed to the isolation which they would often confront in adult jails and lockups.

Policy Implications

These data suggest that the policy of incarcerating children in adult jails and lockups may be contributing to a relatively high rate of suicide among those children. Further, in our data, eleven of twenty-two children who killed themselves while in jails and lockups had not committed a felony, which implies that many of those juveniles who are imprisoned in jails pose little threat to their communities. These findings also indicate that the problem of juvenile suicide is no more acute in juvenile detention centers than it is in the general population.

As noted earlier in this report, environmental and staffing limitations are common situations in adult jails and lockups. The effects of such living conditions worsen when isolation also occurs. This study has determined that the suicide rate for juveniles held in adult jails is about 4.6 times greater (12.3 per 100,000) than the suicide rate among youth in the general population (2.6 per 100,000). This high rate cannot be attributed to secure confinement alone since the suicide rate in separate juvenile detention facilities is well below that of the general youth population. Given this disparity in secure settings, it must be assumed that the high rate of juvenile suicides is attributable to the environmental and staffing conditions present in most adult jails and lockups.

The important point here is that nearly 500,000 juveniles experienced these detrimental conditions each year. If the physical and emotional well-being of juvenile offenders is to be a matter of concern, every effort must be made to prohibit the jailing of juveniles. The identification of these detrimental conditions should be the subject of continued investigation.

References

Bakwin, Ruth Morris, "Suicide in children and adolescents." *Journal of American Medical Women's Association*, 1973, 28: 643-50.

Barter, J. T., D. O. Swaback, D. Todd. "Adolescent suicide attempts." *Archives of General Psychiatry*, 1968, 19: 523-7.

Beall, Lynnette. "The dynamics of suicide: a review of the literature, 1897-1965." *Bulletin of Suicidology*, 1969 (March): 2-16.

Beigal, Allan and Harold E. Russell, "Suicidal behavior in jail: prognostic considerations." *Jail House Blues,* ed. by Bruce L. Danto, 1973, pp. 107-17. Orchard Lake, Michigan: Epic.

Cashion, Barbara G., "Durkheim's concept of anomie and its relationship to divorce." *Sociology and Social Research,* 1970, 55: 72-81.

Children's Defense Fund, "Children in Adult Jails," 1976, Washington, D.C.: Washington Research Project, Inc.

Danto, Bruce L., "Suicide at the Wayne County Jail: 1967-70," 1973, *Jail House Blues,* edited by Bruce L. Danto, Orchard, Michigan: Epic.

Danto, Bruce L., "The suicidal inmate," 1973, *Jail House Blues,* edited by Bruce L. Danto, Orchard Lake, Michigan: Epic.

Dorpat, T.L., J.K. Jackson, H.S. Ripley, "Broken homes and attempted and completed suicide," 1965, *Archives of General Psychiatry,* 12: 213-6.

Faigel, Harris C., "Suicide among young persons." 1966, "Suicide among young persons." *Clinical Pediatrics* 5: 187-90.

Fawcett, Jan and Betty Marrs, "Suicide at the county jail," 1973, *Jail House Blues* edited by Bruce L. Danto, Orchard Lake, Michigan: Epic.

Finch, S.M. and E.O. Pozanski, "Adolescent Suicide," 1971, Springfield, Illinois: Charles C. Thomas.

Fishman, Joseph F., "Crucibles of crime: the shocking story of the American Jail," 1969, Montclair, New Jersey: Patterson Smith.

Gibbs, J. "Stress and self-injury in jail," 1978, Unpublished dissertation, State University of New York at Albany.

Gibbs, J. "Psychological and behavioral pathology in jails: a review of the literature." 1978, Paper presented at the Special National Workshop on Mental Health Services in Local Jails; Baltimore, Maryland: September 27-29, 1978.

Gould, R.E., "Suicide problems in children and adolescents." *American Journal of Psychotherapy,* 1965, 19: 228-46.

Heilig, Sam M., "Suicide in jails: a preliminary study in Los Angeles County," 1973, *Jail House Blues* edited by Bruce L. Danto, Orchard Lake, Michigan: Epic.

Holinger, P.C., "Adolescent suicide: an epidemiological study of recent trends," *American Journal of Psychiatry,* 1978, 135: 754-56.

Jacobs, Jerry, *Adolescent Suicide.* 1971, New York: John Wiley.

James Howard, *The Little Victims: How American Treats its Children.* 1975, New York: David McKay.

Johnson, Robert, *Culture and Crisis in Confinement.* 1976, Lexington, Massachusetts: D.C. Heath.

"Youth hangs self in W. Va. jail that routinely ignored making cell-block inspection rounds." *Juvenile Justice Digest,* 1979, 7: 10.

Litman, R.E., "Police aspects of suicide," *Police,* 1966, 10: 14-18.

Looking Glass: The Newsletter of the Youth Policy and Law Center at Madison, Wisconsin, "Children in Wisconsin Jails," 1980, 4:7-11.

Lowell, Harvey D. and Margaret McNabb, *Sentenced Prisoners Under 18 Years of Age in Adult Correctional Facilities: A National Survey.* Washington, D.C.: The National Center on Institutions and Alternatives., 1980.

Mulcock, D., "Juvenile suicide: a study of suicide and attempted suicide over a 16-year period," *Medical Officer,* 1955, 94: 155-60.

Peck, Michael, "Suicide motivations in adolescents," *Adolescence,* 1968, 3: 109-18.

Peck, Michael, "Research and training in prevention of suicide in adolescents and youth," *Bulletin of Suicidology,* 1970, No. 6: 35-40.

Poulin, John E., John L. Levitt, Thomas M. Young, and Donnell M. Pappenfort, "Juveniles in detention centers and jails," *National Center for the Assessment of Alternatives to Juvenile Justice Pro-*

cessing, 1979, Chicago, IL: University of Chicago, The School of Social Service Administration.

Prentice, Ann E., *Suicide: A Selected Bibliography of Over 2,200 Items.* 1974, Metuchen, New Jersey: Scarecrow.

Sarri, Rosemary C., *Under Lock and Key: Juveniles in Jails and Detention.* 1974, Ann Arbor, Michigan: National Assessment of Juvenile Corrections.

Schrut, A., "Suicidal adolescents and children." *Journal of the American Medical Association,* 1964, 188: 1103-7.

Seiden, Richard H., "Suicide among youth: a review of the literature, 1900-1967." A supplement to the Bulletin of Suicidology, (December): 1-61.

Shaffer, D., "Suicide in childhood and early adolescence," *Journal of Child Psychology and Psychiatry,* 1974, 15: 275-91.

Shafii, Mohammad, Rick Oliphant, Kay Lutz, "Suicide in children and adolescents: incidence and patterns," 1979, Unpublished working draft; Department of Psychiatry, University of Louisville School of Medicine, Louisville, Kentucky.

Teicher, J.D. and J. Jacobs, "Adolescents who attempt suicide: preliminary findings," *American Journal of Psychiatry,* 1966, 122: 1248-57.

Toch, H., *Men in Crisis: Human Breakdowns in Prison.* 1975, Chicago: Aldine.

Toolan, J.M., "Suicide and suicidal attempts in children and adolescents." *American Journal of Psychiatry,* 1962, 118: 719-24.

U.S. Department of Commerce, Bureau of the Census. Criminal Justice Agency List. 1978, Unpublished but available on tape or printout from the Law Enforcement Administration (LEAA), Washington, D.C.

U.S. Department of Commerce, Bureau of the Census. Current Population Reports, Population Estimates and Projections, Series P-25, No. 870, 1980. Estimates of the Population of the United States by Age, Race, and Sex: 1976-1979. Washington, D.C.: U.S. Government Printing Office.

U.S. Department of Health, Education, and Welfare; Public Health Service; National Center for Health Statistics. 1979, Monthly Vital Statistics Report, Provisional Statistics, Annual Summary for the United States, 1978. Washington D.C.: U.S. Government Printing Office.

U.S. Department of Health, Education, and Welfare; Public Health Service; National Center for Health Statistics, 1980. Vital Statistics of the United States; Annual Summary, 1978: Mortality. Unpublished data available from the National Center for Health Statistics, Washington, D.C.

U.S. General Accounting Office, "Conditions in Local Jails Remain Inadequate Despite Federal Funding for Improvement: Report to the Congress by the Comptroller General. 1976, Washington, D.C.: U.S. Government Printing Office.

U.S. Senate Committee on the Judiciary. Hearings Before the Subcommittee to Investigate Juvenile Delinquency (91st Congress, 1st Session); Part 20: Conditions in Juvenile and Young Offender Institutions. 1971. Washington, D.C.: U.S. Government Printing Office.

Wilmotte, J.N. and J. Plat-Mendlewicz, "Epidemiology of suicidal behavior in one thousand Belgian prisoners," 1973, *Jail House Blues,* edited by Bruce L. Danto. Orchard Lake, Michigan: Epic.

Wooden, Kenneth, *Weeping in the Play Time of Others: America's Incarcerated Children.* 1976, New York: McGraw-Hill.

Woolen, J. M., "Suicide among Indian convicts under transportation," 1913, *Journal of Mental Sciences,* 59: 335-43.

14

Treatment of the Violent Incorrigible Adolescent

Vicki C. Agee

Within the population of disturbed youth there is a growing percentage of youth who, as a group, cause more problems than all other adolescents combined. These are the youths that combine hostile, aggressive, acting out behaviors with an amazing resistance to change, usually to the point that some frustrated treater terms them "incorrigible" or "untreatable." Compared to other problem adolescents, they engender a totally disproportionate cost in money, time, and effort to those agencies charged with educating, apprehending, and treating them. They hurt, and occasionally kill, people. They steal and/or destroy a great deal of property, and they repeatedly harm themselves. At the very least, they are extremely disruptive to the people they are around—in their homes, in schools, in placements, and in institutions. Schools and social agencies exert much effort trying to meet their needs, police occupy much of their time trying to apprehend them, and the legal system spends enormous amounts of money in prosecuting them. Further, there are high costs to social agencies for treatment attempts and placements in a variety of institutions and placements. In addition, the majority of these youths graduate into the adult institutional system, where they continue to be a significant drain on society's resources all their lives.

It is as difficult to label this group of youths as it is to treat them. They cross not only all psychiatric diagnostic categories but also the various differ-

Reprinted by permission of the publisher, from *Treatment of the Violent Incorrigible Adolescent* by Vicki L. Agee, (Lexington, Mass.: Lexington Books, D.C. Heath and Company, Copyright 1979, D.C. Heath and Company).

ential diagnostic systems. The only commonality of diagnoses is that they usually fall in the "severe" end of each diagnostic continuum. The psychotic and neurotic disorders are less often diagnosed in this population, but the character and personality disorders are well represented.

Because of the difficulty in psychiatric diagnoses, in this book, *aversive treatment evader* has been coined as a descriptive term for the typical behaviors of this group of youths. The term *aversive* refers to the effect these youths have on the people with whom they interact. Their habitual aggressive and often violent behavior makes most people attempt to avoid them. *Treatment evaders*, of course, refers to their ability to sabotage or resist attempts at intervention.

Following is a representative case history of an aversive treatment evader (ATE). It is obvious that there is no typical ATE. The following case history is cited to show the early onset of difficulties and a typical pathway through the system.

Tony. *Tony and his brother were abandoned by their parents when Tony was two and his brother was four. No one knew what happened prior to that time, only that the parents were transients. The boys were placed together in a foster home, where they stayed until Tony's brother was seven and was adopted by another family. Tony has never seen him since. At that time, Tony began showing problems of hyperactivity, immaturity, and distractibility. As soon as he entered school, he was reported to be disruptive and quite assaultive with the other children. When the social agency that had custody was notified, they decided to move him to another foster home.*

At age seven, Tony was sent to another foster home where he would remain the longest time. Unfortunately, the foster parents immediately began to see problems. He started developing effeminate behaviors and a liking to play in girls' clothes. He also increased his assaultiveness, and particularly attacked little girls. At one time he was discovered choking a little neighbor girl, and at another time he was caught choking a dog. In school, Tony was in a special program for behavior-problemed children, but he was becoming increasingly worse. His nemesis was peer relationships, as he was thoroughly disliked because of his aggressive "tough guy" facade, his immaturity, and his homely appearance. He also began running away from the foster home because "no one loved him."

At age twelve, Tony refused to go back to the foster home after one of his runaways, and they, in turn, refused to have him back. Tony was sent to his first group home. He promptly encountered his usual problems with peer relationships and began running away frequently. His behavior was also becoming bizarre enough that it was felt that he needed psychiatric care. He was placed in the children's division of the local state hospital. After four months, they felt he was improved enough to be placed again, and he was sent to a boys' ranch-type facility.

Whatever improvement that had taken place in the psychiatric setting did not generalize to the ranch, as his behavior was similar to his previous behavior. He was rejected by his peers because of his verbal and physical assaults and his immaturity. He also began running away. After a few runaways, the ranch decided they did not want him back. Since they were running out of placements and seemed to be making no headway, the social services agency brought court proceedings against Tony, and he was adjudicated as a status offender. He was placed in an open camp setting where he stabilized enough for six months that he was placed in another group home. As usual he began running away. During these runaways, however, his behavior took on a new twist, as he began selling his sexual favors to older homosexual males. A few months later, reportedly in a homosexual panic, Tony went to the emergency room of a local hospital and asked for psychiatric care. He stated that he felt he was going to kill himself because he was depressed because his parents and twelve siblings had been murdered, although he retracted the latter when questioned more closely.

Tony was transferred to a state hospital, where he assaulted staff and tried to run away from the adolescent treatment center the day he arrived. He fought continuously and had to be restrained for the rest of the night. The next day he began complaining of strange symptoms but was fairly cooperative for about a week, when he again assaulted staff and threatened to kill himself. A few weeks later he ran away but was apprehended fairly rapidly and returned. Again he had to be restrained several times for being out of control and violent. Two weeks later he attacked a staff member on the night shift and began beating her. He would have been successful in killing her had he not been interrupted by staff from another unit who were alerted by another patient. The nurse was unconscious when the other staff entered. Tony dropped her and managed to escape. He was picked up the next day in another state. He was charged with assault, adjudicated a delinquent, and was referred to the Closed Adolescent Treatment Center.

As can be seen from this representative case history, the ATE in this book is multi-symptomatic. Tony, during his childhood, showed hyperactivity, schizoid tendencies, sexually deviant behavior, depression and suicidal threats, chronic runaway, and violence toward others. By early adolescence, his disturbance was so severe that he was essentially untreatable in any but an institutional setting, and even institutional settings were unsuccessful in preventing his continuing deterioration.

Early Childhood

Although there are a few exceptions, the majority of ATEs show symptoms of disturbance in early childhood. These are not the situational-emotional reactions of adolescents to some situational trauma, as described by Marguerite Warren.[1] If there were someone around to tell the story, it is obvious that even prior to entry into the school system there were significant problems. Often there is no clear history, however, because the family situation usually is so chaotic that the disturbance of a small child does not stand out.

Typically, the early concerns revolve around behaviors that indicate the child is attempting to push people away or to reject control by others, usually in a violent manner. The acting out behaviors vary, but often include one or more of the following: physically attacking others, firesetting, frequent temper tantrums, cruelty to animals, vandalism, and running away.

Many, but not all, fit the description of the criminal child in Yochelson and Samenow's analysis of the criminal child.[2] The behaviors are different in quality and quantity from the normal independence-striving of a preschool child. The ATE child is punished often, in most cases with no significant change in behavior. This makes the role of punishment very difficult to interpret. As the punishment is often extreme and violent, it is easy to assume that it is a causative factor in the behavior problems. However, it can be assumed also that it is the intractable behavior that provides the stress on the parents, resulting in their loss of control. Yochelson and Samenow's review of the literature clearly indicates the lack of substantive answers to the question of what causes this type of behavior. Whatever the cause, from early childhood ATEs choose to behave in highly aggressive ways.

The following excerpts from the early childhood portion of the case history of "Tricia" are illustrative of the chaotic and destructive situations that one often finds in the background of the ATE.

Tricia *Tricia's mother is a prostitute, and her father is unknown. According to her maternal grandmother, Tricia's first year of life was extremely turbulent. She was often abused by her mother, who was reportedly schizophrenic and addicted to both drugs and alcohol. The grandmother described one incident when Tricia was crying and her mother tried to strangle her. The neighbors would frequently call the police because they heard Tricia and her younger sister, Dolly, crying. The grandmother would usually respond and find the children unfed, dirty, and their diapers unchanged. When Tricia was about one year old, her mother left town and left her with the grandmother. This was not unusual, because Tricia has a total of six siblings, all of whom are in foster care or some other setting.*

The grandmother also had the responsibility for Tricia's younger sister and her older sister. According to the grandmother, Tricia was the most disturbed of the three girls, and she felt it was because Tricia was the most severely abused of the three. She had severe temper tantrums if she did not get her needs met immediately. As the grandmother stated, "Tricia had to be first and most important."

It is really not certain what kind of care Tricia was given by her grandmother, but it is sure that she tried very hard to get other families to take Tricia and her younger sister, Dolly. Finally, when Tricia was six and Dolly five, their nursery school teacher and her husband (a very young couple) decided to adopt them because they felt the girls needed help. From the beginning both girls adjusted to the new family poorly, although Tricia was by far the worse, mainly because of her uncontrollable temper tantrums. The Browns sought professional help to no avail, and they finally put Tricia in the children's division of the local state hospital. She was there for six months, when the adoptive parents withdrew her against medical advice because they felt she was getting worse. After withdrawing her from therapy, apparently extremely severe methods were used for discipline. The neighbors reported that Tricia was locked in the basement for months and never allowed out. The Browns were also described as very rigid and controlled, and the children were required to sit still with their hands folded when visitors were in the house, and they were not allowed to play with the neighborhood children.

When Tricia was eleven, the Browns contacted the Welfare Department and asked to relinquish her for adoption. The authorities tried to work with them, but their rejection of Tricia was total; they told Tricia they wished they had never seen her. Three years later, they did the same with Dolly.

Predictably, by the time she was fifteen, Tricia had been in a total of ten different placements after the Browns rejected her. She was also acting out quite seriously and was considered highly assaultive and uncontrollable.

Again, this case history is fairly representational, as actual physical abuse and deprivation are not uncommon. Unlike Yochelson & Samenow's population, however, it is unusual to find both parents to be responsible people. In fact, it is quite common for at least one of the parents to have behavior very similar to the child's. An alcohol- or drug-abusing parent seems most likely to produce an ATE, and parents with various mental and character disorders come a close second. Occasionally one can look back through the generations and see, for example, grandparents and parents having identical behavior problems as the child. Whether this is due to genetic or environmental factors, or a combination of both, is not known.

The Early School Years

Public attention is usually first focused on the child when he or she enters school. Prior to that time they are too small to do much damage and are not impinging on so many people. Neighbors, for example, may be able to deal with assaultiveness with a preschool child by teaching their children to avoid the child. This does not work in the school setting, as the classmates are unable to avoid the acting out child, and parents and teachers necessarily move into protector roles for their children.

In addition to the behavior problems—hitting people, temper tantrums, chronic lying, low attention span, and impulsivity—it is not unusual for an ATE to be a fairly unattractive child. This may be contributed to by parental neglect or abuse, but, for whatever reason, it is another strike against the child. Much research has been done on the effects of personal attractiveness on others, and it is clear that both teachers and peers are more likely to reject an unattractive child.

The question arises as to what percentage of the ATEs is minimally brain damaged, as their symptoms are difficult to separate from the symptoms of minimal brain damage. The answer is that probably very few have identifiable organic problems. This, of course, may reflect difficulty in diagnosis rather than a normally functioning central nervous system. Nevertheless, it is crucial that these children be specially tested for learning disabilities, as their presence immeasurably compounds the problems.

Along with the obvious acting out, and the possible perceptual problems, the young ATE has major problems in relating to both peers and adults. In regard to peers, it is not infrequent that an adolescent ATE has never had a genuine friend. If they have acquaintances, they are what will later be referred to as "sliding partners"—or peers who find themselves in the same circumstances and get some reinforcement in having company in their misery. The shared activities are always negative ones, and the ATE may be a leader or a follower but is seldom just "one of the boys"—an average gang member. His behavior is far too erratic and untrustworthy for him to be included in such a well-structured group.

The teachers are confronted with an enormously problematic child, who often takes more time and attention to just control than the rest of the class. Before the days of strict controls over the schools' disciplinary systems, the young ATEs probably encountered much corporal punishment. In lieu of that, some teachers attempt to effect control by such methods as verbally confronting them in front of their peers. Unfortunately, this usually results in an unexpected effect. Since the young child probably has already experienced derision and hostility from his peers, he eventually becomes accustomed to this and gets some reinforcement out of negative attention—if one cannot do things right, there is some satisfaction in doing a thorough job of doing things wrong.

The next major tactic in attempting to deal with a young ATE in a classroom of normal children is to exclude them, first from the classroom, secondly from the school. Often, they will first be sent regularly to the principal's office, which is unfortunately a reinforcement for both child and teacher. The child is reinforced by the opportunity to briefly escape from an anxiety-producing situation—the classroom. Even though the discipline received from the principal's office is also anxiety producing, there is a gap in time before consequences are received, which makes the expected behavior very difficult to learn. Also, there is not the added factor of the peers witnessing the situation.

When visits to the "office" do not work, the next step is usually to assign the youth to a classroom designed for youths with similar behavior problems. With many youths, the individualized attention received in such a setting is helpful; with the ATE there is a stronger likelihood that the behavior will get worse. For one thing, the child has many new behaviors to model from peers; secondly, resistance to adult control often increases as they perceive that they can evade consequences for their behavior because they are in a class for "crazies."

The final exclusion is from the school itself, and most ATEs begin to experience suspension from school at a much earlier age than other acting out children. Again, this proves to be very reinforcing for both the child and the school personnel. The child is reinforced by being able to escape the unpleasant situation. The teacher and classmates are reinforced, of course, by the child's absence, and that becomes an easy solution when the situation arises.

In brief then, during the early school years, the clearest lessons learned from school by these children are: (1) they are different from their peers; and (2) by continuing to act out, they can escape from bad situations.

The Placement Years—Pre and Early Adolescence

During the early school years, various social agencies usually begin to get involved in an attempt at treating the ATE and find their efforts unsuccessful. The ATE's behavior problems, which have been slowly escalating during the first nine or ten years, begin to skyrocket in pre and early adolescence. This is for many reasons—the disruptive hormonal changes occurring, the increased importance of peer pressure, and the increased opportunity to learn negative behaviors and act on them. It is also at this age that law enforcement and court personnel begin to feel more comfortable in filing criminal charges. A seven year old hitting somebody is one thing—at twelve, depending on the circumstances, it can certainly be considered an assault. It is usual that most ATEs have essentially been breaking the law for years in one way or another, but the consequences are delayed until they seem old enough to accept some responsibility for their actions. Also, as stated previously, new opportunities present themselves. Although young children have fairly free access to various toxic vapors, they usually are fairly restricted from narcotics of various sorts. These become plentily available in most urban junior high schools. Although some sexual problems may be seen in early childhood, it is in early adolescence that sexual offenses begin to occur. Prior to this age, most out-of-home placements are attributed to parental neglect. It is at sometime during this stage that the ATE is first removed from home for his own unacceptable behavior, and the series of unsuccessful placements begins.

Unlike most disturbed children who enter the system, the ATEs obviously not only do not get better, they get worse. The usual progression through treatment in the community, out-of-home placements, and institutional placements is attempted and fails.

In regard to the first step, treatment in the community, the major dilemma is how to treat the patient in the setting that is presumed to have induced, or at the very least, added to the problems. There is great reluctance to remove a child from his or her home without considerable cause, so a concerted effort is made to treat the child and the family "in the community" via community mental health centers, school counselors, social service workers, and private psychiatrists and psychologists. This involves serious drawbacks. The percentage of mental health professionals trained to work with children and youth generally is quite small in any area of the country. Those who are trained to specialize in this age group are usually trained to work with fairly motivated children and their families. The majority of families who seek out professional help in the community are middle-class families who are "hurting" and will cooperate at least minimally in alleviating the problem. This is seldom the case with the ATE's family. The rejecting message they receive from their parents usually includes no desire to be involved in any attempt at alleviating the problems; parents may even actively sabotage attempts at doing so.

Secondly, most therapists are trained primarily in "talk therapy" techniques, which require a level of verbal, interpersonal perception and abstract thinking beyond most ATEs. This decreases the ATE's already abysmally low motivation for treatment. The hapless community treater is thus confronted with a hostile child and an equally resistive family, and must attempt the impossible—designing and carrying out a treatment plan with no control whatsoever over the environment. What frequently happens is that treatment attempts cease after a few sessions with either a silent or attacking child, missed appointments, and more. It is a rare community therapist who continues treatment with this type of child for an extended period of time.

The initial out-of-home placements are destined for failure, because the foster or group home parents are not prepared to handle the constant unpleasant testing of limits (and/or runaways) from very unlovable children. Also, the child is not prepared to leave the home. Rejected children very often have strong desires to remain with rejecting parents. Not only are the parents the only ones they have known, but also there seems to be a desperate need to undo the rejection ("I'll be good this time"). Reasons for ejection from placement vary. Sometimes it is the child's behavior, for example, running away, verbal or physical assault, stealing, truancy, sexual acting out, drug or toxic vapor use. At other times, the parent manages to get the child out of placement for brief periods of time, and the space in the foster or group home is promptly filled in the child's absence.

Unfortunately, with each placement several things occur. For one thing, the child becomes more resistive to establishing new relationships. Secondly, it is harder to find placement for children who have failed in previous settings.

Finally, the child has learned practically foolproof methods of getting out of settings they do not want to be in. Running away is the most common technique; few settings will tolerate a child for long who drops in for an occasional stay. Being hyperactive, assaultive, uncooperative also are very effective techniques for terminating a placement. Whatever the technique, or combination of techniques, with each placement the child gains a feeling of invulnerability—that no one can or will control him for long.

ATEs' lack of sequential planning is an important factor in the numerous placements. Most adults are rather amazed that the youths do not conceptualize that each time they get ejected from placement, they end up generally in a more restrictive one—a "regressive move" in adult correctional terminology. This is expected to be an effective deterrant and, in fact, is frequently used as a threat: "If you do not behave here, you will get sent to _____." Neither the threats nor the regressive moves can overcome the effects of the immediate reinforcement the child receives on terminating a placement. For one thing, the pain of being forced to relate to adults and peers is instantly removed as are restrictive rules and regulations. Secondly, there is often a significant time-gap in placements, wherein there is much freedom to act out without adult control. ATEs' problem with sequential planning prevents them from seeing "the larger picture." The only connection that is made is that between the immediate behavior and its results. For example, the thought process might be "If I run away, I get to go home." The next step, "and then I'll get picked up and sent to a detention center," does not figure into the ATE's cognitive processes. Each new placement becomes a new challenge to resisting control.

After a series of failures in community placement, the next step is an institution. This may be a private or public mental health institution, or a correctional institution. Often a child's social class will determine whether he goes through the mental health system prior to entering the correctional system.

The Mental Health System and the ATE

The mental health movement of the sixties with its well-meant, but not well thought out emphasis on deinstitutionalization, resulted in numerous problems when providing services to the ATE. With the basic tenet that all institutions are bad for people, most adolescent programs were designed to provide short-term "crisis intervention," usually in an unlocked setting, with prompt return to the community. Unfortunately, those youths who could not benefit from such a program (or those who had already experienced much of the same sort of thing in various community settings) had to be excluded from consideration—much as if they did not exist. With a similar sort of logic that resulted in chronic adult patients being herded to boarding homes and nursing homes so that they wouldn't be "institutionalized," ATEs (among others) were excluded from mental health institutions because they did not or would not "benefit from treatment." At this time, the long smoldering argument about the difference between a disturbed youth who needs treatment and the bad youth who needs structure and limits (usually meaning punishment) began to surface into a clarion call. (This will be discussed further later in the chapter.)

Leaving the area of exclusion from treatment for a moment, those ATEs that were admitted to treatment often found a treatment program that was ill-designed for youths with their problems. Again, the most popular mode of treatment emerging during the mental health movement of the sixties was a rather free, unfettered approach often described as a "therapeutic community." This widely used, and highly adapted version of Maxwell Jones' "Therapeutic Community"[3] revolved around a basic tenet that patients were to be responsible for themselves. Unfortunately, in the worst of situations, this meant that there was essentially no treatment program. What there was was an individualized approach based on each youth deciding what he or she needed to do to change and then deciding how to go about doing it. Most of the "real treatment" would take place not in one-to-one relationships with a therapist or in intensive group therapy, but in an environment of peers and adult staff members that would be designed to be conducive to good mental health. Again, in many settings, the environment could better be described as nontherapeutic. The peers, having no experience in being positive models for anything, were negative models for learning new "crazy" and/or acting out behaviors. The staff seldom intervened, partly because of the "individual responsibility" philosophy and partly because, in the era of encounter groups, they were often quite involved in treating each other.

This is, of course, an indictment of mental health settings that is unfair as all simplistic generalizations are unfair. Possibly many good efforts at treatment could be cited. Nevertheless, in general, the mental health institutions were of little help to the ATE, and, because ATEs were effectively eliminated from the system, most mental health settings continue to be of little help to them.

The Youth Correctional System and the ATE

In every society there are "dumping grounds" for those who persist in not fitting in. Prior to the mental health movement of the sixties, the correctional and mental health systems shared jointly in this responsibility. With the movement of mental health patients from institutions back into the community, however, the correctional system began to get more than its share of "dumpees." The undefinable, but oft-cited, community received right back in their laps many of those it wished to reject. In spite of all the rhetoric, they were ill-prepared for this responsibility, and the only way to reject again the deviate was to expand the possibilities for ending up in the correctional system. In the juvenile justice system, for example, a movement which was intended to decrease the population in the institutions increased it for quite a while before people were aware of the results. The "status offender" laws were created in most states to treat differently the youths who had committed crimes that would not be crimes if they were adults—truancy, runaway, and not obeying parents. The laws then provided for court custody and often placement in a correctional institution. There was usually little difference in the provisions of the laws between status offenders and delinquents, except the label, which was imagined to be of grave importance to the child. Unfortunately, in many states it seemed easier for courts to adjudicate a child as a status offender than a delinquent. Many times the petition to commit came from a mental health institution or a social services agency. Thus, rather than protecting status offenders, as the original intention was, the laws often resulted in more commitments to correctional institutions. Although there was also a movement in youth corrections toward "community corrections," the fact that these youths were court committed to institutions made this very difficult. Many ATEs made their first contact with the court as status offenders.

Along with attempts to establish community programs, another revolution was occurring within the youth correctional system. Because of both legal precedents and a "new wave" of correctional approaches in the sixties, traditional youth correctional institutions were expected to provide treatment to their clients, rather than the previous expectation of custody (with the unspoken expectation of some punishment thrown in). The youth correctional institutions found themselves in a serious predicament. Traditionally very low staffed, with untrained personnel in subaverage facilities, the correctional institutions were faced with providing treatment, not only to the "average delinquent" (a serious enough task) but also to the status offender on one end and the ATE on the other. The decade of the sixties saw gargantuan efforts to do so all across the country, with some success. Unfortunately there was none with the ATE. The ATE generally proceeded to do exactly what had been successful in previous placements—act out, run away, disrupt the program for everyone, and assault people. As with all previous settings, attempts were made to exclude them from the system—not an easy job with court commitments. First, attempts to transfer them to mental health settings were attempted, with incredible resistance on the part of most mental health institutions. In the rare circumstance that an ATE was accepted into a mental health institution, the situation was definitely short-term. The caustic joke among youth correctional workers "We drive them there, they beat us back" became a byword. Another avenue was to attempt to transfer the ATEs to the adult correctional system—the final dumping ground. This avenue was cut off or severely interfered with by legal opinions requiring legal hearings before transfer to adult correctional systems. When all else failed, they were occasionally released back to the community on parole. The joke that one could "flunk reform school" was not as far-fetched as it sounded.

One very positive result of the pressure on youth correctional institutions to provide treatment was the emergence of the first significant differential diagnostic models, most notably the Interpersonal Maturity Level System[4] and the Quay System.[5] This was an impressive step in two ways: first in that it emerged from youth corrections, traditionally not conceived of as progressive, and second, that the philosophy clearly elucidated that different types of youth need different types of treatment. This is a simplistic concept but one that had long been ignored. Whatever new treatment fad appeared traditionally would have been applied "carte blanche" to all types of youth, as traditional psychiatric diagnoses did not generally lead to differential treatment approaches. Also, traditional psychiatric diagnoses were quite unreliable and open to the abuses now described.

The Name Game

One of the most effective ways of avoiding having to treat the ATE youth is by selective admission policies. Since youth corrections admissions are controlled by courts, not by diagnostic staff as in mental health, the "game" is controlled by a mental health orientation.

The "name game" of course refers to the process of selectively admitting youths to treatment programs via their psychiatric diagnostic label, or certain diagnostic characteristics. Certainly this is a realistic factor in program design; no one can be expected to treat everybody. Also, each treatment program would like to work with those clients that have the highest probability of success. Unfortunately, ATEs almost always lose out in this process.

A major part of the name game is the diagnosis itself. The usual tactic is to attempt to differentiate between the "emotionally disturbed" and the "character-disordered youth." The neurotic and psychotic diagnoses lump in the first category (along with miscellaneous "wastebasket" categories such as adolescent adjustment reaction). The second category is mainly for sociopathic disorders and aggressive personality syndromes. In the former category, one of the positives is that there are very few psychotic adolescents, and neurotics, by virtue of their overt anxiety and guilt, are presumably easier to treat. The latter category has no real positives. Character disorders are unpleasant types who are generally thought of as having no consciences, little if any human emotions such as warmth and caring, an inability to profit from experience, illogical thinking, and a deep resistance to treatment. In fact, in many settings a diagnosis of some type of character disorder is tantamount to a diagnosis of untreatable. Although a few ATEs may be diagnosed as psychotic or neurotic, the majority have a label of character or personality disorder.

Many mental health professionals feel that the place for all character disorders is some sort of correctional setting, implying that they need punishment, "structure," and custody, and that they do not need treatment. This implication can be couched in very sophisticated mental-health-ese, such as "the patient needs to learn to accept the consequences for his actions in the correctional system," or "the patient has benefited maximally from treatment and needs to be in a structured setting where firm controls can be set over his behavior."

This differentiation can be carried to the absurd to the point that youths who act out or have behavior problems are excluded from treatment because they have no "underlying emotional disturbance"—which would presumably indicate that their behavior is more or less motivated by an empty organism, with no feelings or thought processes. The author was present when a board member of a psychiatric hospital planning a new adolescent treatment center said, "We must be certain that this is for emotionally disturbed adolescents and not for those with behavior problems." When asked if behavior-disordered youth did not also have some underlying emotional disturbance, the answer was that there was a big difference: "Some kids are sick and some are just bad."

This introduces another reason that ATEs are usually excluded from treatment—they are often lower-class or minority group youths. The mental health system is designed by and for bright, verbal, middle-class whites. In some cultural groups, most notably black and Chicano, it is much preferred to be termed "bad" than "crazy." In the Anglo culture, prison has more stigma than a mental health institution. Therefore, to question a black or Chicano about what problems they need to work on in an institution (which is a fairly routine question in admission evaluations), is suggesting that they are "crazy" and the response will probably indicate that there is "little motivation for treatment." There are several other characteristics of intake or admission interviews that are really only appropriate to a fairly circumspect group of people. Many hospitals send an evaluation team of several people to question the prospective patient. This is, of course, overwhelming to many people, particularly lower-class and minority group youth. The questions themselves often imply a high level of abstraction: "What do you plan to work on while you are in the hospital?" Again, a vague or concrete answer to this question will result in a diagnosis of "not motivated for treatment," which is ample reason for exclusion in many institutions.

Another problem which now is not quite as prevalent, is the practice of insisting that family members participate in treatment—otherwise the patient will not be accepted or will be discharged. With maddening logic, the philosophy was that they could not help the identified patient if they could not change the family; therefore they wouldn't try if the family wouldn't cooperate. As stated earlier, the families of ATEs many times effectively blocked treatment for their children by refusing to cooperate.

Following is an excerpt from a case history of a female ATE showing a transition into a youth correctional setting by a youth who had essentially never broken the law.

Susie. *Susie began to be very difficult to handle somewhere between the ages* *of three and four, a few months after having had a high fever and convulsions* (there was some question of meningitis). *She had febrile convulsions until age four and was given Phenobarbital to control the seizures. This possibly contributed to her increasingly out-of-control behavior. She was hyperactive, had violent mood swings, seemed not to learn from experience, and refused to work in school. Even as a small child she seemed obsessed with sex. In addition, she was eneuretic (day and night).*

Susie's school career began with her assaulting other children in Headstart. She was placed in "transition classes" after a stormy kindergarten and remained in them throughout elementary school. Her behavior continued to be poor, and she was reported to have many emotional problems. Her third-grade teacher described her as having a hard time getting along with peers, lying frequently, using foul language, and being constantly out of her seat. Her sixth-grade teacher described periods of average behavior and at other times unacceptable behavior much like that already described.

The year that Susie started junior high she was transferred to classes for the educationally handicapped. Because of increasingly poor behavior, she was placed at a private institution for children with learning problems and organic disorders, along with behavior problems associated with organicity. After seven months, Susie was discharged from the institution as being "not ameable to treatment."

Within a week after being discharged from the institution she was taken to a juvenile detention center by her parents. They insisted that she be placed outside the home because they could not control her. The detention center placed her in a group home where she lasted a week before being returned to the detention center as "uncontrollable." The detention center diagnostician then referred her to the local state hospital's adolescent treatment program. The evaluator from the state hospital refused admission, but stated that a treatment program could be initiated there "if and when Susie has acquired sufficient behavioral controls and motivation for treatment." For lack of an alternative and with essentially no record of delinquency, Susie was sent to a juvenile correction institution on a status offender's petition.

At the juvenile institution, Susie was every bit as uncontrollable as she had been in the past. She was very defiant of rules, did not trust peers or adults, had temper tantrums, and ran away. Once she cut her hand by putting it through a window. She was finally referred to the Closed Adolescent Treatment Center. Unfortunately, a case history like Susie's is not uncommon, and, in fact, both juvenile institutions and adult correctional institutions across the United States have inmates whose case histories are fairly similar.

The Dumping Syndrome

Avoidance is a commonly used method of dealing with ATEs, and when they are not successfully avoided, a rather prompt subsequent step is to attempt to get someone else to take responsibility for them as soon as possible. Usually, the more physically assaultive the ATE, the faster this process becomes. This is not a habit pattern that is limited to the mental health field—it is also fairly common in youth corrections (although made more difficult by legal commitments).

Following are several excerpts from a psychiatric case record on an ATE girl in a mental health institution:

Ruth. Course of Illness and Summary of Treatment. *On admission, Ruth frequently isolated herself from the others. As she did begin to interact, her behavior became more belligerant and demanding. This habit of being isolative or belligerant continued throughout her stay. When Ruth's disruptive behavior earned her restriction, she generally was able to do it and was pleasant for a short time afterward. It appears that Ruth finds close relationships threatening and extremely difficult to handle . . . Her behavior was also evident in her peer relationships. At times, she would interact appropriately and then for no apparent reason set up a hassle, leading her to rejection.*

At the end of her first month, Ruth left the cottage without permission and went home. She was allowed to stay for the weekend. When she returned, her behavior was bizarre. She handled her restriction well. In early June, Ruth left the cottage again without permission and went home. She was placed in Juvenile Hall, pending a filing of a status offender petition. Staff of Juvenile Court refused to file, but did agree that one more run would necessitate a petition. Ruth appeared to understand this, and she never again left the hospital without permission.

Ruth had difficulty with the behavior modification program and the token economy. She was frequently in debt or on restriction for her combative or disruptive behavior. Ruth's physical combativeness had decreased during her stay here. She continues to be isolative and to sleep whenever she is allowed. She is seen as irritable and at times preoccupied with her thoughts. She has used group meeting to explain some feelings, and this usually leads to some acting out behavior . . . her thinking becomes loose and her behavior bizarre as pressure is put on her.

Ruth attended school and there her performance fluctuated greatly. . . . She was chosen to attend a two-week backpacking trip during July. She did very well, and a decrease in her disruptive and isolative behavior was noted for approximately two or three weeks following the experience.

The plan was for Ruth to be placed, and referral was made to a residential treatment setting.

Disposition and Aftercare Plans. *After several discussions with Mrs. Smith of Child Welfare and Ruth's mother, plans were made for Ruth to be placed at the*

Blank Children's Home. She expressed reluctance to go, but a week later she was transported there by staff. Ruth seemed reluctant to leave, crying and refusing to leave the car. She was persuaded to try the placement for a week but she ran away as soon as the car door opened. Ruth was running from Blank Children's Home when staff had to leave. She will be discharged as of this date. Both her mother and Mrs. Smith were notified of this fact. (Note: on the actual case history, the following note was penciled in after the typing: "It was felt Ruth needed to learn to relate to the staff at Blank Children's Home.")

Ruth's behavior is similar in its frustration-potential to all ATEs. The results are also similar: an attempt was made to transfer her to the juvenile correctional system via a status offender petition, which was eventually successful; after a very short period of time (two to three weeks) of what was probably barely adequate behavior control, she was placed precipitously—so precipitously that she had to be forced from the car—and the staff left as she was running down the street. (The penciled note at the end of the Disposition and Aftercare Plans makes the hurried placement seem even more ludicrous, as it is difficult to image how Ruth could "learn to relate to the staff" as she was running down the street.)

Following are the last few sentences from a psychiatric case record on a thirteen-year-old male, called Ralph, whose behavior was almost identical to Ruth's.

Ralph. *Ralph was taken off his medication, and on several occasions, when things were going badly for him and he was getting upset, he asked to be placed back on the medication, which did not happen. Following discussion of plans to place him on extended leave with parents in December, Ralph exhibited hostile and negative behavior. Nevertheless Ralph was placed on extended leave status with his parents at _____. He was then discharged from leave status.*

Again one has the strong suspicion that the primary motivation was Ralph's removal from the program, rather than the best possible placement. In this particular case, both parents had been severely abusive.

At times, the institution that is unable to find an alternate placement is successful in returning the child, essentially untouched, to the referring institution. Following are brief excerpts from a psychiatric case record of a twelve-year-old ATE.

Sean. *Sean was brought to the state hospital because of his extremely aggressive behavior in the detention center, where he had been placed because of running away from home and stealing.* (Note: the next several paragraphs describe the serious acting out in the hospital setting, including assaultiveness on female staff and a peer, fantasies of killing his mother or himself, sexual problems, and severe "authority problems.")

Termination came about as Sean ran away from the hospital and was caught by the police while breaking into a private home. The decision was made to return Sean to the Detention Center and the courts rather than permitting him to return to the hospital.... At the time of termination, we had been in touch with Welfare in terms of arranging a foster placement for Sean. Inasmuch as it appeared that a placement was going to be at least a month away, it was decided not to permit Sean to return to the hospital following his second runaway. This decision was made due to the lack of Sean's responsiveness to our program after three months in residence.

Sean is a very hostile, angry child, whose acting out and antisocial behavior is related to his anger at mother's rejection. It is thought that if he were in a long-term placement in a benign setting where he would have structure, limits, and controls, then he might be helped. If he does not receive such help, however, it is thought that he will continue to develop along antisocial lines, which ultimately will probably lead to placement in a correctional facility.

Not surprisingly, Sean did end up in a correctional facility rather shortly after this report was written. There are several rather obvious indications of irresponsibility in this report. Most obviously, he was returned to the place which had sought help in controlling him, with no real rationalization for doing so nor help offered. Since the average detention center is a court-related facility designed to hold youths awaiting trials, the usual situation is one staff member on duty (who is not a trained treatment person), and the necessity for much of the time spent in locked rooms, with essentially no treatment. Although detention centers vary greatly in their degree of humaneness, they are essentially designed to be "mini-jails." The average mental health institution, on the other hand, has at least a one-to-one staffing ratio, and the staff is highly trained. Therefore, the dumping process seems all the more ludicrous, since in effect they are asking the "dumpees" to do something they are unable to do. The reasoning that the fault lies with the child's "lack of responsiveness to treatment" is also a frequently used excuse for ejecting a youth from the setting. The illogical part involves the premise that the mental health centers are the "experts" in providing treatment; therefore, if the patient is not benefiting, he is not treatable. This circular reasoning is a very effective way of preventing mental health professionals from having to question the effectiveness and quality of the treatment they provide.

A final note on the case of Sean is the empty recommendation for a "long-term placement in a benign setting where he would have structure, limits, and controls." Again, this is a common tendency, to recommend a utopian placement which obviously does not exist. Again, if the setting the child was in was not a "benign" one and did not provide structure, limits, and controls they claim the child needed, then how could they claim to have provided the expert treatment?

Footnotes

[1]C.E. Sullivan, M.Q. Grant, and J.D. Grant, "The Development of Interpersonal Maturity: Applications to Delinquents," *Psychiatry,* 20 (1957): 373-395.

[2]Samuel Yochelson and Stanton Samenow, *The Criminal Personality, Vol. I: A Profile for Change* (New York: Jason Aronson, 1976), pp. 55-152.

[3]Maxwell Jones, *The Therapeutic Community: A New Treatment Method in Psychiatry* (New York: Basic Books, 1953).

[4]*Op. Cit.,* Sullivan *et al*

[5]H.D. Quay, *"Personality Dimensions in Delinquent Males as Inferred from Factor Analysis of Behavior Ratings" Journal of Research in Crime and Delinquency,* 1 (1964): 33-37.

15

The Exploitation Matrix in a Juvenile Institution

Clemens Bartollas, Stuart J. Miller
and Simon Dinitz

Victimization of juveniles in institutions has received little attention in the criminological literature. Fisher[1] was the first to deal specifically with victimization, defining what it means and developing the various types of victimization which took place in the institution he studied. Davis[2] raised disturbing questions about the extent to which juveniles were the victims of stronger inmates in the Philadelphia Van System. In his study, he pointed out that inmates of all ages and degree of criminality were stored together in vans awaiting disposition of their cases. The consequence of this was that younger boys had no chance as older, predatory males took advantage of them by beating and homosexually raping them, sometimes en masse. Polsky[3] mentioned that homosexuality is a concern in juvenile training schools, but failed to go into depth about it. Huffman[4] reported that 62 youthful offenders had to be transferred for psychiatric observation because of homosexual involvement over a three year period in the state of Illinois. And Barker and Adams, in describing the social organization of a juvenile institutions, portrayed how inmate leaders victimized inmates lower in the pecking order.

The purpose of this study is to explore the types of exploitation which took place at the various levels of the peer hierarchy, the social processes of

Reprinted with permission from *International Journal of the Sociology of Law,*
1976, 4, 257-270.

exploitation, the stimulus qualities related to exploitation, the ranking of the various types of exploitation, and the varieties of sexual behavior.

The Institutional Setting

The institution studied is considered end-of-the-line and is reserved for overly hostile and aggressive males ranging in age from 15 to 18 years. These boys, 51% black and 48% white, are considered to be the hard core delinquents in the state. The majority of these youths have committed serious personal and property offenses with 2.4 being the average number of previous commitments to state institutions. Additionally, one-half have been diagnosed as dangerous to others and 20% more as emotionally disturbed. As one administrator put it, "There is no innocence here."

The boys are housed in eight cottages joined by corridors connecting school, vocational, and recreational areas. Each cottage has a living, dining, and recreational area, offices for the youth leaders and a social worker, two four-bed dormitories, and 16 single rooms. Although only 149 boys were in residence at the time of the study, the institution can accommodate 192 boys. The youth leaders, who have more contacts with boys than anyone else, are 97% black.

Methods

Initial interviews with several experienced staff members who work directly with inmates indicated that food, clothes, and cigarettes were the major form of material exploitation, whereas masturbation of others, oral and anal sodomy were the forms of sexual exploitation.

Additionally, we administered a number of in-depth interviews with three line staff members which were tape recorded; and, as soon as we discovered the most blatant exploiters and the most extreme victims, they too were formally interviewed using a tape recorder.[5] Also, every one of the 62 line staff (youth leaders and social workers) as well as three-fifths of the 149 inmates were talked with informally throughout the year of data collection.

Since we wanted to be able to differentiate the exploiters from the exploited, we analyzed the demographic, criminal history, psychological, and physical characteristics of all residents. Specific factors examined included the number of previous commitments, number of previous offenses, and the seriousness of the offense leading to the present commitment. Further, data on other characteristics including age at admission, I.Q., and the weight and height of the boys were collected.

One of the most helpful methods in discovering the exploitation matrix was four years of participant observation by one of the authors. Employed by the institution in varying capacities, this author was able to delve into the behind-the-scenes processes of cottage living from the viewpoint of the inmates, and this ethno-methodological approach yielded an in-depth description of institutional life. It also gave a much wider perspective to victimization in this particular institution than the one year of data collection could have possibly given.

This combined method revealed that 72% of the boys were exploited by other inmates (some of these also exploited others), that another 18% were exploiters only, and that, taken together, the figures indicated that a total of 90% of the residents were either exploiters or exploited. Thus, 90% of the boys found that their lives revolved around either exploiting others or avoiding exploitation. Some staff felt that about 50% of the boys' waking hours were spent in figuring out how to take advantage of others, and other significant portion of their time must be spent in determining how to protect themselves.

The Exploitation Matrix

The exploitation matrix which emerged in each cottage typically was composed of four groups. At the top was an inmate leader called a heavy. Almost always black, this heavy was assisted by three or four black lieutenants who make up the second ladder of the matrix. The third group was made up of 8 to 16 black and white residents. This third group was divided into a top half of mostly blacks who were called alright guys, with the bottom half composed mostly of whites who were referred to as chumps. The lowest group in the pecking order was made up of one or two boys called scapegoats. Generally white, they were the sexual objects for boys further up the ladder. Finally, one or two boys managed to remain independent of the matrix, for they neither exploited others nor were exploited themselves.

In general, the form of exploitation at each level of the hierarchy was fairly clear cut.[6] The power of the inmate leaders protected them from victimization and also enabled them to attain whatever they wanted from peers. These heavies were divided into aggressive and cooperative types, and varied considerably in their interaction with peers.[7] For example, the cooperative heavy was more of a mediator of cottage conflict and was involved in little overt exploitation. When he became aware that someone had stepped out of line and was creating problems in the cottage, he would then pass an order to bring the offender into line to one of his lieutenants. Or, if he desired something (usually food) from the youth leaders or social worker's office, orders were given to one of the lieutenants who either carried it out or passed the order on down the line to someone in the third level. The aggressive heavy, on the other hand, differed in that his power and control were based on the open use of brute force and violence. He felt no reservation about the fact that others were aware of his exploitative acts, and both peers and staff resisted his ascension to power because of the disruptions caused by his aggressive behavior. For instance, he took food, clothing, cigarettes, and sex from weaker youths. Since his power rested upon his ability "to use his hands," all youths were kept in a constant state of tension, fearful of a confrontation.

On the second ladder of the exploitation matrix, lieutenants had to manage their roles very carefully. While on one hand they needed to prove that they were tough and smart enough to become heavy, they lessened their chances of acceptance by peers and staff if they were too aggressive. Victimized somewhat because they carried out the heavy's wishes, which may result in a staff's "bust," they were generally able to exploit almost anything they wanted from those further down the ladder. Since staff did not regard the exploitation of minor material items (food, cigarettes and pop) to be serious, lieutenants were usually permitted considerable leeway in extorting these items from weaker peers. Sexual exploitation, nevertheless, involved much more risk because it could prolong their institutionalization and decrease their chances of becoming a cooperative heavy.

The sexual exploiters, whether they were aggressive heavies, lieutenants, or from the next rung down the ladder, were called booty bandits. Directing most of their sexual activities toward whites and an occasional willing black, no affection—especially with whites—was involved. The sex play was done simply to relieve sexual frustration; in spite of the risks involved, there appeared to be a sense of commitment to this type of behavior. Potential victims were harassed physically and psychologically, and the target was beaten upon, teased, and coerced in all possible ways. Although a few white booty bandits were found in this institution, they directed their predatory activity toward whites. In terms of motivation, they, like black booty bandits, defined sexual exploitation as an acceptable means of satisfying sexual desires.

In comparison to the first two groups, there was little upward mobility manifested in the third group. The major exception to this was the youth new to the institution who aspired for the top leadership positions. However, in terms of exploitation, there were significant differences in the alright guys and chumps. All-right guys, for example, gave up some material items, but very seldom were peers able to convert them to sexual victims. Usually well liked and willing to fight to protect themselves, they simply were not given the higher status awarded more aggressive peers. Conversely, the chumps lost many of their material possessions, and were sometimes physically pushed around by fellow residents. Even though they lacked respect and had poor interpersonal relationships, they maintained their social status on the third ladder of the pecking order until they were sexually exploited. Then, if discovered, the chump could become the cottage scapegoat.

Cottage scapegoats ended up on the bottom of the pecking order because they were sexually victimized. But for inmates to be assigned this lowly status, it was necessary for them to submit several times to anal sodomy or become involved as the passive victim in oral sodomy or masturbation of others. Still, their sexual victimization must become known to peers. One factor protecting them was that sexual exploiters did not usually publicize their sexual exploits, even to their closest friends. But once labelled as the scapegoat, this youth became an amenable sexual victim, and inmates reacted by "putting him on a shelf" and making him a social outcast. Feeling that his sexual victimization had changed him, peers refused to have anything to do with this social pariah. For example, they acted as if he were not present with them in the same room, and were even reluctant to take his food, cigarettes, and other material items.[8]

Independent of the exploitation matrix were two groups of boys in each cottage. Infrequent in number, the first group was made up of youths who thought more about their futures, interacted more with staff, and were quite concerned about their community adjustment. Their obvious physical prowess enabled them to thwart attempts to victimize them. And, in fact, this first group sometimes helped scapegoats get "off the bottom." The second group was different in that they avoided the matrix simply becaue they wanted to "do their time and get out." Their size and physical strength deterred aggressive peers from exploiting them.

Varieties of Homosexual Behavior

Indeed, the impression gathered from the data was that material exploitation was almost incidental—even though it contributed to feelings of resentment and poor self esteem on the part of victims—and that boys' actual ranking on the matrix depended on how far away they were from being sexually exploited. When it became obvious that sexual exploitation was unlikely or out of the question, then attention was focused on how many material goods could be extorted from victims. Further, only victims were labelled as homosexuals in this institution, regardless of their motivation.

The first type was made up of youths who willingly had homosexual encounters in other institutions, but came to this institution hoping to leave their past behind. Nevertheless, once their peers became aware that they had been victimized sexually in other places, great pressure was placed on them to continue this sexual behavior. Finally submitting to the persistent pressure from their peers, these youths sometimes became committed to homosexuality as a life style before leaving the institution.

The second type was the youths who gave up sex in exchange for something else. Inmates out of cigarettes, for instance, would occasionally masturbate another for a pack or two. Also, a few whites bought protection from a strong black peer because they did not want to be slapped around or sexually victimized by several peers. Thus, they exchanged sexual privileges for protection.

The third group of labelled homosexuals was the passive and dependent boys who submitted strictly out of fear. Afraid of being physically attacked and mentally fatigued from the harassment received from black peers, these residents were simply overwhelmed by their environment. Usually middle-class whites, they felt lost and alone—very much in a state of anomie. In addition, there was some indication on the psychological tests that these youths had some need of self-abasement and humiliation.

The fourth group, moreover, was quite different, in that they were lower-class whites who came into the institution with reputations of being "tough guys." But either in gang rapes or an encounter with an extremely aggressive black, these youths were sexually victimized. Few in number, these boys sometimes experienced a drastic change in personality after the incident, becoming passive and losing their confidence. In one incident, a lower-class white who had pushed others around became quite passive after a gang rape, and ended up becoming the cottage's scapegoat.

The fifth group was made up of white or black youths who "trade-off" with another white or black because they liked and wanted to feel close to each other. Intra-racial in nature, most of these sexual affairs were characterized by the exchange of friendship, rather than the coercion or exploitation. Consequently, their voluntary behavior would come close to what is considered to be true homosexuality. But even here, the relationship appeared to be temporary and a function of institutional living.

A final group was made up of youths called queens. In contrast to scapegoats who were white, queens were almost always blacks. And, in spite of the fact that their numbers have been small over the past several years, the disruptions caused by their presence far outweighs the importance of their numbers. Playing the role of women both in dress and mannerisms, booty bandits, in particular, vied for their favor and attention. Sometimes, aggressive inmates were caught kissing the queen, and it was not unusual for aggressive boys to fall in love with a queen.

Ranking of Exploitation

Compared to what was available in the community, institutional living represented deprivation. Subsequently, the politics of scarcity became a way of life, and every item has a value blown out of all proportion to what it would have in the community. Not surprisingly, each item available ended up rank-ordered according to its importance. Boys, thus, became quickly aware of the status importance of each item and what it would mean to them providing they were willing to give it up. Consequently, boys decided to draw the line where they would permit themselves to be exploited, but vigorously resisting victimization beyond that. Certainly, this point usually changed over a period of a boy's stay because he generally gave up more early in his stay than he would later. Situationally, too, a predicament might arise when he felt a compromise was necessary, but then would revert, if possible, back to what he felt was acceptable. Obviously, this ranking was important because peer respect was greatly affected by how much a youth was willing to give up.

Figure 1 shows the rank ordering of the various items and sexual acts found in this institution, and is set up so that items of least value are listed first.[9]

Item 1 refers to cake and other desserts served for lunch and supper and was one which boys had little reluctance in giving up. Item 2 had a little more value because certain foods were highly desired when available and boys exhibited more resistance in giving them up. Item 3 refers to pop and candy brought back from the canteen on Saturday morning. Belonging to boys and purchased by their money, these items were seen to have more status than the best institutional food. To be expected, item 4 had even greater value because "mom" brought it from home. The next item resulted in greater loss of status, since it created conflict with staff for wearing dirty institutional clothing and this conflict could prolong institutionalization.

Institutional dessert 1	Institutional favorite foods 2	Canteen pop and candy 3	Parents' pop and candy 4
Institutional clothing 5	Toilet articles 6	Cigarettes 7	Personal clothing clothing 8
Radios 9	Physical beating on 10	Anal sodomy 11	Masturbation of others 12
Oral sodomy 13			

Fig. 1 Ranking of material and sexual exploitation.

Item 6 is again concerned with personal property; and in this impersonal and sterile setting, soap and lotion were highly esteemed items. Item 7, cigarettes, was a valued commodity, for they were used for trading, gambling, and buying sexual favors. Therefore, the familiar white and green "Kool" pack was a significant status symbol. Item 8, which is personal clothing, had even greater status because boys had few nice clothes; in addition, clothing was rarely returned when "borrowed." The giving up of one's radio connoted even greater loss of status due to its expense and the fact that it was sent from home. Item 10 involves permitting oneself physically to be beaten upon by other youths, which certainly resulted in greater social degradation than the first nine items. Item 11, anal sodomy, is looked down upon so much that being a passive participant would place a boy on the bottom of the pecking order. Similarly, items 12 and 13 were considered so undesirable that a youth was considered a social outcast and excluded from all cottage interaction once he committed them.

Stimulus Qualities

Impression Management

Impression management was a major key to success in escaping the pressures from other inmates, and some boys were able to adopt consciously the mask they wanted others to accept. The tools of impression management primarily included tone of voice, facial expression and posture, and confidence in interpersonal relations. Also, social characteristics were important, and will be explored in the next two sections. Through impression management, boys projected to others either the image of strength (ability to take care of self) or of weakness (amenability to exploitation). Strong images resulted in positions of leadership, whereas weak images resulted in extensive exploitation. Thus, stimulus qualities were the clues by which all were judged and evaluated.

The impression management of heavies and lieutenants consisted of looking others directly in the eye when answering questions, discussing the seriousness of the crimes they committed, holding their "ground" when talking even during an argument, and reminding others throughout their stay how tough they were. They were able to communicate successfully that they were not afraid of anything or anyone, and these characteristics drove home the point that they were not to be "messed with." When asked what he thought kept him from being victimized, one boy said:

> People respect me because of the charge (bank robbery) and they feel that I'm a lot rougher than what I let on. I have wrestled an awful lot of guys and I'm not that big, you know. There's a lot of power here that

people just can't understand where it comes from. There will be a boy twice my size and when we go down to the gym, we'll put the mats off the wall, and maybe I'll flip the dude or slam him. And he says, "hey, I under-estimated your little ass," you know all the other guys see me do it once or twice and that keeps them off right away.

On the third ladder of the social hierarchy, youths were not able to project the appropriate images as well. Their impression management was characterized by being less forceful, less direct eye contact, backing away from arguments, incarcerated for less serious crimes, and less able to "use their hands." Thus, peers did not give them the same status which they gave those at the top of the hierarchy. Although not devoid of strength, these youths only possessed it in a lesser degree than the heavy and lieutenants. In fact, the alright guys, in particular, projected a reasonably good impression management to others.

Finally, others boys came into the cottage with fear written all over them. These youths were soon on the threshold of victimization with their heads hung low, nervously shifting from one foot to the other, backing up when talking with others, not holding eye contact, answering questions with a weak projection of voice, and appearing too anxious to develop relationships with others. A youth described one of these boys:

> ...He was a younger dude who would let people take his cigarettes, candy, anything he got. If there's going to be any sexual exploitation at all, this is the cat. They give him a lot of stuff, too, because he would be unwary. They give him stuff left and right. Then, they come at him with the old approach — you owe me something, right. Now, come on. That's the type of person who gets exploited.

Race as Stimulus Quality

With 97% of the line staff black and 51% of the inmates black, the stage was set for race to be a major factor as a stimulus quality. Thus, with black inmates at the top of the inmate social hierarchy and black staff in charge of the cottages, power was identified with blackness. For whites coming from middle-class suburbs and rural areas, this minority relationship was confusing and threatening, resulting in their exploitation. The picture that emerged then consisted of blacks exploiting both whites and blacks and of whites exploiting whites. In spite of the fact that some whites sexually exploited their weaker peers, interview data indicated that whites seldom or never exploited blacks in this setting. Youth leaders, for example, could remember no incident in recent institutional history where a black youth was sexually victimized by a white.

Of importance also in this black dominated institution is the fact that blacks were much more cohesive than whites. Feeling resentment toward whites because of their victimization from white society in the community and from the white dominated criminal justice system, especially judges and parole officers, blacks felt unified and justified in exploiting whites. This cohesiveness was particularly identifiable when a black resident had a confrontation either with a staff member or white inmate. In addition, when a strong white youth physically handled a black inmate, black "brothers" made a point to "get even" with this white.

Also germane in understanding black exploitation was the feeling of some whites that certain black staff were prejudiced against them. White inmates tended to single out one staff member in each cottage for this charge. Representative of the feeling against certain staff is the following statement from a white youth.

> I tell you this that the white dudes need a white man. Those black leaders eat our food. The suck asses in the kitchen give them the best food....is the worst one. He always took our food. He is a real fuck up; he will burn you.

> He was the one that caused me to go AWOL. When I returned from trade school the night before, I lit a cigarette and...was all over me. He called me a white bastard. I decided then that I was not going to school the next day, that I was not coming back to the institution. He would not even let me go back to my room to take a shower.

Social Class as Stimulus Quality

Four basic classes of youths were incarcerated in this institution: the lower-class, ghetto black; the middle-class black; the lower-class white who lives near the ghetto; and the middle-class white. Youth leaders felt that these youths were further divided into the haves and have-nots, with the have-not blacks in control of whites who were similarly made up of haves and have-nots. These social economic backgrounds also helped set the stage for those who became victims.

The lower-class white, for example, was not as easy to exploit as the middle-class white because of his physical and mental toughness. Generally, he was a youth who was used to fighting and was not easily intimidated. Further, perceiving of himself as capable of taking care of himself, he may, in fact, be looking for a good fight to improve his status in the cottage. His exploitation was made even more difficult because he never had much to begin with and therefore was extremely reluctant to give up any of his material possessions.

But in comparison, the middle-class white youth seldom had little savvy on how to survive in this institutional setting. Generally, a troublemaker in his own community, he usually felt totally inadequate to defend himself against ghetto blacks and whites. Furthermore, the enormous amounts of food brought by his parents created jealousy from peers, and made them even more determined to strip him of his goods. Although the middle-class black youth rarely was sexually exploited and generally could defend himself more adroitly than his white counterpart, he, too, was pressured to relinquish some of his food, cigarettes, and pop brought by his parents.

Obviously, no one pointed to a newcomer and said, "Here comes a middle-class punk; let's get him," nor did they say, "That kid comes from the ghetto and looks tough, we had better stay away from him." Rather, living in a middle or lower-class environment simply provided each youth with behavioural patterns, fighting ability, access to material goods, and manners which made them different from the youth from a different class. Consequently, while middle-class "virtues" were viewed as signs of weakness to the ghetto youth, the "strengths" of the ghetto came across as vulgarities and animal-like conduct to the more protected, reticent youth from a white and blue collar area. Impression management, race, and social class, then, set the stage for who became the victim and the aggressor by providing the appropriate clues.

Other Stimulus Qualities

Originally, it was thought that other factors would have a significant effect on victimization. But no significant differences appeared between the sexual and non-sexual exploiters on the factors of age, height, weight, I.Q., number of previous commitments, or number of previous offenses. Size and age apparently were not important in the process of sexual exploitation.

Moreover, in analyzing the data in terms of "how the boy was leaned on" (exploited), a significant difference was found among the three categories — "not at all," "items only," and "sex" — only on the variable "number of commitments to other institutions."

The youths who were not leaned on at all (28% of the sample) had more previous commitments than the other categories. They were slightly older than the others and were actually lighter in weight than the sexually victimized. But they were slightly taller than the other boys. They, in addition, had slightly fewer previous offenses than those exploited on items only.

In terms of the exploited, sexually victimized boys were slightly younger, heavier, shorter, had a fewer number of previous commitments to institutions, and a fewer number of previous offenses than their stronger peers. Those exploited on items only were somewhat between the other two age groups on age at admission, number of previous commitments and height, while they weighed less and had more previous offenses than the other two categories. Surprisingly, then, only the number of previous commitments was statistically significant among these various variables.

Conclusion

A reciprocal exchange is one in which both parties are mutually satisfied. But in this end-of-the-line institution, victimization — where one party is clearly the loser — is the more typical relationship as 72% of the inmates were victimized in some way. While some boys were exploited for such material items as food, cigarettes, clothes, soap, and radios, others were sexually victimized. To understand this victimization, an exploitation matrix was examined. The hierarchy which emerged consisted of a black heavy, several black lieutenants, a third group made up of alright guys and chumps, and a white scapegoat at the bottom of the pecking order. These four groups, along with one or two boys who remained independent of the exploitation matrix, made up the social organization of each of the eight cottages in the institution. In terms of understanding the social processing of inmates by inmates, it would appear that various stimulus qualities separated the boys in the different levels of the exploitation matrix. The most important of these stimulus qualities, at least in this institution, were impression management, race, social class, and number of previous commitments to institutions. Through these qualities, boys projected to others either the image of strength or weakness.

Acknowledgements

We are very indebted to the Ohio Youth Commission, its research staff and institutional officers for their permission to conduct this particular study. We would also like to thank the Office of Research as well as the Program for Study of Crime and Delinquency of the Ohio State University for their financial support throughout the various phases of the project.

This paper on the exploitation matrix is based on data presented in full in Clemens Bartollas, Stuart J. Miller & Simon Dinitz, *Victimization: The Exploitation Paradox of a Juvenile Institution,* New York, Halsted Press; a Sage Publications book, 1976.

Footnotes

[1] Sethard Fisher, "Social organization in a correctional residence," *Pacific Sociological Review* 1961, 4 (Fall), 87-93.

[2] Alan J. Davis, "Sexual Assaults in the Philadelphia prison system and sheriff's vans," *Transaction* 1968, 12, 9.

[3] Howard Polsky, *Cottage Six — The Social System of Delinquent Boys in Residential Treatment.* New York: Russell Sage Foundation. 1956.

[4] Arthur V. Huffman, "Problems precipitated by homosexual approaches on youthful first offenders," *Journal of Social Therapy* 1961, 7, 170-81.

[5] James Roberts, Edward Redd and Donald Jennifer were three staff members who were of special assistance in this study.

[6] The constant shifting of power and the resulting flexibility of the matrix meant that the extent and type of exploitation changes as youths shifted positions in the hierarchy.

[7] Stuart J. Miller, Clemens Bartollas and Simon Dinitz, "The 'Heavy' and social control," *Proceedings of the Fourth Annual Alpha Kappa Delta Sociological Research Symposium*. Richmond, Virginia Commonwealth University. 1974.

[8] Clemens Bartollas, Stuart J. Miller and Simon Dinitz, "Becoming a scapegoat: a study of a deviant career," *Sociological Symposium* 1974, 11 (Spring), 74-89.

[9] In our initial scale on "how the boys were victimized," we did not ask staff about each of the items separately, but simply on food, clothing, cigarettes, and the various forms of sexual exploitation. Although we were not therefore able to demonstrate the present ranking empirically, we have done so on the basis of our experience with institutional life.

Section V

POLICY CONSIDERATIONS

The last section of the reader addresses several important policy issues for the future. The most serious problem area in the area of juvenile justice, and corrections in general, is the absence of careful policy development. Far too often individuals responsible for policy development have little grasp of the problems faced by the youth affected, or by the practitioner who must carry out the policy through program implementation. Additionally, the administrator is constantly caught between the policy "ideals" and the realities of limited budgets, undertrained staff, staff burnout, and a host of additional problems. Finally, the juvenile justice system, not unlike the adult criminal justice system, is caught between the demands for punishment on the one hand, and the conflicting demands for rehabilitative and reintegrative programming on the other.

Lloyd Ohlin, in "The Future of Juvenile Justice Policy and Research," provides a number of insights into the broad area of policy development in juvenile justice. Ohlin points to the fact that the rhetoric and scope of proposed programs often exceeded the resources and talent available to direct the changes called for by new policies. Because the achievable does not measure up to the ideal, the result is disillusionment, alienation and ultimately, abandonment of the programs themselves. Ohlin's "challenge of the future" reflects the problems that have deep roots in society and a permanence that has lasted for generations. At the same time, to ignore the issues he has raised is to invite further escalation of the problems he has identified.

James Hackler's "The Need to Do Something," echos the earlier arguments raised by Frank Tannenbaum. Hackler notes that the demands to do something are always there, and once we conclude that our intentions are good, there is virtually no limit to the harm that we can accomplish. Persons of good will also often attempt to impose their own ideologies in the policy development process; concurrently, they resist new knowledge which might point them in different directions. At the same time, Hackler raises some optimistic issues which have the potential of leading policy development in new directions. However, his discussion on the resistance of knowledge probably provides a more accurate indicator of the future, and barriers to the development of realistic and successful policies in juvenile justice.

In the last article in this section, Shirley M. Hufstedler asks, "Should We Give Up Reform?" While the obvious answer for Hufstedler is no, she also provides the reader with a series of philosophical and procedural problems that must be addressed if we are to work our way out of historical dilemmas that constantly plague whatever we do. Her arguments against incarceration are strong and persuasive. However, she may have overlooked one of the most serious barriers to reform — the deep philosophical divisions hidden in the debates between those who would punish and those who would treat. From time to time, each side of this debate wins, and as a consequence, juvenile justice programming is much like the pendulum on a clock. Swinging back and forth between different ideologies and resisting new knowledge, the juvenile justice system is reformed with each new generation. And each time the children seem to lose.

16

The Future of Juvenile Justice Policy and Research

Lloyd E. Ohlin

Examining the Past

The federal government has played an increasingly dominant role in fostering policy directions during the past two decades. At the risk of oversimplifying complex social developments, we can identify three major shifts in federal policy that have been made in response to public concern about youth crime.

Federal Policy in the Early 1960s

The first federal act to focus directly on the problem of juvenile delinquency was passed in 1961 under the aegis of the President's Committee on Juvenile Delinquency and Youth Crime. This committee, which included Secretary Abraham Ribicoff of the Department of Health, Education and Welfare and Secretary Arthur Goldberg of the Department of Labor, was chaired by Attorney General Robert Kennedy. It sought a fresh initiative to deal with the emerging and potential growth of youth crime.

The committee adopted a comprehensive community development model

Lloyd E. Ohlin, "The Future of Juvenile Justice Policy and Research," *Crime and Delinquency,* Vol. 29, No. 3 (July 1983), pp. 463-472. Copyright ©1983 by Sage Publications, Inc. Reprinted by permission of Sage Publications, Inc.

being tested by the Mobilization for Youth project on the lower east side of Manhattan in New York City. This model stressed prevention of delinquency through the creation of better opportunities in the world of work, school, family, recreation, and social services. It sought to build community participation and competence to deal with delinquency by more active control of the institutions for the socialization of youth. It drew on the experiences of the Chicago Area Project developed by Clifford Shaw and Henry McKay in the 1930s and on the later community organization strategies in Chicago of Saul Alinsky. In breaking with the casework treatment approach, it redirected attention to the key role of community relationships in achieving better delinquency prevention and control. The President's Committee wished to test this model of community development in the high crime-rate areas of several cities. The model was to serve as a device for integrating and maximizing the impact of several federal agency programs.

Needless to say, many problems developed in the implementation of this policy. First, many community agencies believed that delinquency prevention and control was too limited a target to justify the broad scope of the proposed reforms in youth services, and they resisted adopting the committee's plan. Second, some of the assumptions underlying the committee's recommendations appear now to have been naive. We are much more aware today that juvenile justice depends on the successful operation of a broad formal and informal network of social relationships that guide youth development. We are also more aware of the need for better knowledge of how to bring about large-scale community and institutional change in the high crime-rate areas of large cities. We know that providing resources and goals for change is only part of the job. There are limits to what can be achieved through a large-scale project which funds both institutional reforms from within and social movements demanding such changes from the outside. The ensuing conflict quickly becomes politically inflamed and too threatening to the funding sources.

We should also note that those early efforts at community development for youth escalated too rapidly as the delinquency programs were combined with other community programs such as the war on poverty, housing and area development, and the model cities program. The accompanying rhetoric and the scope of redevelopment exceeded not only the resources but also the talent and knowledge available to direct changes of such complexity. The growing gap between expectation and achievable results fostered disillusionment, alienation, social unrest, and ultimately, abandonment of the programs themselves.

However, there is much that we can yet learn from those early federal initiatives to foster community responsibility. The experiences of the early 1960s can yield lessons about the importance of indigenous leadership, the power of entrenched institutions to resist change, the political character of major reforms, and the pace of community change in relation to social movements and conditions in the nation as a whole.

Presidential Crime Commissions: Focusing on Control

The second major shift in national juvenile justice policy was spearheaded by a series of presidential commissions that addressed problems of crime and violence. Their agenda was set initially by the 1967 report of the President's Commission on Law Enforcement and Administration of Justice. Unlike the efforts of the early 1960s, the mandate of this commission required a much tighter focus on control of rising crime rates. Although the task force on juvenile delinquency made many broad recommendations about prevention, its primary task was to suggest better methods of controlling identified delinquents and status offenders. This focus led to six major strategies later identified as: (1) *decriminalization* of status offenses (such as running away from home), (2) *diversion* of youth from court procedures into public and private treatment programs, (3) extending *due process* rights to juveniles (in anticipation of the Gault decision that guaranteed those rights), (4) *deinstitutionalization* (use of group homes or non-residential treatment facilities rather than large training schools), (5) *diversification* of services, and (6) *decentralization* of control.

These strategies were variously endorsed or expanded by a series of governmental commissions dealing with such varied topics as the rise in violent crimes and riots in large cities, the unrest on college campuses, and the issues of pornography and obscenity. The second major presidential crime commission, the National Advisory Commission on Criminal Justice Standards and Goals (appointed in 1971 to address again the surging crime problem), also supported the thrust of the 1967 report.

Despite broad concensus among experts about the validity of these strategies to deal with delinquent youth, implementation has been spotty and the results difficult to assess. Statistics cited by Barry Krisberg and Ira Schwartz[1] indicate that the decriminalization of status offenses has had a significant impact in most states. The number of status offenders committed to institutions has declined substantially in response to support from the Office of Juvenile Justice and Delinquency Prevention in the U.S. Department of Justice. There is still some question, however, that we have simply traded control by correctional officials for welfare supervision.

The diversion strategy, in which community services are substituted for correctional facilities, has also had some impact. But a recent assessment by James Austin and Barry Krisberg has pointed to potentially troublesome consequences of using community-based alternatives to juvenile incarceration. Austin and Krisberg call attention to three possible effects of diversion: (1) wider nets in which more youth are officially processed, (2) stronger nets that hold more youth in the system, and (3) different types of nets other than corrections (such as mental health and welfare placements).[2]

The due process revolution is still in progress, but in the direction of increased criminalization of the juvenile court process. In some instances, it has even led to suggestions that juvenile courts be abolished—a result which would go far beyond that intended by the national commissions interested in better protection of the rights of juveniles.

Efforts to deinstitutionalize juvenile treatment have met with mixed results. Greatest success was achieved under the direction of Jerome Miller in Massachusetts. Miller reorganized and ultimately closed five correctional facilities in that state, retaining only a small percentage of the beds for juveniles requiring incarceration.

Purchase of services from the private sector has increased diversification and decentralization of services in varying degrees in different states. However, there is increasing evidence that major private vendors (group and residential care facilities) are "skimming" the more treatable cases, leaving the more difficult to the public institutions. There is also evidence of more resistance to location of small, diversified facilities and programs in the home communities of delinquents.

The 1970s: A "Law and Order" Reaction

The third major shift reflects a strong conservative reaction to the liberal policies advocated by the national crime commissions. This reaction has occurred in spite of recent endorsement of those policies by the Juvenile Justice Task Force of the National Advisory Commission on Criminal Justice Standards and Goals (1976) and the standards issued by the Institute of Judicial Administration and the American Bar Association (1980).

The conservative trend originated in efforts to reexamine fundamental assumptions of the adult criminal justice system by a series of special study groups beginning, ironically, with the American Friends Service Committee publication *Struggle for Justice* (1971).

The American Friends Service Committee was guided by a desire to improve the plight of prison inmates. The committee perceived rehabilitation programs as thinly disguised measures for asserting greater control over inmates. The 1971 report suggested that indeterminate sentencing and decisions about parole were capricious and, moreover, that they permitted biased judgment and improper criteria to control the length of time served by inmates.

The original motives for rejecting rehabilitation programs and indeterminate sentencing were lost as public demand increased for "just deserts" (an eye for an eye) punishment and as sentencing and imprisonment were explored as a means of incapacitating offenders and deterring others from committing similar offenses. Growing fear of crime and increasing demands for repressive action have led to more punitive sentencing and to a rapid escalation of both the number of prisoners and the time to be served.

This approach is now spreading to juvenile justice. In many states we see increasing incarceration even as delinquency rates decline. Juvenile reform legislation now calls for more mandatory sentencing and more determinate sentences for juveniles, lowering of the upper age of juvenile jurisdiction, greater ease in obtaining waivers to adult court for juvenile prosecution, and greater access to juvenile records.

There is also a greater preoccupation with chronic, violent offenders that has led to redirection of resources for their confinement. In the absence of reliable criteria for identifying such offenders, this preoccupation tends to stereotype all delinquents and is likely to raise the level of precautionary confinements. It is also likely that due process reforms, which make the juvenile system look much like the adult system, will also lead to the same result.

Thinking about these major shifts in juvenile justice policy inspires a fresh appreciation of the power and depth of traditional beliefs about the causes and cures of crime in our society. The system can bend for a time in the direction of new approaches to prevention and control. But implementation is likely to be tentative and skeptical. Vested interests in traditional views surface quickly as problems arise. We are now in one of those periods of conservative reaction where the prevailing views about crime express beliefs about retribution, deterrence, and incapacitation that are deeply rooted in our religious and cultural heritage.

Our policies are now being developed by those who believe that the traditional system of punishment can be fine-tuned to control offenders by increasing the predictability and certainty of punishment. My own view, however, is that our society is unwilling to sustain the levels of repression and incarceration needed to make more than limited incremental gains in crime control. Yet I am not bitterly opposed to this effort. The process of change has a rhythmic character. Reaction and retrenchment occur as both new and old ideas are tested for their relevance to our deep-seated beliefs and values. It is time, then, to take a fresh look at the challenges and opportunities the next wave of reform must deal with when the current reaction has run its course.

The Challenge of the Future

Confronting the Alienation of Youth

I would like to suggest six policy issues that will require new perspectives and approaches over the next decade or two. The first major challenge lies in the increasing isolation and alienation of youth in our society. Historians are beginning to document the social processes by which adolescent youth have been progressively excluded from meaningful participation in the work force. Economic isolation becomes especially obvious in times of economic recession as unemployed men and women displace adolescents from low paying, unskilled jobs.

The reaction of youth has found expression not only in public disorder, vandalism, and crime but in the resurgence and increasing violence of gangs. It has also led to greater use of drugs and alcohol and more chronic youth offenders — children who are in trouble with juvenile justice and other social control agencies from an early age.

In addition, the key issues in youth crime have changed. The pervasiveness of delinquent acts among all youth has shifted our attention away from attempts to distinguish delinquents from non-delinquents. Instead, we must now explain why some young people persist in delinquency while others do not. What circumstances and experiences distinguish them from one time or occasional offenders? More importantly, why do most chronic offenders also eventually cease their criminal activities?

We lack adequate theories not only of *persistence* but of *desistance* from crime. To develop them will not only require fresh ideas and data but also integration of some of the current theories. Theories of social control, economic and social strain, cultural conflict, and deviance all address somewhat different aspects of the crime problem. Progress may be made by thinking of these theories as complementary rather than competing. In any case, a greater concern with issues of persistence and desistance from crime may influence policy significantly. Should we not, for example, concentrate our resources at those points where youth are making critical choices in their lives, so that they will be more likely to avoid careers in crime?

Building Community Resources

The second major policy issue relates to the role of local communities in prevention and control of crime. The local community is of central importance in the socialization of youth through the formal and informal networks that help to shape behavior. What are the characteristics of a community capable of encouraging its young people in constructive behavior? And what does it take to raise a high delinquency rate community to this level of competence? We have gained significant breakthroughs in theories of organization and personality development by studying competent and healthy organizations and personalities instead of only those that break down. We should be able to make similar gains by contrasting effective communities with ineffective ones.

At our center for Criminal Justice in the Harvard Law School, Alden Miller and I have been examining some Boston neighborhoods as an extension of our study of the Massachusetts Department of Youth Services. We have been especially concerned about identifying any linkage between correctional programs and other youth services in high crime-rate neighborhoods. Not surprisingly, we found very little connection between the two. Once a young person is in a delinquent track, it is hard to get out. Though we have yet to examine other communities, it seems evident that training schools or group homes isolated from community life have little sustained impact on delinquent tendencies.

Clearly, we need to know much more about community responses to delinquency. We especially need to know what high crime-rate communities can do without additional financial resources, because this is the situation these communities are likely to face under the "new federalism" policies that reallocate responsibility but provide fewer resources.

I have been encouraged by observing the increased control of crime in a public housing project in Boston, where a tenant council has been granted primary responsibility and resources for improving conditions. Once plagued by a high vacancy rate, vandalism, and crime-ridden elevators and buildings, the project is now making progress through effective demands for prompt police service, building maintenance, citizen patrols, a crime watch, and constant attention to youth problems and needs. Well organized residents with a stake in their neighborhood and the responsibility and authority to command essential resources are an important ingredient in constructive change.

Allocation of Federal State and Local Resources

The allocation of responsibility among federal, state, and local governments is in a state of uncertainty and transition. We need to learn more about the best ways to divide and coordinate these responsiblities. Over the past twenty years, the federal government provided increasing resources, although often in an erratic and unstable pattern. It now seems likely that such resources will be substantially reduced and the federal role confined to research, statistics, and dissemination of information to states and local communities. Problems of employment, education, welfare, and housing will undoubtedly require federal involvement and will affect the ability of local communities to deal with crime. However, crime control and prevention will become more of a state and local responsibility. We are now at a critical stage in defining what allocations will best bring about effective crime control.

Employment

The fourth issue concerns problems of employment and education that contribute to the isolation and alienation of youth. In the 1970s, we saw an enormous growth in the 18-34 age group, the population from which new workers are recruited. The 1980s will be a decade of sharp decline in the 15-24 age group and significant reduction in the growth of the 25-34 age group. We are likely to see a labor shortage and a decline in population in the high crime-risk ages. This combination of factors may provide an unusual opportunity to foster more effective involvement of youth in the work force. We should be thinking now of ways to capitalize on that situation before it is upon us.

Similarly, with the reduced school population, there is more opportunity to experiment with changes that will enhance involvement by young people now estranged from traditional school practices. Over the past decade, the growing literature on educational policy has documented prospects for increasing achievement scores through changes in the organization of schools and the roles of administrators, teachers, and students; and through redefining expectations, tasks, and rewards. Strategies for change involve such practices as breaking large schools down into subschools or clusters (schools-within-a-school), infusing the curriculum with work and career oriented exercises and opportunities, instituting cooperative learning in mixed-ability groups, encouraging more democratic decisions and tasks in the classroom, and fostering changes in school governance.

These are just a few of many innovations now being tested for their impact on delinquent conduct and school achievement in a joint project funded by the Office of Juvenile Justice and Delinquency Prevention and its National Institute of Juvenile Justice and Delinquency Prevention. The project is conducted by the Westinghouse National Issues Center in Columbia, Maryland, and the National Center for the Assessment of Delinquent Behavior and Its Prevention at the Center for Law and Justice, University of Washington, Seattle, Washington. While many of the program elements have been tested in other contexts, there is reason to believe that the controlled evaluation of this project and similar experiments will yield new insights into more effective learning environments for school-age youths.

Fear of Crime

The fifth challenge for the coming years concerns the fear of crime. Public attitude surveys indicate that the link between fear of crime and actual risk is not as direct as one might assume.

Why do national survey samples show that respondents perceive juvenile crime as increasing rapidly when juvenile arrest rates are actually declining? Inaccurate information purveyed by sensationalist media sources is an oversimplified explanation. Part of the answer may lie in the national and international scope of violent crimes reported by the media. These crimes are then perceived as happening close to home as well. Furthermore, crime is now reported in areas once perceived as remote and safe.

Some studies suggest that the fear of crime by the elderly arises as much from a pervasive sense of social disorder and lack of control of youths as from objective perceptions of risk. Idle, noisy youth hanging about obstructing and harassing passers-by, vandalized empty buildings, and trash-strewn lots produce a sense of communal loss of authority and inability to preserve order. The sources of fear are complex and variable, but we need to know more about them if we wish to mobilize support for community action. It is through cooperative, organized community programs to reduce crime that a sense of safety and control is restored, rather than through the barriers of locks, bars, and dogs.

The relationships of class, race, and gender to crime are potentially explosive issues which we must confront directly in the years ahead. For example, the disproprotionate representation of ethnic and racial minority groups throughout the criminal justice system is a cause of great concern. This era is similar to the 1920's, when the combined impact of immigration, prohibition, and the growth of organized crime caused lengthy public debate. Concern about crime led to the studies and reports in the 1930's by the National Commission on Law Observance and Enforcement, commonly known as the Wickersham Commission. This commission quieted fears that "foreigners" were creating a crime wave and pointed instead to the social and economic systems of large cities where new arrivals were forced to reside. To some extent, the crime problem today also provides a focus for unresolved racial and ethnic conflicts that once again must be sorted out and dealt with more directly.

Creating Cooperation

The sixth issue relates to the establishment of some mechanism by which a sustained attack on the problems of juvenile delinquency can be mounted. One useful possibility would involve the establishment of several centers which would pull together already assembled data, undertake carefully designed longitudinal studies and critical short term studies, and analyze the results systematically for their policy and theoretical implications. In the past, we have looked to the federal government to provide such initiatives in addition to training, technical assistance, and dissemination of information. But it is likely that in the future, we will have to look to private initiative for policy oriented studies of this kind.

I wish to stress the view that juvenile justice policies cannot be successfully dealt with outside the context of a more general youth policy. We have seen enough evidence of the diffuse sources of delinquency and the variety of responses to it to realize the need for a more comprehensive and coordinated youth policy to deal with youth alienation and delinquent acts. We must also think of ways to open up more challenging opportunities for youth in our society. We need a cumulative program of research and policy analysis, for there is much to be done. Like many others, I see resorting to incarceration as a confession of bankruptcy of ideas and initiative in this field. I believe there is a large body of latent public support for less repressive, more creative solutions to the problem.

Finally, I would also like to call attention to a persistent, nagging problem — the emphasis on job security of professionals in the field as a major obstacle to change in the years ahead. We must meet this problem head on, be honest about it to begin with, and then see what has gone wrong. What are the positive as well as negative effects of professional treatment of youth problems? How do we combine the strength and motivation of community leadership and participation with the trained sensibilities, experience, and counsel of professionals? This issue intersects and confounds all the others I have suggested are challenges before us. Workable solutions to it would immeasurably ease their resolution.

Footnotes

[1] See "Rethinking Juvenile Justice," this issue.
[2] James Austin and Barry Krisberg, "The Unmet Promise of Alternatives to Incarceration." *Crime and Delinquency,* National Council on Crime a' ' Delinquency, 2 28:3, 1982.

17

The Need to Do Something

James C. Hackler

It is time you knew of Tagoona, the Eskimo. Last year one of our white men said to him. "We are glad you have been ordained as the first priest of your people. Now you can help us with their problem." Tagoona asked, "What is a problem?" and the white man said, "Tagoona, if I held you by your heels from a third story window, you would have a problem." Tagoona considered this long and carefully. Then he said, "I do not think so. If you saved me, all would be well. If you dropped me, nothing would matter. It is you who would have the problem."

—Margaret Craven

Responding to Delinquency

It is appropriate to ask how society selects and responds to those features that are seen as troublesome. Social problems change from time to time. Frequently these changes reflect the current concerns of the public as much as the "problem" itself. For example, the Ruhr Valley in Germany has suffered from pollution for many years, but the workers at the Krupp factories and other heavy industries in that area have not complained about the "pollution" problem. Those most concerned with pollution do not

James C. Hackler, "The Need to Do Something," *The Prevention of Youthful Crime: The Great Stumble Forward,* Methuen Press, Toronto, 1978, pp. 8-23. Reprinted by permission of the author.

necessarily live in areas where this problem is the most threatening. Similarly, these concerns change with time. At an earlier period in this century, pollution was viewed as a major concern. Then interest faded. In the 1960's interest was revived. Now it seems that this particular "social concern" is again losing its grip on the public imagination.

Although there is always much public interest in delinquency, different aspects attract attention at different times. In the late 1950's gang wars received much publicity. In the 1960's drug use attracted great attention. In the late 1970's these aspects have been the focus of less public interest, even though these activities have probably continued with only modest changes. In other words, delinquency, or any other social problem, cannot be isolated and studied outside of its social context. Since we cannot study everything at once, we have to focus on different aspects of the delinquency problem, viewing the situation from one perspective and then another. Our first task is to note how society responds to delinquency and distinguish which responses are temporary and which are enduring. This may help us to understand the dynamics of societal responses to juvenile delinquency.

Even though the definition of a social problem varies from time to time and place to place, we should not treat all social ills as simply being "in the eye of the beholder." Rather, social problems are deeply woven into the fabric of society and cannot be understood without taking into account the reaction of the public, the social structure of the society, the relations between various elements in the society, and the social characteristics of human beings. It is difficult to recognize many aspects of this complex pattern and to discern which behaviour patterns are the most important. The actors who "cause" the problems or who initiate action are not always easy to identify. Those who stand at centre stage may actually be less important than those in supporting roles or those who operate the lights, write the scripts, or prepare the make-up. However, we have a tendency to provide simplistic answers to most questions concerning social problems. This is also understandable. The news media want to cover a topic in a few minutes; political leaders need to present issues in clear, unambiguous terms. One characteristic of society which influences social problems is that the public demands straightforward answers to questions concerning topics such as delinquency and crime. Before attempting to recommend some reasonable responses to delinquency and crime, we need to review the dynamics of societal responses and the settings in which these responses take place.

The "We've Got to Do Something" Syndrome

After an outbreak of vandalism, purse snatching, or other malicious behavior by local juveniles, there is usually a public demand for action. Under such circumstances it is unwise for some academic to point out that the harm done to life and limb by juveniles is a tiny fraction of the injuries caused by the automobile or that the economic losses are trivial compared with those resulting from cheating on income tax, and the variety of crimes committed by more affluent members of society. Enduring certain nuisances while concentrating on vital problems has never characterized human society. Down through the ages our literature is filled with comments of how the younger generation is going to hell. While other social problems come and go, attempts to "reform" the young continue. Although juvenile delinquency may be receiving more attention than it deserves, in terms of its danger to society, it is clearly a legitimate social problem. Yet we should keep in mind that this concern is heavily tempered with emotionalism and confusion, which in turn influence the problem itself. Individuals and agencies working in the delinquency field are a product of these factors and their responses are conditioned by them.

Clearly, then, we've got to do something—not because delinquency is objectively a tremendous threat to society, but because the demands for action are always there. Since we must act, it is normal to ask the "experts" to research the problem, analyze the causes, generate reasonable proposals, launch programs based on these proposals, evaluate these programs and rationally select the programs that "cure" delinquency. Many believe that this scientific approach will lead to the "solution" of the problem. Although a scientific perspective on understanding human behaviour is valid to a degree, there is a growing belief that this "rational" approach to problem solving is oversimplified and not as revealing as was initially hoped. Therefore, I will devote considerable attention to such factors as the problems connected with the launching of delinquency prevention programs and their evaluation. Some of these activities, I will argue, are self-defeating.

Hans Mohr, a sociologist at York University who was with the Law Reform Commission of Canada for three years, argues that the logic of social science practices and the logic of social practices are not the same and therefore should not be used interchangeably. The strategy for dealing with a scientific problem is not the same as that directed toward a social concern. The response of a community to delinquency will not be "rational" in terms of "curing delinquency" if we judge it by scientific standards. However, community behaviour makes more sense when one understands that there are many different forces pulling in different directions. Community action will be a compromise response to these pressures. The public response will "make sense" even though it ignores relevant scientific knowledge. Similarly, the activities of those doing research on delinquency, launching programs, conducting evaluations, or drafting legislation will have their own dynamics. It is erroneous to believe that deductions that arise out of social science research will or should automatically be transformed into social policy. Nor should we assume that a supposedly reasonable social policy will automatically influence delinquent behaviour. Many researchers in delinquency continually complain that social policy fails to incorporate social science findings. Actually, social policy does utilize social science research, but how and when this occurs is contingent on a number of other factors.

This does not mean that science research is unimportant. Rather, it might be wiser to see the social scientist as a person who provides a smorgasbord of facts and ideas. The policy maker must choose from this selection to put together a reasonable meal. The scientist may recommend spinach because it has lots of vitamins, but if people hate spinach, they will overlook its benefits. In other words, as a strategy to obtain social action researchers should generate many alternatives. What is finally selected for public policy is based not just on what is "correct" but also on what will be acceptable to a wide portion of the public. It is clear that when the government official expects the scientist to draft legislation or when the scientist expects the public official to enshrine research findings in legislation, both of them will be disappointed.

The Ineffectiveness of Men of Goodwill

The confusion which exists in our attempts to develop a clear social policy regarding delinquency prevention is the product of neither a deliberate strategy nor ignorance. True, these two components may contribute, but the facts of delinquency are difficult to distinguish from plausible hypotheses and myths. One of the major stumbling blocks to effective social policy is the persistent belief that the intentions of "men of good will" surely result in progress.

This faith in the power of good intentions is a common response to the "we've got to do something" syndrome. However, developing courses of action on the basis of good intentions does not automatically lead to effective social policy. Just as the best will in the world, combined with the best existing knowledge, has failed to cure cancer, so the best intentions and the best existing knowledge have failed to rid the world of delinquency.

An appropriate first step, then, to a discussion of policies related to delinquency, may be to examine the various perspectives and orientations which people have toward the problem of correcting or treating people who are considered deviant. Different orientations will naturally advocate different courses of action. These orientations and recommended courses of action are a product of prevalent ideologies and beliefs. Any action program should be viewed within the context of the larger social milieu.

Societal Attitudes Toward Treatment

During the nineteenth century in Italy, public officials were concerned because people kept urinating in the street. Public urination was illegal and people guilty of it were punished. A famous criminologist of that period, Cesare Lombroso, suggested that such criminals be confined for their actions. Reflecting his own conclusions about crime, Lombroso logically argued that people who commit crimes are inherently different from others and there is little that one can do to change these innate characteristics. Therefore, society should simply confine those who commit criminal acts. However, a young student of Lombroso, Enrico Ferri, who was to become a famous criminologist in his own right, suggested an alternative: public urinals.

The point is, it is possible that no action program is needed, at least in terms of correcting deviants. Changes made elsewhere in the social milieu may be more meaningful. The need for action and the nature of both prevention and treatment programs come out of our image of man and society. For Lombroso the problem lay in the make-up of human beings. Ferri saw it as the result of a specific deficiency in society. Regardless of the correctness of any social perspective, its simple existence is a social fact. We must maintain a critical attitude toward our images of man and constantly reevaluate any policy proposals in this light.

The Resistance to the Acceptance of New Knowledge

Let us begin with two questions: does knowledge have any impact on social policy and would we recognize a solution if it was in fact discovered?

The story of Ignaz Semmelweis, a Hungarian physician working in Vienna in the nineteenth century, is revealing. This young doctor noted that women who gave birth to children in hospitals died more frequently than those who gave birth in rural areas or even in the streets next to the hospital. He performed many autopsies on victims of "childbed" fever and observed the practices of his colleagues with the hope of finding an answer to this problem. He noted that doctors examined cadavers, wiped the blood and pus on the lapels of their coats, then without washing their hands, proceeded to probe the vaginas of pregnant women.

It dawned on Semmelweis that doctors were somehow transferring the infection which they contacted in their surgical activities to healthy patients. His conclusion was that it would be wise if the doctors washed their hands before examining pregnant women. It seemed like an obvious solution, but the medical profession at that time showed little inclination to change its habits. It is difficult for us to imagine how a professional mentality could be so obtuse. In spite of remarkable declines in the death rate of pregnant women in Semmelweis' care, other doctors refused to acknowledge the demonstrated connection between dirty hands and infection. They clung to their filthy coats as status symbols in a professional hierarchy, and it was some time before they adopted Semmelweis' suggestions.

Likewise our programs dealing with juvenile delinquents frequently ignore vitally relevant knowledge. Social change takes place for a variety of reasons, and the discovery of new knowledge may be only *one* of the less important contributors. For those who set great store in public education this is an uncomfortable thought. Although we must not abandon our pursuit of knowledge, perhaps we should not be surprised when society does not utilize what we consider relevant knowledge until *other* dynamic processes have come into play.

Just as the customs and status-determining characteristics of medicine were more crucial than knowledge in Vienna in the middle of the nineteenth century, the benefits derived by those who administer the criminal justice system may outweigh academic knowledge. For example, certain ideas about "law and order," although based upon acknowledged ignorance and half truths, may form an enduring psychological base for the majority of the population.

When a policeman is killed in a shootout with a criminal, there is usually increased public demand for the death penalty. However, capital punishment may be irrelevant to the problem of protecting policemen. Most policemen, like the rest of us, risk their lives in auto accidents much more often than they do on the job. Also, intervention in family arguments is more frequently the cause of police injuries than confrontation with criminals. But the public is not always interested in objective knowledge. Justice, revenge and many other concepts may be more important. We must accept the reality that the application of knowledge plays a minor role in influencing social policy when emotions are involved and other social processes are operating.

Our mistake is in assuming that the knowledge *should* be applicable to such policy decisions, or that it should be more relevant than other factors, such as the needs and biases of those who administer a system. For example, the evidence that counseling or psychiatric treatment are irrelevant to the success or failure of delinquent rehabilitation programs is unlikely to influence the behaviour of those who are in charge of delivering the services. Unless those in authority are satisfied that their needs for security, power and prestige can continue to be met under the proposed policy change, they will resist such changes. The actual effectiveness of counseling is but one of many factors that will influence the persistence or change in delinquency prevention practices.

In addition to arguing that knowledge influences social policy only when certain conditions exist, we might well be cautious about applying new knowledge immediately. Let us speculate on the long-term consequences of any obviously sensible recommendation. Let us assume that Semmelweis had been successful early in convincing his colleagues to wash their hands. Let us further assume that the five million or so mothers who died of childbed fever survived instead. Would Europe have had a population explosion which would have depleted its resources, led to starvation, etc.? Of course, one could speculate in the other direction. The increase in fertility could have led to the discovery of reliable birth control methods sooner and a response to population pressures at an earlier level in our technology. This in turn might have influenced the rest of the world and led to the stabilization of world population early in the twentieth century. Today's wisdom may be tomorrow's folly.

Is Knowledge Always Useful?

Let us provide another illustration. When juvenile corrections in Alberta were transferred from the Attorney General's Department to the Department of Health and Social Development, changes were made in one of the training institutions. A high wire fence topped by barbed wire which circled the perimeter of the grounds was removed in an attempt to create a new image for the training school as a place conducive to rehabilitation. Soon the rate of escapes soared. The police were annoyed. The staff had to pay more attention to locking outside doors. Conducting activities out in the yard became a problem. After a few years many people wondered whether removing the fence actually restricted the freedom of the juveniles because of the need for compensating measures.

Obviously, hindsight is more accurate than foresight. Applying current knowledge is not always the "wisest" choice. For example, it would now be difficult to rebuild the wire fence around that institution even if new knowledge suggested that its advantages outweighed its disadvantages. The point is that the conservative manner in which knowledge works its way into policy decisions may have certain positive attributes, even though this delay causes frustration and arouses charges of incompetence.

True, humility should not paralyze us. Many reforms make sense. Unforeseen negative consequences may occur, but such risks should not be used as a reason for opposing all change. On the other hand, since the consequences of reforms may be negative, change should be approached cautiously.

We might benefit from looking carefully at research and ideas which try to trace the consequences of programs that have been launched. Instead of asking, "How does one prevent delinquency?", we should be asking, "What have been the unanticipated consequences when carefully reasoned delinquency prevention programs have been introduced?"

Treatment Versus Justice

In the above section I have tried to show that delinquency prevention programs will be influenced by the social milieu. Current beliefs, which may be considered "knowledge" by some but not by others, will play a role, but not necessarily a direct one. A number of factors will influence the way knowledge is used or ignored. Let us now turn to the question of what might happen when certain ideas are polarized. For several decades North America has favoured a philosophy advocating help or treatment rather than punishment as a means for changing delinquent behaviour in juveniles. At the same time counter pressures to the treatment approach have been growing. These criticisms have arisen from disappointment with the effectiveness of treatment programs. Another source of pressure against the treatment approach is generated by some of the questions raised by the neo-Marxists. Some argue that the institutions generated by the "child-saving movement" were created to meet the needs of those who wanted to do the saving rather than those to be saved (Platt, 1969; Dahl, 1974). There is a further suspicion that juveniles may not have benefited from a juvenile court philosophy that pays little attention to legal safeguards in its efforts to help rather than punish the child. Some scholars argue that the child is presently getting the worst of both worlds (Lemert, 1971).

Let us assume, however, that society has resolved some of the issues raised above and government programs are moving forward in a coordinated manner. Are there other pitfalls and unanticipated consequences that require our vigilance?

The Dangers of Doing Something

Improving Illegal Skills

One of the most carefully evaluated programs in Canada was a treatment program at Matsqui Institution, a federal medium-security prison for delinquent drug addicts, located at Abbotsford, British Columbia. The treatment involved a therapeutic community setting, daily group therapy, and an academic upgrading program to grade 10 (Murphy, 1972). Surprisingly, the control group did better than the group receiving the sophisticated treatment. The findings indicate that the treatment made no difference in terms of changing the amount of time legally employed or the dollar value of legal earnings; however, compared with the control group, the treated group spent more time illegally employed, had more illegal earnings, and used more drugs after completion of the program.

It seems that treatment group members learned to express themselves in ways more likely to be pleasant to others. This social ability combined with academic skills learned by the treatment group made little difference in the legal employment sphere but gave them an edge over other delinquent addicts in the competition for scarce illegal opportunities and drug supplies.

Sophisticated Crime Disguised as Success

Another study in British Columbia by Tony Parlett and Eric Linden focused heavily on upgrading education (Parlett, 1974). While it may have been effective in terms of achieving higher levels of educational skills, Parlett notes that there could have been some unanticipated consequences.

> One of our most successful graduates from the programme has now spent more time on the street, i.e., less time in jail, than at any time in his adult life. If we did not know his background quite intimately we would consider him a successful citizen. However, the amount of money which we know he spends is very much greater than he earns. (8 or 9 times greater). Thus we are aware that he is successfully dealing in the heroin trade. He was, before we educated him, a minor, unsuccessful trafficker. Now he is a major, successful dealer. (Parlett, 1975)

This last study is particularly relevant because it illustrates how some subjects would normally be rated "successful" if the researcher did not know the truth of the situation. It is important to realize that we can get into various kinds of trouble when reacting to the demand to "do something." First, the program itself can have a negative impact on the clients; second, skilled researchers can be led astray; and third, attempts to evaluate a program, instead of simply observing it, can create a distorted picture of the program's success.

Ignoring Relevant Knowledge

Do action programs launch activities which are contrary to present knowledge? The desire to do good is often so overwhelming that it is easy to ignore present knowledge. For example, a sociologist was invited to advise a project which was designed to motivate underprivileged students to want to go to college. The consulting sociologist noted that one of the popular theories of deviance emphasized the discrepancy between desire to have certain things and the actual means available to reach these goals. When the gap between the aspirations and the means to achieve those goals is large, it is claimed that there would be an inclination toward deviant behaviour to achieve those goals (Merton, 1938). Therefore, the visiting sociologist asked if the program would also provide the means to achieve the new goals; that is, would it provide scholarships so the increased aspirations would be realized.

No, he was informed that the project was not designed to provide scholarships; it was designed to motivate underprivileged students. The sociologist argued that increasing aspirations without increasing means could lead to a rise in frustration and delinquency. Perhaps it would be better to lower aspirations and decrease frustration. The sociologist was not invited back.

Knowing the cause, of course, will not necessarily provide a cure (Nettler, 1970: 168). Some causes might not be alterable. If low I.Q. led to delinquency, there might be little we could do. If in fact the "causes" of delinquency are largely unalterable, our tendency to "do something" should be examined even more carefully.

In their study of delinquency in a birth cohort, Wolfgang, Figlio and Sellin (1972) have noted that many offenders tend not to repeat their delinquency. In fact, their data suggest that there is little to gain by treating first, second or even third offenders. Those with a fourth offence or more might profitably be the target of intervention. This recommendation differs markedly from the more frequent comment, "We must intervene earlier, so we can help." The same study also notes that offenders who were punished severely had worse subsequent delinquent careers than those who were punished mildly, even after controlling for the category of offences.

True, there may be situations where only dramatic changes can bring about any changes, and this may apply to some aspects of juvenile programs in some parts of North America. It is also possible that loud voices crying for drastic changes will help set the stage for more cautious reforms; but despite the criticsm from the Left that a policy of gradualism will automatically be ineffective, I would argue that none of the advocates of revolutionary changes has demonstrated the superiority of their recommendations. The same judgement applies to law and order advocates on the other end of the political spectrum. There may be times when a situation is considered so serious that we are willing to accept the gamble of an extreme policy, but we should be acutely aware that it is a gamble. An alternative strategy is to see delinquency as a trade-off for other features in our society. How much are we willing to pay for a highly individualistic society?

Delinquency: The Price We Must Pay for Individualism?

That delinquency is a social evil is a point of view most people would accept; that it may be a necessary one is an opinion many would find abhorrent. In this context the analogy of delinquency and disease can prove useful.

I personally find that treating delinquency as if it were a sickness is a dubious strategy, but let us ask if certain sicknesses are not useful to society. In Africa, sickle-cell anemia is common in certain areas. It is inherited through a recessive gene; that is, some people in the population carry the disease in their genes but show no symptoms of the disease themselves. Africans with recessive genes for sickle-cell anemia have a greater resistance to malaria and are, therefore, able to live in areas where that disease is common.

A second category includes those individuals who inherit genes for sickle-cell anemia from both the father and mother. Under these conditions the recessive trait becomes dominant. These people will be anemic and it is likely that they will not live very long.

A third group of individuals will not inherit genes for sickle-cell anemia from either the father or mother and will be incapable of producing offspring who have the disease or passing on the characteristics. However, such individuals will have a relatively low tolerance to malaria and will die more easily in infested areas.

As we can see, this particular disease has certain positive effects. It enables some persons to live in malaria-infested areas. On the other hand, approximately one-quarter of the children born to a population where this gene is widespread will be anemic and will die young. A primitive society without the technology to eliminate malaria might look upon sickle-cell anemia as a "price" paid for protection against malaria.

Can juvenile delinquency be seen in a similar manner? Is it the price we pay for a creative and individualistic society? Those who are treatment-oriented will resist such a philosophy. Perhaps it is necessary to accept that random delinquency is preferable to organizing these deviants for the purpose of social improvement. After all, Hitler was successful in turning hoodlums into soldiers by giving them uniforms and letting them go around assaulting citizens and breaking up printing presses. Drastic and over-simplified cures have failed to work in the past, yet they continue to attract supporters. Even a past president of the Canadian Psychiatric Association, Keith Yonge, has suggested that special work camps be established for young people who use drugs and refuse to take advantage of the educational opportunities in our society (Edmonton *Journal,* November 21, 1969). The possibility that the cure could be worse than the disease is relevant to a balanced perspective on delinquency. A little delinquency may be essential to a healthy society. Thinking of delinquency as a disease that can be eradicated or a war that can be won is nice-sounding rhetoric for politicians; however, it is unlikely that delinquency will be cured, solved, or conquered in battle.

The Great Stumble Forward

Given the debate between those who wish to "treat" and those who wish to return to a more legalistic approach, we can anticipate a greater demand for evidence that a specific program works or does not work. Hence, there will be an increasing demand for the evaluation of programs. Those of us in the research business should welcome this increased interest in evaluation. However, it is possible that some of these efforts could consume vast amounts of scarce resources and have a variety of negative side effects.

Yet stumble forward we must. Society demands it and the reasons for proceeding outweigh those for doing nothing. Our rather trivial accomplishments should make us hesitant, but the momentum is great. Despite loud and seemingly confident voices, the direction is not clear. There is good reason to believe that some of the seemingly promising routes will in fact be long detours. Even if we correctly identify some of the routes which will bring us closer to the goal, the path will probably be bumpy. There may be tremendous forces dragging us down certain roads, and usually it will be difficult to distinguish the cries of those who are wise and courageous from those who are simply frightened and confused. A reasonable strategy suggests that we should study the experiences of those who have stumbled on ahead of us. Therefore, let us look carefully at some of the more sophisticated delinquency prevention programs and their evaluations to see if we can chart a reasonable course.

References

Dahl, Tove Stang, "The Emergence of the Norwegian Child Welfare Law," *Scandinavian Studies in Criminology,* 1974, 5: 83-98.

Lemert, Edwin, M., "Instead of Court: Diversion in Juvenile Justice," 1971, National Institute of Mental Health, Rockville, Maryland.

Merton, Robert K. "Social Structure and Anomie," *American Sociological Review,* 1938 3: 672-682.

Murphy, Brian C., "A Quantitative Test of the Effectiveness of an Experimental Treatment Program for Delinquent Opiate Addicts," Research Centre Report 4, 1972. Ottawa: Solicitor General of Canada.

Nettler, Gwynn, "Explanations," 1970, New York: McGraw-Hill.

Parlett, T.A.A., "The Development of Attitudes and Morality in Adult Offenders," 1974 Unpublished Ph.D. Dissertation, University of Victoria, B.C.

Parlett, T.A.A., Personal correspondence, 1975.

Platt, Anthony M., "The Child Savers," 1969, Chicago: University of Chicago Press.

Wolfgang, Marvin E., Robert M. Figlio and Thorsten Sellin, "Delinquency in a Birth Cohort," 1972, Chicago: University of Chicago Press.

18

Should We Give Up Reform?

Shirley M. Hufstedler

We Americans are dedicated reformers and problem solvers. We tend to believe that for every problem, there must be a solution, if we just put our minds to it. We are also an impatient people. We want our problems solved quickly and with little or no personal costs. These attitudes are strikingly evidenced by our responses to education and to crime and punishment.

When our republic was founded, we inherited our judicial system and a great body of law from England, including traditional English views of criminal punishment. Leaving aside the peculiar aberration of witch burning, like England, we hung people, had them whipped, ducked them in ponds, maimed them, branded them, banished them, and exposed them in the village stocks. We had no dungeons in which to place political prisoners and no prisons. We had jails. To the gentle quakers, we owe the creation of prisons. The belief was that a criminal could be reformed, if he or she would be confined to a prison and left alone in his or her cell with a copy of the Bible. Solitary meditation with the "good book" doubtless drove more prisoners mad than drove them to virtue. Nevertheless, the idea quickly caught hold, not only at home, but also abroad.

From that day to this, the criminal justice system has been a favorite target for the reformers' zeal. None of the systems that we have developed have worked very well, so there is a constant search to make them better,

Shirley M. Hufstedler, "Should We Give Up Reform?", *Crime and Delinquency,* Vol. 30, No. 3 (July 1984), pp. 415-422. Copyright © 1984 by Sage Publications, Inc. Reprinted by permission of Sage Publications, Inc.

always marked by unintended consequences that often prove more costly than the problems that reformers set out to cure. Then, as now, we are torn by doubts about what the system is supposed to accomplish. Do we imprison convicted law breakers because we want to reform them, punish them, incapacitate them, or take revenge upon them, or deter others by demonstrating the consequences that will happen to them by the misdeeds they may be contemplating? Sometimes one of these theories is an ascendency and becomes dominant, then another wave of reformers popularizes a different theory. Perhaps more often, the public simply checks "all of the above," even when some of the aims are antithetical to one another.

The concept of juvenile justice is a latecomer to the justice system. Because it seems so common to us today, it is easy to forget that the concepts of childhood and adolescence did not emerge until well into the nineteenth century. We recognized infancy, but children were thought of as small adults. They were dressed accordingly, and were expected to become members of the labor force when they emerged from swaddling clothes. In an aggrarian society, or even during our period of cottage industry, no more sophisticated ideas of education and human development were necessary. It was the industrial revolution together with increasing urbanization that led us to change our concepts of childhood. We did not invent adolescence until well into the present century, when, for the first time, we had excess unskilled labor and our industrial development required a better educated labor force.

Shortly before the turn of the century, the exploitation of children in mills and factories arose as a social issue, and the first stirrings towards a juvenile justice system began to take shape. When the juvenile court was founded at the turn of the century, it was conceived as a specialized institution for dealing with dependent, neglected, and delinquent children. Its purpose was to permit the state, acting through a court, to take the place of the child's natural family whenever the child's welfare was imperiled. The court was to be the loving, benign, but firm parent, who acted in the child's best interest.

In its early manifestations, the juvenile court probably was relatively benign. Although there were surely instances of violent behavior by some youngsters brought to juvenile court, society did not then have at the children's disposal either our cornucopia of temptations of consumer goods or our arsenals of evil, such as drugs and handguns. Moreover, at the time there were far fewer children.

As the population of our country grew, urbanization increased, and the traditional social constraints of home, family, church, temple, and small town recognition decreased. So too did the opportunities for productive labor by juveniles decrease. At the same time, the juvenile justice system expanded very rapidly.

The image of the juvenile judge as the wise and good father began to change when the harsh realities of violent behavior by juveniles grew and the volume of all kinds of juvenile crime rose. The judges could be neither paternal nor wise as caseloads expanded leaving juvenile judges with only minutes to look over a case, or to develop a record or to decide an appropriate disposition. Nevertheless, the rehabilitative ideal still glowed brightly. In the thirties and early forties the idea was embodied in apothegms that seem almost quaint today. "There is no such thing as a bad boy." Retrospectively, it is easy to view sentimentally the difficult issues of juvenile crime, when we recall that the same era had an unusually low crime rate for all elements of the population. The country's overwhelming concern was the economy, and later the Second World War. Crime had not become politicized and fear of crime was very low on the list of national problems. As we became economically robust, it was believed that we could afford to recognize injustice and try to do something about it, whether in the arena of civil rights or in that of juvenile justice. In its most extreme libertarian form, the entire responsibility for criminal behavior of juveniles was placed on society as a whole and removed from offending youth. It is futile to deny and potentially dangerous to fail to acknowledge the connections between poverty, unemployment, racism, and juvenile crime. At the same time, those relationships are far more complicated than some reformers realized and those perceptions have led many to the cynical conclusion that nothing can be done in juvenile justice until all of the ills of society had been vanquished. The surest way to reach paralysis on any movement is to assure ourselves that if everything cannot be done, nothing can be done.

Parallel to these developments was the widespread assumption that juvenile courts could be used, not only to address criminal behavior of the young, but also to correct behavior that was not criminal, but that was deemed deviant by the dominant society. Deviance in this sense was an invitation to many juvenile courts to punish youngsters for failing to behave according to a particular judge's perception of appropriate social norms and gender roles. The standards were as elusive as the definitions of common law vagrancy, and the social control aims were more varied and often masked. The original purpose of vagrancy laws was to keep cheap labor bound to the land. The purposes of the status offense was to accomplish more diverse and vague social goals; as variously perceived by individual juvenile judges.

During the last 30 years, perhaps affected by our growing enchantment with the miracles of modern medicine, as well as by the continuing ideal of rehabilitation, juvenile justice moved toward a medical model. Institutionalization—sometimes for very long periods—was equated with "treatment" of the "disease" of delinquency. Many juvenile judges convinced themselves that sentencing adolescent girls with active sexual lives to long terms in reformatories was good medicine and that the girls would undoubtedly benefit from the "treatment." It is still very difficult to convince those who adopted the medical model that it does not fit, that the results are often dreadful and always destructive. Juvenile reformatories are prisons, not benign medical sanatoria and juvenile judges are lawyers, not doctors.

In the last 15 years, crime of all sorts for all age groups has been at the top of the list of national anxieties. Criminal issues have become highly politicized. During this era very few candidates for public office have failed to make promises that he or she is "going to do something" about crime. We vote out judges who are "soft on crime." Observers who have tried to tell the public that the crack down on crime ranging from resurrection of the death penalty to mandatory prison sentences of great length, did not and could not reduce crime, were rarely heard, and even more rarely heeded. On those rare occasions when the words were heard, the speaker was often denounced as a "fuzzy-minded liberal."

The combination of these forces, and others, has moved the country almost to abandon completely the rehabilitative goal for offenders. The trends have been toward increasing long sentences to prisons, increasing use of determinate sentencing, with the result that prisons are bursting at the seams with inmates and being maintained or warehoused at huge public costs.

The same forces continue to converge on the juvenile justice system. More and more pressure is building to be increasingly punitive: to impose incarceration more frequently and for longer periods; toward punishment and incapacitation and toward waiver of serious juvenile cases to adult courts. Additional pressure has been applied to this situation by advocates of expansions of procedural protections to juveniles. These reformers won the first important round with the decision of *In re Gault* (387 U.S. 1; 1967), in which the Supreme Court observed that, all too often, juveniles ended up in the worst of both worlds—with none of the protections accorded an adult and with incarceration as long or longer than an adult. Moreover, juveniles can be incarcerated for behavior that would not be regarded as criminal by adults.

As juvenile courts came to look more and more like adult courts in procedural protections, those who wanted to dismantle the juvenile system and abandon the rehabilitative ideal gained renewed impetus. When one cannot tell the difference between a juvenile court and an adult court, except for the absence of a jury, and when juveniles were routinely committed to institutions housing both adults and juveniles, it becomes harder and harder to justify the maintenance of two different tracks of justice.

Criminal statistics generally, and juvenile statistics in particular, are both suspect and misleading. As anyone familiar with these systems understands, we do not have uniform methods or criteria for collecting the data. Moreover, the statistics are skewed for many reasons, including the fact that poor or minority youth, when arrested, are far more likely to be booked and detained than middle-income, white youth. The arresting officer is more likely in the latter case, if the infraction is relatively minor, to let the youngster go with a reprimand, or a trip to the station with a call to the parents, than he or she is to make a formal arrest and to put the youngster's name on the police blotter. Even with allowances for these deficiencies in record keeping, it is clear that juvenile crime is decreasing. The "get-tough" enthusiasts will claim the triumph as their own. But the fact is that the hard liners cannot take credit for the drop in youth crime. The answer lies in demographic changes that have dramatically affected many elements of our lives. The age cohort that will reach 18 years old in this decade, is 15% fewer than in the last decade. Within the next 10 years there will be 20% fewer youngsters in this age cohort. Moreover, during this same period of time about 30% of these young people will be of Black and Hispanic origin.

The diminution of the age cohort that is most criminogenic in terms of number of offenses, but not in severity, easily accounts for the drop in youth crime. Anxiety about crime is nevertheless undiminished, and the emotional and political volatility of the subject remains undiluted. As a nation, we like to believe that we care about our children; the reality is not as rosy. We have shown little indication that we care deeply about other people's children, especially if those children do not look like the majority of us in terms of social class background and ethnic origins.

From this brief retrospective, it should be evident that a reassessment of where we are in juvenile justice is in order. It is time to rethink old "truths"; time to preserve the best of the system, eradicate the worst, and develop innovative ideas that make a positive difference.

First, it is exceedingly important to renew dedication to the goal of rehabilitation. To be sure, there are not many convincing demonstrations that particular rehabilitative methods completely reform the individual or reduce recidivism. However, we do know that when judges, jailers, social workers, probation officers, and parents—to name a few—give up on the idea that rehabilitation is possible, they then think so poorly of themselves and the job they are trying to do that almost any hope for success is lost. The keepers are damaged perhaps as much as the kept.

Incarceration—no matter how euphemistically described—is still imprisonment. Maintaining the rehabilitative ideal does not offer an excuse for deluding ourselves into the belief that imprisonment is therapy or medical treatment.

At the same time, no matter how thoroughly we may agree that a particular delinquent is a victim of society, we must recognize that we all are

accountable for our actions. We do no one a favor, particularly the convicted by suggesting that he or she has no responsibility for his or her
criminal conduct. It is the case that we have many youngsters in our society
who have been terribly abused by their parents or surrogates and by the
conditions in the communities in which they live, but neither our outrage
about their mistreatment, nor our guilt in failing adequately to deal with the
social situations in which they live excuses us from ignoring the misbehaving
youngsters. Those facts, however, should not blind us to the reality that the
disposition of an 8-year old who has killed his Stepfather with his Stepfather's gun should not be the same as a 15-year old who has done the same
thing. Justice must be fair to be just.

The facts supply little nourishment to the belief that long periods of incarceration either benefit the offender or have any significant effect on the
population who are supposed to be deterred. The public costs of lengthy
incarceration are huge. We know that it costs more to keep one person in
prison for a year than it would to send that person to Princeton University.
The collateral costs are also very large — including aid to dependent families
and other expenses. To the extent that prison serves neither as a deterrent
nor as an appropriate punishment, short sentences are preferable, and jail is
preferable to prison, if incarceration is necessary. Long prison sentences
should be reserved solely for those intractable cases in which incapacitation
of the violent offender is deemed necessary for the protection of the public.

The trend to remove status offenders from incarceration is heartening,
but it is not proceeding as fast as it could and should.

The practice most prevalent today in the juvenile courts of giving first,
second, and third time offenders little punishment, but merely probation to
the home, should be reexamined. Silberman (1978) makes an excellent case
for eliminating this common practice. He does not advocate that sanctions
be heavy. Rather, he recommends that the young offender perceive that
something has happened, as a consequence of his or her actions — that he or
she has not had a "free ride." Offenders should receive punishment that
tells them that they must pay for what they have done. In seeking to provide
alternate disposition, the juvenile court must bring to bear the variety of
resources in the community. A youngster who has vandalized his or her
school room will understand very well why he or she is assigned to clean up
school rooms for a month. But, that alternative is not available to a juvenile
judge, unless the youngster can be made to do penance under supervision.

Another option frequently used in juvenile courts is required
participation in certain academic and vocational classes, both during and
after incarceration. Perhaps this system actually does some good. Informed
intutition, however, suggests that when a course of study is not connected to
a job, forced attendance at these courses does very little for the youngster.
Before we send more youngsters through the same system, we need to know

a lot more than we know about what kinds of programs are effective with which sorts of youngsters.

Resistance must be much stronger to attempts to remove discretion from juvenile judges. We should offer more resources to judges, especially for alternative placements and dispositions in the community. We should also offer greater opportunities for juvenile judges to become better acquainted with programs throughout the country that have shown promise. Programs should not be labeled promising without an adequate evaluation by skilled persons who are drawn from outside the justice system. Anecdotal evidence of the value of a program is useless, and, in many instances, misleading.

The rehabilitative ideal now exists primarily as rhetoric. When a court sentences a youngster to many years of confinement for relatively minor offenses, the judge may tell you that he or she is rehabilitating the individual, and sometimes even he or she does not know that is untrue. It is conventional practice to consider a program as rehabilitation if its avowed purpose is to reduce recidivism, no matter what results have been achieved from the program.

> The state of the art in delinquency treatment today is such that no particular techniques or approaches have proven superior to any others. That statement includes recent well-intentioned innovations: a broad range of experiments conducted over the past two decades failed to demonstrate than any particular forms of innovative community or institutional programs were consistently more effective than traditional approaches. ... juvenile correctional staff, although they have considerable treatment resources at their disposal, are not held accountable for the outcome of their efforts. Programs are routinely evaluated by administrators based on input, not outcome. There is no incentive to keep searching for improved techniques, since there is little optimism that can be found, and no evidence that the system is prepared to recognize them if they are [Greenwood et al., 1983: XV]

I would add to this set of observations that due to the fact that no single program has proven superior to others is not to say that some techniques or approaches are definitely poorer than others or good results are not obtained at least some of the time by some of the better approaches.

Locking up people has not been successful in reducing crime; locking up more people will be just as unsuccessful. The more humane and community-based methods have thus more attractions and less costs (human and dollar) than incarceration.

We must remember first that we are dealing with human beings, not numbers, when we adopt reforms or changes in our juvenile justice system.

References

Greenwood, P., A. Lipson, A. Abrahamse, and F. Zimring, "Youth crime and juvenile justice in
    California: a report to the legislature." 1983, Rand Corporation Report, R-3015-CSA.
Silberman, Charles E., *Criminal Violence, Criminal Justice*, 1978, New York: Random House.